WINGS OF WAR

Fighter Over Finland is the epic tale of a little known but savage air war, the heroic struggle of a tiny Finnish air corps against the powerful forces of the Soviet Union. Eino Luukkanen, whose fifty-four victories made him the Finns' third-ranking ace, writes with elegance and feeling about five years of bitter battles in two separate wars.

America's strong affection for the Finns, engendered in part because they alone had paid their World War I debts, increased enormously when on November 30, 1939, the brutal Goliath, the Soviet Union, invaded Finland after months of increasing diplomatic and military pressure. The world expected the enormous Soviet military forces to win a quick victory. Instead the Finns, fighting with skill and courage in what became known as the Winter War, inflicted grievous losses on the aggressors that had repercussions within both the Soviet and German High Commands.

Within the first few hours after the invasion, Lieutenant Eino Luukkanen, an experienced fighter pilot with more than a thousand hours flying time, made his first combat sortie. One day later, flying a Dutch-designed Fokker D XXI fighter, he scored the first Finnish aerial victory of the war when he shot down a Soviet SB-2 bomber.

Flying foreign equipment was common in many air forces, but none had the strange mixture that Finland was forced to use over the next years. Although the Finns had a small indigenous aviation industry, they took airplanes where they could find them, employing planes built by their German allies as well as captured U.S., British, French, Italian, and Russian aircraft that were sold to them by Germany. Luukkanen himself achieved great success in the Brewster Buffalo, an American-made aircraft widely reviled by every other air force to use it.

Besides their numerical inferiority (they were sometimes outnumbered by as much as fifty to one) the Finns had to contend with weather that would have grounded any other air force in the

TIME-LIFE BOOKS INC., ALEXANDRIA, VIRGINIA 22314

FIGHTER OVER FINLAND

The author in the cockpit of a Messerschmitt Bf 109G-2 fighter.

FIGHTER OVER FINLAND

The Memoirs of a Fighter Pilot

EINO LUUKKANEN

Translated from the Finnish by Mauno A. Salo
Edited by William Green

MACDONALD : LONDON

FIRST PUBLISHED IN THE FINNISH LANGUAGE AS
HÄVITTÄJÄLENTÄJÄNÄ KAHDESSA SODASSA
BY WERNER SÖDERSTRÖM OSAKEYHTIÖ PORVOO, HELSINKI

This translation and special contents ©
Macdonald & Co. (Publishers) Ltd., 1963

First published in Great Britain in 1963 by
Macdonald & Co. (Publishers), Ltd.
Gulf House, 2 Portman Street, London, W.1
Made and printed in Great Britain by
Purnell and Sons, Ltd.
Paulton (Somerset) and London

"The Fatherland is not just the native soil upon which we tread, nor the water that rinses our shores, but is also the rippling air above us."

MANNERHEIM

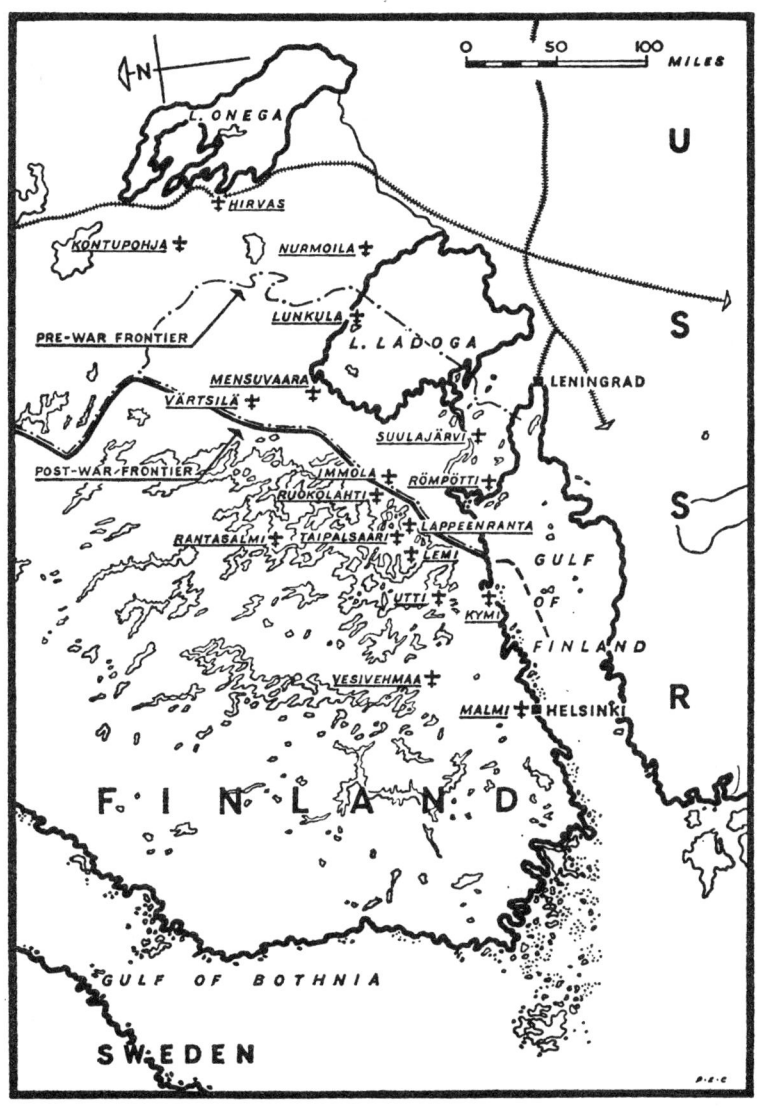

The principal bases from which the author flew during the two Russo-Finnish conflicts.

FOREWORD

A Finnish writer has compared the deeds of human beings to stones thrown into water. They splash mightily and the ripples widen, but as the stones disappear the surface of the water once more becomes smooth. Time is like water. The deeds of man raise splashes and ripples on time's surface, but eventually both men and deeds are forgotten.

Twenty-three long years have passed since that fateful thirteenth day of March 1940 when our so-called "Winter War" came to an end. They were stirring days for we fighter pilots pitted against overwhelming odds, but with the passage of nearly a quarter of a century, memories of their events are already fading from the minds of those who participated in them and survived. To rescue something of these memories before they finally fade into the limbo, I have written about one man's war—my war! It is an account of the activities of the fighter units in which I served, but I believe my experiences to have been typical of those of many Finnish pilots who fought the Soviet Union in two conflicts, and I offer this account as a tribute to all those who fought for their Fatherland; not only fighter pilots, but the crews of bombers, reconnaissance machines and transports, and particularly the mechanics, armourers and other ground personnel whose praises are rarely sung but without whom we would never have got into the air.

The names and dates mentioned in this narrative are entirely correct, and in most cases I have used the nicknames or radio-call names of the pilots rather than their christian names which we rarely if ever employed.

While writing this account of Finland's two wars, I had looked forward to describing the final furious battles fought out in the skies during the summer of 1944. In my mind I had envisaged these as forming the climax of my story, but when I reached that part of the narrative I discovered, to my surprise, that such actions had made far less impression upon me than those first aerial struggles of the "Winter War" in which we, a tiny nation, stood alone. By that last summer the end was already a foregone conclusion; we were fighting bitterly to survive. We asked and gave no quarter. Each fresh battle was just that—a battle. It aroused none of the deep emotion that we all experienced during the conflict of 1939–40.

Having survived both wars, I am only too well aware of the tremendous sacrifices made by those who so readily gave their lives in the defence of their country. May this account help to keep their memories alive.

Oulu, Finland.   EINO LUUKKANEN

INTRODUCTION

The general concept of Finland rarely goes beyond timber and sawmills, sauna baths and the composer Sibelius. Finland is a land of unending forests, a thousand lakes and the midnight sun. Bordered in the north by Norway and in the east by the Soviet Union, Finland possesses an area of 130,085 square miles, approximately one-third more than that of Great Britain and Northern Ireland combined, and a population of some four-and-a-half millions.

Although relatively one of Europe's newer nations, having declared her independence on December 6, 1917, Finland's history dates back to the Finno-Ugors of the Ural Altaic region, forming a part of the Kingdom of Sweden from 1154 until 1809 when she became an autonomous Grand Duchy of the Russian Empire. Civil war followed the Declaration of Independence, and it was during this period that the first steps were taken to organize an air arm.

In 1938 the Russians made their first overtures to the Finns, requesting permission to build both air and naval bases on Finnish soil. Russian requests became progressively demands, and in return for strategic areas of Finland which would have enabled the Soviet Union to turn the Gulf of Finland into a Russian "lake", they offered worthless swampland. The Russians then began to meddle in Finnish internal affairs, and relations between the two countries became increasingly strained until, in the autumn of 1939, the Finnish government ordered mobilization, this action being prompted by the Russian occupation of Estonia, Latvia and Lithuania.

Finally, the Russians brought about the infamous "Mainila Incident", claiming that Finnish border guards had fired across the border, killing a Russian N.C.O. and several troops, and Russian forces began an assault on Finland which was to become known to the Finns as the "Winter War". The Russians encountered unexpectedly fierce resistance from the

Finns who quickly brought the Russian armies to a standstill, but the Soviet Union rapidly strengthened her forces engaged in the attack on Finland until the Finns were finally forced to yield.

Fifteen months of peace followed until June 1941 when Finland was once more embroiled in hostilities, Russian bombers again attacking Finnish territory without any formal declaration of war. Finland now became automatically aligned with Germany, and her forces soon recovered the territory ceded to the Russians in 1940. One of the principal aims of the Germano-Finnish campaign was the cutting of the Murmansk Railway, the vital lifeline for Cash-and-Carry Lend-Lease material. The Finnish and German forces made two separate thrusts in their attempt to achieve this aim; one across the 61st and 62nd parallels and the other across the 66th and 67th parallels. The two thrusts were destined never to link up, and there followed a stalemate lasting nearly one and a half years.

The final onslaught came in June 1944, when the Russians unleashed tremendous forces which trampled their way up the narrow Karelian Isthmus, and Finland was once again forced to yield.

The narrative that follows tells the story of the two wars with the Russians as seen through the eyes of one pilot, Major Eino Luukkanen, the Finnish Air Force's third-ranking ace with fifty-four kills, who roamed backwards and forwards across the battlegrounds, fighting an air war which, in some respects, was not dissimilar to the Battle of Britain.

MAUNO SALO

CONTENTS

Foreword xi
Introduction xiii
1. Gestation of a Fighting Pilot 19
2. The Storm Breaks 25
3. The Weather Worsens 34
4. Two Enemies—Winter and Russians 45
5. Catastrophe 60
6. The End of the First Round 69
7. Lull Between Storms 77
8. At War Once More 86
9. Over the Border 100
10. Nine Months at Nurmoila 108
11. A Nomad's Life 131
12. Au Revoir to Fighters 144
13. Fighters Once Again 150
14. A Hectic Pace 160
15. A Close Call 176
16. The Last Round 181
Appendix I: Official List of Author's Aerial Victories 189
Appendix II: The Principal Types of Aircraft Employed During the Russo-Finnish Wars by the Combatants 191

ILLUSTRATIONS

The author in the cockpit of his Messerschmitt Bf 109G	*frontispiece*
Caudron C.60 and Letov S.218 Smolik at Kauhava	*facing page* 32
Martinsyde F.4 Buzzard and Hansa-Brandenburg A.22	„ 33
Fokker D.XXI	„ 48
Fokker D.XXI at Värtsilä	„ 49
Blackburn Ripon IIF	„ 64
Gloster Gladiator II, the author after promotion to captain and personnel of Fighter Group L	„ 65
Brewster B-239 and ferry pilots at Tröllhattan	„ 80
Aero O/Y Junkers Ju 52/3m "Kaleva"	„ 80
Camouflaged Brewster B-239, Nils Katajainen and the emblem of HLeLv 24	„ 81
Fiat G.50, Captain Lauri Pekuri, Major Olavi Ehrnrooth, the author, and the Curtiss Hawk 75A	„ 96
B-239 after ground loop, Lieut. Kossi Karhila and Morane-Saulnier M.S.406	„ 97
Sergeant Eric Lyly, Sergeant Paavo Tolonen and Flight Master Jätti Lehtovaara	„ 112
Tents at Nurmoila, and the author's B-239 burning	„ 113

xviii   ILLUSTRATIONS

Colonel Riku Lorentz, Lieut.-Col. G. E. Magnusson, the author, and the transfer of Mensuvaara to the Luftwaffe ... ...*facing page*	128
Korppu Paltila and his Tchaika, and pilots of TLeLv 30 ... ... ,,	129
Yak-7A, SB-2bis and the DC-2 "Hanssin Jukka" ... ... ,,	144
The author's Bf 109G-2 and the Dornier Do 17Z-2 ... ... ,,	145
Flight Master Oippa Tuominen and Lieut. Mikko Pasila ... ... ,,	160
Sergeant Pentti Tilli, Flight Master Eino Juutilainen, Joppe Karhunen and Hasse Wind ... ,,	161
Bf 109G-6 at Malmi and one of Karhila's victims, an Il-2 ... ... ,,	176
Ilyushin DB-3, Tupolev SB-2bis and Blenheim I ,,	177
Lieut. Kale Tervo, Lieut. Pege Saalasti, and Lieut. Lauri Nissinen ... ... ,,	192
The author in Bf 109G-6, the emblem of HLeLv 34, and the Pyry II trainer ... ... ,,	193

1

GESTATION OF A FIGHTING PILOT

The splendid month of August 1932, with its long, fine days so ideally suited for flying, had given place to September and the first autumnal signs as I clambered shakily into the elderly Caudron C.60 primary training biplane for that eagerly awaited but painfully apprehended event in the life of every pilot—the first solo flight. I fumbled with my seat harness, my fingers feeling more like so many thumbs, carefully checking and rechecking the instruments and controls, the ancient rotary-type Clerget 9B engine idling and shaking the airframe like a cocktail mixer. As the mechanic whipped away the wheel chocks, I gingerly eased open the throttle a little and slowly taxied from the apron to the edge of the field. Turning into wind, I peered around to assure myself that all was clear and, with my heart hammering like a piston, opened the throttle and was bouncing and swaying across the unevenly mowed grass stubble. The boundary fence raced towards me as my clammy hands pulled back on the stick. Then, miracle of miracles, the vibrating and the shuddering vanished and I was airborne—alone!

Climbing steadily to about a thousand feet, my tenseness slowly eased and my confidence returned sufficiently to allow my gaze away from the instruments. I was truly alone at last in the infinite depth of sky, with the roaring rotary engine and the shimmering airscrew carrying me upwards towards the scattered cottonwool clouds. I began to savour this new and exhilarating experience. The houses, the lakes, the occasional sawmill and the railway station drifted past below, toylike and unreal. I was completely detached from the earth; free of past and future. Yesterday was forgotten and I had no thought of the morrow. My rapture transcended description. I was a part of this frail, vibrating contraption.

The airscrew slipstream beat the streamer attached to the rudder; the "Elves Pennant" warning others that I was a mere fledgeling—a form of aerial learner plate. With new-found confidence, I made what was, to my mind at least, the perfect approach and an equally well-executed landing. I was a pilot! My tunic had still to sport a pair of wings but, nevertheless, I was a pilot! I promptly took-off again for my second circuit of the field, this time with appreciably more aplomb. Five times in all I took-off, circled the field and landed, and as I taxied the Caudron, still intact, back to the apron after my last landing, and chopped the throttle, I could hardly contain my elation.

It was hard to believe that only a few weeks had elapsed since we senior air cadets had left the Cadet School at Munkkiniemi, near Helsinki, and journeyed, after a brief spell in camp at the glorious Pääskylahti, or Swallow Bay, to the Kauhava Central Flying School and the tender ministrations of, in my case, Major Niilo Jusu, a highly qualified flying instructor. But now, as was the custom, my fellow cadets and I celebrated my successful solo in the recreation room, the onus being on me to supply the large quantities of steaming coffee and, more important, the bottle of Scotch.

. . . . .

Six months passed; six months crammed with innumerable hours of classroom and workshop instruction in meteorology, aerodynamics, aircraft structures, engine and armament technology, tactics, radio, and many other subjects, all of which had to find storage niches within our heads. There were also sixty hours of formation flying, cross-country navigational exercises, aerobatics, aerial gunnery and mock combat, mostly in Letov Smoliks, although eleven hours were spent in genuine if somewhat antiquated single-seat fighters—Martinsyde F.4 Buzzards. Powered by a 300-h.p. Hispano-Suiza engine, the Buzzard biplane was a relic of the first world war, a number of fighters of this type having been purchased by the Finnish government from the Aircraft Disposals Company in 1923–24.

At last, in the spring of 1933, our training was complete and, early in May, we returned to Munkkiniemi to check in our training equipment and prepare for the anxiously awaited graduation parade. This event took place on May 16th, and at noon, our spotless parade-ground uniforms outshining the brilliant sunshine, we marched proudly to the President's Palace at Helsinki to receive our wings, our commissions and our assignments.

Together with several other newly-commissioned sub-lieutenants, I was assigned to the 1st Detached Sea Squadron at Viipuri, the principal Karelian metropolis at the far end of the Gulf of Finland and, after two weeks of complete relaxation spent mostly on the shores of Lake Ladoga, reported to my unit. During that summer I undertook a seaplane conversion course on Turkinsaari, or Turk Island, a thirty-minute boat trip from Viipuri, but I felt little affinity with the slow, unwieldy Hansa-Brandenburg A.22 floatplanes. My appetite for the instant response and nimbleness of the single-seater fighter had been thoroughly whetted by my eleven hours on the Buzzard at Kauhava, and driving a floatplane offered hardly more exhilaration than chauffeuring a car! Nevertheless, like it or not, nearly two years were to elapse before I was once again to be found behind the controls of a single-seater fighter; two years of continuous training and practice, both in the air and on the ground. Physical fitness was considered to be almost as important as prowess in the air and, as well as attending two rigorous physical training courses, I took part in the Army ski races at Salpausselkä, Valkjärvi, Kajaani, and Hämeenlinna.

I had almost despaired of achieving my desire to join a fighter unit when, in 1935, some re-thinking on the part of the High Command began to bear fruit in changes in the Air Force. One of the most important developments at this time was the formation of HLeLv 26, or Fighter Squadron 26, at Suur-Merijoki, near Viipuri, this unit, together with a ground organisation, comprising Lentoasema (Air Base) 5. Luckily, I had succeeded in getting myself assigned to a fighter conversion course which I completed favourably and, promoted to full lieutenant on March 21st, was posted to HLeLv 26. The squadron had just received brand-new Bristol Bulldog IVA all-metal fighter biplanes, seventeen of which had been ordered from Britain in May 1934, these actually being the last aircraft of their type to be built, and I was destined to fly this fine little warplane day and night, summer and winter, in fair weather and foul for nearly four years.

We practised continually until we were conversant with every mood, idiosyncrasy and foible of our little Bulldog whose name belied its delightfully sprightly qualities, and the tranquil peacetime years passed rapidly, untouched by shadows of future events. The large air display that we gave at Suur-Merijoki and our most serious peacetime air disaster which occurred when a formation of five Junkers W.34s caught the airscrew wash from six Blackburn Ripons, two of the Junkers colliding with the loss of both crews, seemed important happenings at the time but were soon to pale into insignificance. Our squadron participated in the 1937 winter "War Games" held at Sortavala, exercises dominated by intensely cold weather and best remembered for the pleasurable long winter evenings that we spent in the Officers' Club, a splendid stone castle originally built for Russian royalty. Throughout the summer months the squadron operated from the Käkisalmi airfield, alongside Lake Ladoga.

During 1938 Lentoasema 5 was redesignated Lentorykmentti (Air Regiment) 1, the airfields of Sortavala and Turkinsaari being brought under its command. Increasing tension in Europe had begun to render necessary some modernisation of the Air Force, and orders for new combat aircraft had been placed in Britain and the Netherlands, but although fears of Finland being embroiled in a conflict were undoubtedly being entertained in governmental circles, no such possibilities darkened our days. For about a year I had acted as adjutant to the autocratic and demanding but highly efficient regimental commander, Colonel Yrjö Oppas, but despite the numerous irksome duties that I was forced to perform at regimental headquarters, I succeeded in keeping up my flying time with HLeLv 26, and even managed to wangle some interesting long-distance flights.

・ ・ ・ ・ ・

And so began the fateful year of 1939, the first six months of which I passed at the War College in Helsinki, taking my captain's course. During the spring, HLeLv 24, a squadron based at Utti, had received new equipment in the shape of Fokker D.XXI single-seater fighter monoplanes powered by 830-h.p. Bristol Mercury VIII air-cooled radial engines. The D.XXI retained Fokker's traditional mixed construction with fabric-covered fuselage, and lacked such innovations as the retractable undercarriage which characterised its contemporaries such as the Spitfire, the Hurricane and the Messerschmitt Bf 109. It was a completely orthodox, sturdy monoplane of relatively simple construction which served our needs adequately, and represented a noteworthy advance over the now obsolescent Bulldog biplanes.

Upon completion of my course, I applied for and was granted a transfer to HLeLv 24 as a flight commander, and immediately joined in the very thorough and absorbingly interesting process of evaluating the new fighter's characteristics and assessing its combat potentialities. Most of the training and evaluation flights with the D.XXIs were conducted over the Käkisalmi firing range, and we soon discovered that the little Dutch fighter provided a good firing platform. In general, its flying characteristics were good, but it was not devoid of temperament which could provide dangerous snares for the unwary. Abrupt, high-speed stalls with little or no warning could catch the inexperienced, but landing was the most dangerous feature of the D.XXI as the angle of attack was high, partly blanketing the tail surfaces and resulting in inadequate control. If too much speed was lost on the approach, the D.XXI was not very forgiving and the pilot had to have some luck on his side. Indeed, we were to lose quite a number of our Fokkers in training accidents, but once its idiosyncrasies had been mastered it was a pleasant enough aeroplane, and we were soon to learn that it could absorb a considerable amount of punishment yet stay in the air.

In August the large-scale Karelian war games provided us with an opportunity to discover how our D.XXIs would stand up under simulated operational conditions. We operated from the Perkjärvi airfield and were in the air almost continuously, for the midsummer nights over Finland seldom darken fully. Furious mock combats were fought every day, the results being duly recorded by the gun cameras, and the Fokker passed all its trials with flying colours. The war games terminated in the largest fly-past ever seen over Finland at that time, comprising virtually every combat aircraft possessed by our Air Force in one large formation.

Relations between Finland and Russia were now worsening rapidly, the Soviet Union making no attempt to hide her territorial aspirations in so far as we were concerned, but I now felt as much at home in the cockpit of my Fokker D.XXI as I had in that of my old Bulldog, and I was sure that it would give of its best under any conditions. Thus, belatedly, but with a light heart despite the fact that fighting had already begun in Europe and the knowledge that the fate of my homeland might soon hang in the balance, I began my summer leave, heading once more for the shores of Lake Ladoga.

2

THE STORM BREAKS

Little more than a week of my leave had passed when, on October 6, 1939, a telegram arrived. "Leave cancelled. Report to unit immediately!" I packed hastily and within the hour was aboard a train heading for Utti and the squadron, my mind seething with speculation. I reached the base early the next morning and discovered that, as a result of the continual demands made by the Soviet Union for areas of Finnish territory of strategic importance and military base facilities on our soil, we had begun to mobilize. Our squadron had received instructions to transfer immediately to the Immola airfield, near the vital Imatra power stations, and attain full combat readiness with all possible speed.

The next few days passed in a flash despite the fact that we were all continuously on duty from before dawn until well after midnight. The Mercury engines of the Fokkers were tested and tuned to perfection, the machine-guns were checked and re-checked, ammunition belts were loaded, parachutes repacked, and engine and airframe spares, servicing equipment and personal kit loaded aboard trucks and despatched to Immola. Finally, on the morning of the 11th, HLeLv 24 took-off from Utti for its new operational base.

The Commanding Officer of the squadron was, at that time, Captain G. E. Magnusson, and the squadron comprised four flights, the third of which I led. My flight possessed eight D.XXI fighters with three commissioned and five non-commissioned pilots, and some thirty mechanics, fitters, and radio and armament technicians. From dawn to dusk after our arrival at Immola we were either in the air or in the close vicinity of our aircraft. The younger, less-experienced pilots received additional training in tactical patrol flying and air-to-air and air-to-ground gunnery, but during this programme an unfortunate accident occurred—a young pilot who had just joined us, Sergeant A. Jalovaara, lost control of his fighter at low altitude and crashed to his death in the forest.

Dispersal revetments were constructed to reduce the possibility of our aircraft being damaged by bomb splinters, a task in which we all gave a hand, and one greatly eased by the fine voice of a young assistant mechanic, Sulo Saarits, whose renderings of Finnish traditional songs were magnificent. When we were not in the air, duty periods were passed in the "ready tent" where a portable gramophone played and replayed the same few records from dawn until nightfall. During inclement weather, which kept our fighters grounded, our daily round was varied with physical training, revolver practice, and discussions on tactical problems, but each evening in the mess the conversation invariably centred on one topic—the probability of war.

The future of Finland, as, indeed, for much of Europe, looked ominous. On October 9th, 13th, and 19th, the Russians had made reconnaissance flights over Finnish territory, portents that could not be ignored, and there seemed every likelihood that we would soon find ourselves squinting through our gunsights at Russians. I asked myself time and time again, as did probably every other pilot, if I was ready for combat flying? I had to be! I had been a military pilot for almost seven years and had accumulated nearly a thousand flying hours under all conditions. If I was not ready to fire my guns in anger then I never should be! But once in the cockpit of my D.XXI, savouring the familiar and vaguely comforting cockpit odour, that blend of high-octane fuel, mineral oil and dope, all my misgivings vanished, and I only felt impatience; a desire to be done with this period of waiting. If war was inevitable then why could we not get on with it!

Squadron life continued unchanged, the days being spent mostly on patrols and refresher training, or playing cards in the "ready tent", and the evenings found us grouped around the radio in the mess, endeavouring to listen to the latest instalment in the serialised adventures of Dumas' *Count of Monte Cristo*, increasing interference from a powerful Russian radio transmitter rendering this ever more difficult. Late in November winter descended on us with sudden fury. Raw, cold winds blew from the north, freezing the puddles and bringing with them the first flurries of snow, necessitating a hurried trip to Viipuri to purchase a pair of warm felt boots which were to become my inseparable companions during the months that followed.

Thursday, the last day of November 1939, and the 444th anniversary of the historic Battle of the Viipuri Forts, dawned cold and overcast, the cloud base being at an altitude of little more than two thousand feet. At 06.00 hours, while the night was still as black as pitch, we had gathered around the fighters assigned that morning to alert duty. Icy northern winds shook the branches of the trees, and snowflakes drifted lazily to the ground between the gusts as we inspected our Fokkers. Mechanics were winding the inertia starters, and one by one the engines roared into life, shattering the pre-dawn stillness. We ran up the engines, tested the controls and instruments, and inspected the guns and their ammunition feeds. Our task completed, silence once more descended on Immola. The minutes ticked slowly by, the only movement to be seen being that of the muffled mechanics making last-minute adjustments to their charges. We returned to the "ready tent" to sit around the stove as the sky lightened, a few small gaps appearing in the sombre grey cloud that draped the field. The temperature had risen to 3 degrees C., and at 09.00 hours we flight commanders gathered at the Squadron Command Post for the customary briefing.

With no apparent reason the atmosphere for once seemed charged with electricity, and Captain Magnusson told us to wait. Something was certainly in the air, and after ten minutes the usual buzz of conversation died away. At 09.20 hours, the regimental commander, Colonel Riku Lorentz, the "father" of Finland's fighter forces, hurried into the Command Post, fired his revolver into the air, and announced, "This morning at 06.15 hours Russian forces crossed our country's borders! At this moment a number of enemy aircraft are reported to be heading in the direction of Viipuri!" Captain Magnusson immediately gave orders for the Alert Flight—my flight—to attempt an interception over Viipuri.

I had grabbed my flying helmet and had started for the door before he had finished speaking. I raced across to our aircraft. The mechanics, sensing what had happened, were already winding the starters. Shouting orders to the other pilots, I clambered on to the wing of my Fokker, levered myself into the cockpit and, within five minutes of Colonel Lorentz's dramatic gesture with the revolver, we had formated over Immola Lake and were heading in the direction of Viipuri. I glanced around to ensure that every member of my flight had joined the formation, and it was only then that it dawned upon me that I was leading the first actual combat flight of the war.

Could we reach Viipuri in time to intercept the intruders? We were flying just beneath the cloud base at two thousand feet, cruising at 186 m.p.h., and I estimated that we would arrive over our destination in about twenty minutes. But twenty minutes were ample for the Russian bombers to make their bombing run and turn for home. At 09.45 hours the familiar old city appeared below and to starboard, and my fears were immediately proved well founded. I could see fires burning among the wood sheds of the Maaskola railway yards. We were too late! The Russians had already dropped their bombs and departed. We veered southwards and I spotted two bombers disappearing into the clouds a considerable distance away, over Ura.

We climbed above the cloud layer into the bright sunshine at about five thousand feet, but there was no sign of the enemy. Our quarry was evidently taking full advantage of the cloud to make good his escape. For an hour we patrolled south of Viipuri to Kuolemajärvi without seeing a sign of other aircraft apart from a few of our own Bulldogs, and as our fuel was beginning to run low, we could do no more than head for home, disappointed by our failure to come to grips with Ivan.

The return flight was made through drifting snow clouds which thickened as we neared Immola, until a snowstorm forced us down to virtually the tops of the trees where visibility was little more than a half-mile. Once back at Immola our chagrin was complete when we were told that Viipuri had been bombed at 09.42—three minutes before our arrival! The snowstorm worsened so that further flying was impossible, and our first day of war darkened to a wintry night, relieving us of the need to remain on alert status.

After dinner in the mess we were, for the most part, absorbed in our own thoughts, considering the circumstances in which our little country now found herself. The future would obviously not be easy for we were opposing an enemy possessing more than fifty times our strength, but we could not allow this to discourage us. Right was on our side, although it would have been nice had we possessed a few more squadrons to help us defend what was rightfully ours! This first day of what was to become known as our "Winter War" had been disappointing, but perhaps the next day would allow us to show Ivan our mettle.

. . . . .

The next morning, the second day of the war, I was aroused at 05.30 hours and, only pausing to climb into my furs and without waiting for breakfast, I stumbled across the pitch-black airfield towards my flight's revetments. The Fokkers were swathed in white camouflage covers, and with my mechanic I pulled away the sheets. My D.XXI, which bore the Finnish serial number FR-104, might well find itself in action that day, so I carefully inspected the aircraft, paying special attention to the machine-guns and their ammunition belts. I swung the rudder with my feet on the pedals, rocked the stick, watching the ailerons, and signalled to the mechanic. The starter whined, the Mercury coughed, I caught it with the throttle and it burst into a comforting, deep-throated bass. I checked the instruments and then, satisfied, chopped the throttle.

Now began the period of waiting so familiar to fighter pilots of all nationalities. Gradually the darkness gave place to a murky grey, and the sky began to turn a yellowish-pink in the east. The telephone in the "ready tent" rang shrilly. We were to maintain a continuous patrol of two fighters[1] over Vuoksenlaakso. I decided to lead the second patrol, accompanied by Vic Pyötsiä, a dependable and experienced pilot, as my wingman. We relieved the first patrol over Imatra. Our predecessors had seen no sign of enemy air activity during their ninety minutes patrolling. There was a considerable amount of cloud,

[1] The Finnish Air Force had followed the lead of the Luftwaffe in abandoning the close "V" in favour of a loose pair, or *rotte* as it was known by German pilots. It had been discovered during the Spanish Civil War that a tight formation of a larger number of aircraft was not practical for combat purposes, the pilots having to pay more attention to avoiding collision than watching for enemy aircraft.

the base of this being as low as thirteen hundred feet, and we began our patrol at an altitude of about a thousand feet, flying a roughly triangular route with Imatra, Enso and Jääski forming the corners.

While flying over Enso during our second circuit of the patrol area two bombers appeared. They were flying north-east at about three thousand two hundred feet at roughly two o'clock. I gave Vic the signal to attack, rammed open the throttle and, engine roaring, attempted to position myself on the tail of the closest of the two bombers. Our intended victims, sleek, twin-engined monoplanes, had evidently spotted our approach, for they banked sharply to the south-east, but this was a serious mistake for it only helped to close the distance between us more swiftly.

Quite rapidly the nearest bomber grew in my sights. Four hundred, three hundred, two hundred, one hundred yards. Never had my feet been planted more firmly on the rudder pedals, my hands gripped the control column so tightly, or my eyes been glued so closely to the gunsight as at that moment. I depressed the firing trigger and saw my tracers curve in towards the bomber. Simultaneously, brilliant orange flashes danced in front of my windscreen. The dorsal gunner was pumping away at me for all he was worth! The target now completely covered my sight and I was forced to break sharply to starboard to avoid a collision. Pulling the Fokker around I again lined up the bomber in my sight. The dorsal gunner was still blazing away at me, his tracers winking all around my fighter, but in the excitement of the moment I felt no sense of danger. I edged in to make absolutely sure of my opponent.

Our altitude was down to five hundred feet by this time, and suddenly several large objects tumbled away from the bomber. The pilot had decided to jettison his load to lighten the aircraft, and the blast from the bombs tossed my little Fokker around like a piece of straw in a high wind. Once again I positioned myself on the bomber's tail. A little more throttle and he was squarely in my sight. Now, I could not possibly miss! I depressed the firing trigger, but just as my burst began raking along the rear fuselage, the pilot of the bomber lowered his undercarriage which, acting as an air-brake, slowed the aircraft immediately, forcing me to pull up the nose of the Fokker to avoid ramming the Russian amidships. This pilot evidently knew his stuff. I had no intention of being caught a second time, however, and I swung in to the attack once more, throttling back to match my speed with that of the bomber. I loosed a long burst into the starboard engine from a distance of no more than fifty yards, and dirty grey smoke belched back from the cowling. The airscrew windmilled momentarily, came to a standstill, and the bomber nosed down, just cleared a clump of trees and pancaked in a small field.

I could hardly believe my own eyes. My first kill! I had acted purely by instinct throughout the conflict, not giving a thought to tactics or firing angles. In fact, it seemed that my mind had been a blank throughout the incident; my reactions had been automatic. Then an awful thought struck me. Had I actually shot down a *Russian* bomber? I had made no attempt to identify the nationality of the aircraft or its type. I had only *assumed* that it belonged to the enemy! I spiralled low over my victim and, to my intense relief, saw that the bomber, a Tupolev SB-2, sported the red star insignia of the Soviet Union. The three crew members climbed from the aircraft as I roared past, waving white cloths and evidently scared that I might intend to administer the *coup de grâce* by strafing them with my remaining ammunition.

Until that moment it had not really occurred to me that there were men aboard this machine which now straddled some poor farmer's potato field, its back broken. An air battle is somehow detached and impersonal. One hears no cries of pain, sees no despairing faces of the dying, no blood, no agony, no human wretchedness. The sight of a stricken plane arouses only elation. Its human occupants are remote, and pity for them does not trouble the victor's conscience. A childish scheme entered my head. Could I land alongside my victim and take its crew prisoner? I had even throttled back the engine and begun my approach when I realised what a damned fool idea it was, and opened the throttle once more.

During the heat of the fight I had had no time to note my position, and now I had only the vaguest idea of the direction of Immola. Then I saw a railway line and a tiny station just two or three miles away. Flying low over the station, I managed to make out the name "Koljola". Several people were staring up at me from the platform, and I made several turns over the station, pointing in the direction of the crashed Russian bomber. Not knowing if they had understood my signals, I turned northwards towards Immola, anxious to feel terra firma once more beneath my feet, and to relate my experience to my friends. This, my first combat, was obviously destined to remain one of the most profound experiences of my life. Later, more hectic battles would never produce an effect so lasting as this exhilarating yet sobering experience.

While lost in these reflections, I found myself once more over the Immola Lake, and began preparations for landing. Such was my excitement that my approach speed was too great, forcing me to go around again like a learner! My Fokker trundled over towards the members of my flight grouped around their machines, and as I cut my ignition switch, I tried vainly to hide my elation, and climb from the cockpit with some nonchalance, but it was no good, and my fellow pilots and the mechanics were soon tossing me in the air. Who can remain dignified when tossed in the air? They were as excited as I. After all, was this not an historical event? This was the first Finnish victory in the air, and it was only later that I realised that to me had gone the honour of becoming the first Finn to have destroyed an enemy aircraft in combat. Vic had apparently made two firing passes at the other bomber, but these had had no visible effect, and the enemy had eluded him by slipping into cloud.

· · · · ·

Ravenously I attacked my belated breakfast in the mess while my Fokker was being refuelled and rearmed, and I was just strolling back to the field when the alarm rang. Almost simultaneously came the roar of many powerful aero engines, and above, but quite low, several twin-engined aircraft appeared, their bomb doors agape. The noise of exploding bombs and the staccato rattle of machine-gun fire coupled with the pounding of engines was deafening and confusing, but it was immediately obvious that the Russian bomb-aimers were no experts at their trade, for most of the bombs fell outside the airfield perimeter, the only damage being that suffered by the roofs and windows of an empty hangar!

(*Above*) Caudron C.60 and Letov Smolik S.218 trainers on the apron at Kauhava. The Caudron in which the author soloed, CA-32, in August 1932 may be seen at the far end of the hangar doorway.

(*Right*) The author flew a total of sixty-one hours in the rotary-engined Caudron. About a dozen of these had been purchased from France in 1923, and another thirty-four had been built in Finland in 1927. The Smolik S.218 (*below*) with the 120 h.p. Walter Gemma I engine could hardly hurdle the fence at Kauhava on take-off, so the Finnish-built model was equipped with a 145 h.p. engine.

The Martinsyde F.4 Buzzard (*above*) was a relic of the First World War purchased in 1923-24 from the Aircraft Disposals Company. Used primarily for gunnery training, the Buzzard was a sprightly little aircraft with a 300 h.p. Hispano engine, and the author logged eleven hours in this type. The Hansa-Brandenburg A.22 (*below*) was normally equipped as a seaplane but is seen here on skis. The author flew twenty-five hours in the A.22 after being assigned to the 1st Detached Sea Squadron at Viipuri, and the Finnish State Aircraft Factory built no less than one hundred and twenty-two machines of this type, the largest number of any one type of aircraft manufactured in Finland to the present time.

This low-altitude attack by ten SB-2s had evidently taken our warning system completely by surprise, and only the fourth flight managed to get airborne. Nevertheless, they succeeded in catching the Russian formation, bringing down four of its number. We even got a prisoner from this incident, his acquisition providing a good example of the low standard of training of the Soviet units with which we were faced. Over the edge of the airfield the pilot of one of the SB-2s had signalled his bomb-aimer to release the bomb load, but the bomb-aimer misunderstood the signal and, believing something to be wrong, promptly bailed out! Fortunately for the young Russian lieutenant, his parachute opened immediately despite the low altitude at which he had jumped, and he landed near one of the hangars, none the worse for his experience.

3

THE WEATHER WORSENS

Just as we had begun to put heart and soul into this new and exciting life, a tremendous snowstorm smothered our operations. Our airfield was temporarily out of action, and we were unable to make any further retaliatory efforts. From December 2nd the snowstorm continued unabated for several days, and all aircraft were grounded. This provided an opportunity to search for the remains of our first victims, examine their defensive weapons, armour protection and fuel cells, and ferret out their weaknesses for future reference. Several of us found our way to Koljola, and it did not prove too difficult to ascertain the whereabouts of my SB-2. We found that it was a brand-new machine, and the manufacturer's plate in the cockpit revealed the fact that it had been completed earlier that year.

The fuselage of the bomber appeared to have more holes than a colander. We counted no less than one hundred and eighty-seven! This appeared to be an exorbitant number of hits to bring down one bomber, but a close examination of the wreckage revealed the fact that the fuselage was fairly heavily armoured. However, the fuel tanks in the wings aft of the engines were entirely unprotected and, had I known this and aimed at these tanks, I could no doubt have brought the bomber down with a very much smaller expenditure of ammunition. We all learned much from this expedition, and we now knew the Achilles' heel of the SB-2.

Returning to Koljola we happened to meet the stationmaster who told us of the events following my shooting down of the bomber, and the fate of its Russian crew. This comprised a major and two sub-lieutenants who promptly drew their sidearms when the Finnish villagers approached to take them prisoner. A pitched battle ensued in which two of the Russians died. The third member of the crew thereupon put a bullet through his own brain. I wondered what might have happened had I heeded my childish notion to land alongside the bomber and take the crew prisoner!

. . . . .

Most conversations in the mess now centred on the few battles in which we had participated before the snowstorm had brought a temporary lull in the air war. We compared each other's experiences and formulated tactics to be tested once missions were resumed. We now had a better idea of what we were up against, for our intelligence people had informed us that the Russians had concentrated some eight hundred aircraft for use against Finland. To oppose this armada we had barely a hundred operational machines of all types, and this strength included such antiquities as Ripons and Bulldogs which, from the performance viewpoint, were all but worthless. The misty, grey, snow-filled days followed monotonously in the wake of each other, our only consolation being the knowledge that the weather was also curbing Russian aerial activity. From the radio reports and newspaper accounts we followed assiduously the Finnish Army's heroic resistance in the face of overwhelmingly powerful Russian forces, yielding ground only yard by yard. The weather rendered us powerless to help our countrymen.

On December 18th the snow at last ceased to fall, and the freeze set in. Heavy layers of snow clouds still hung low in the sky, and the snow was now so deep that we had to replace the wheels of our fighters with skis. Shortly before 11.00 hours a coastal artillery battery at Saarenpää, near the fortress of Koivisto, reported that a Russian spotter aircraft above them was directing fire from warships. My flight was immediately detailed to undertake the destruction of the aircraft, and so Illu Juutilainen and I took off to perform the mission.

Owing to the low cloud base, we were forced to fly at an altitude of little more than three hundred feet, but within thirty minutes the Gulf came into view and we were soon flying over Saarenpää. There was no sign of any spotter aircraft. We searched the area thoroughly, but our quarry must have slipped into the clouds. We were just crossing the eastern section of the island when there was a sharp explosion in the belly of my Fokker! Involuntarily, I gave a startled shout as the aircraft seemed to sway, then right itself again! I quickly checked my instruments but nothing seemed amiss. Illu was still flying serenely alongside. I made a sharp turn and glanced behind me. A long thin stream of fuel was trailing behind my Fokker. My fuel tank had been punctured by ground fire.

Telling Illu to continue the search for the intruding Russian, and since there appeared to be no immediate danger of fire, I turned homewards, hoping to reach base before my fuel ran out. There were more than sixty miles to cover at low altitude over terrain totally unsuited for a forced landing, and I had no way of knowing how rapidly the fuel was pouring out of the tank! I flew with the knowledge that the D.XXI, with its fixed undercarriage, was hardly the most suitable aircraft in which to attempt an emergency landing, particularly in heavily wooded countryside, and few pilots who had made such an attempt had walked away from the scene.

I flew in a straight line at maximum cruising speed in an attempt to reduce the time factor as well as keep the loss of fuel through the hole in the tank to a minimum. I passed over the small communities of Johannes, Säiniö, and Tammisuu, one eye constantly on the clock. My ears were carefully attuned to the roar of the engine, wary of any change of note, and several times my heart jumped when I thought that I detected a falter. Thirteen minutes and I had passed the halfway point. I crossed the Viipuri-Antrea railway line and was just passing south of the Kavantsaari station when what I had been fearing happened. The Mercury engine faltered, coughed a couple of times, petered out and then picked up again. My fuel was all but gone. Already the Fokker was slowing down, and I had no alternative but to look for somewhere in which to make an emergency landing. Luckily, there were no thickly wooded areas directly ahead but, nevertheless, the terrain was anything but promising. I had no choice but a ploughed field traversed by drainage ditches and bordered by telephone lines and power cables.

By this time my altitude was a mere five hundred feet, and there was no time to search for a more hospitable landing area. The engine coughed once more and then died completely. I approached the field in a steep glide but my calculations were thrown out by some telephone lines which suddenly popped up in front, forcing me to jam down the nose of the Fokker to scrape beneath them. The skis hit the ground with a tremendous thwack, shaking every bone in my body, my straps cutting into my shoulders. The aircraft bounded a hundred feet into the air, then dropped back on to the skis with a second jarring crash. With the rudder I tried desperately to keep the fighter running in a roughly straight line, but bouncing and swaying over the partly snow-covered furrows and ditches, I had about as much control as I would have had over an unbroken horse.

Gradually, the aircraft began to slacken its erratic rush across the field. The rudder no longer had any effect, and the nose plunged into a deep drainage ditch. Everything was suddenly eerily still. The Fokker's wings straddled the ditch, its tail pointing skywards, and I hung from my safety belt about ten feet from the ground, afraid that any hasty move on my part would disturb the precarious balance of the aircraft which could well fall over on its back, pinning me beneath it. Hardly daring to breathe, I gingerly unsnapped my straps, carefully wriggling from the cockpit and dropping to the ground.

Shaking from my experience, I sat on my parachute pack on the edge of the drainage ditch and considered my predicament. Beside me, standing on her nose, was my sorely damaged D.XXI. It seemed hardly fitting that this faithful friend which had brought the Finnish Air Force its first victory should, temporarily at least, end her operational career in so undignified a fashion, with her proud nose in a ditch. To add insult to injury, the anti-aircraft bullet that had brought about her discomfiture was obviously not the product of some Russian factory tucked away behind the Urals but one hastily fired by the very forces that had requested our aid in removing the Russian spotting plane.

My "landing" had obviously been seen from a nearby house for, as I sat miserably smoking, two men began walking extremely stealthily towards me, both carrying shotguns. They had evidently not recognised the blue swastikas on my Fokker and, assuming that I was a Russian, were now bent on making me prisoner or despatching me to Hades. I realised that I had better make my nationality known to them before they started blasting away with their shotguns, and, hurriedly, I shouted, "Hyvää päivää". As soon as they heard me calling "good day" to them in their own tongue, they lowered their guns and hurried forward to offer their assistance. I took one last look at the Fokker. Although she would fly again some day, it was obvious that the aircraft would have to spend some time in the factory at Tampere. The airscrew was a total write-off, the port wingtip needed replacing, the undercarriage was badly damaged, and heaven knew what other damage she had suffered, so, with my 'chute slung over my shoulder, I accompanied my "escorts" to the nearest house. After telephoning the base to inform them of my mishap, I sat with my hosts drinking coffee and discussing the war until a car arrived to take me back to Immola.

. . . . .

The loss of my D.XXI was a serious blow for the third flight. We had already lost two D.XXIs and two pilots to the second flight which was operating from Suur-Merijoki. Both had been exceptionally fine combat pilots; Sub-Lieutenant Pekka Kokko, who was later to be killed in an accident during the "Continuation War", and Sergeant Lauri Nissinen who was to lose his life on June 17, 1944, when the wing of a falling aircraft struck his machine which was flying at a lower altitude. Now, with the loss of my aircraft, our strength was down to five fighters and six pilots.

The morning of December 20th dawned cloudless with the promise of excellent flying weather. At 09.00 hours my flight was assigned an interception mission over the Vuoksenranta-Antrea sector, and our five remaining Fokkers took-off with my deputy flight commander, Tatu Huhanantti, leading them. I did not have the heart to deprive someone of his personal aircraft so that I could accompany this sortie, so stayed behind at Immola, silently cursing that misdirected Finnish anti-aircraft bullet that had found its billet in my fuel tank. The boys were highly elated when they landed. It appeared that just as they arrived over the sector, they ran straight into an enemy bomber formation, dispersing it in a furious mêlée. They had chased the Russian bombers all over the sky, and several running battles had ensued, but when all five pilots had landed safely, I was delighted and proud to learn that they had raised our total by no less than five kills.

As we sat around steaming cups of strong coffee in the mess, I am sure that I felt as much excitement while listening to the retelling of their adventures as they had in experiencing them. However, I had noticed that young Sergeant Pentti Tilli displayed an ashen face when he clambered from his cockpit and still looked rather seedy. He was not the type of youngster to suffer from combat nerves, and on taxing him for the reason for his apparent discomfiture, he related the details of a singularly unpleasant experience.

It appeared that he had managed to get on the tail of one of the bombers and, after a short chase, had despatched his quarry with a few bursts. He noticed several aircraft in combat above and to port, but as he turned towards the battle he felt a terrific shock on his starboard wing, and the aircraft swerved violently. Tilli's eyes were hardly prepared for the horrible sight that met them. Less than three yards from his cockpit was the body of a crew member of one of the Russian bombers transfixed by the protruding barrel of one of the Fokker's wing guns! Undoubtedly the Russian had been killed instantaneously, but the contorted features of the Russian seemed to grimace at Tilli no matter how he attempted to dislodge the body, and control was extremely difficult with the Russian's parachute streaming back from the wing. Gradually the parachute disintegrated and, finally, the body dropped from the gun barrel, leaving only a large tear in the wing fabric to remind Tilli of his unwelcome passenger, but he told us that it would be many a long day before he would forget the face of that dead Russian.

The next day was again bright and clear, although the temperature had fallen to minus 20 degrees C. During the moonlit night an air-raid alert had sounded, but no enemy aircraft had found their way to our base. I borrowed another pilot's Fokker and led an interception sortie over Taipalejoki. We cruised at an altitude of ten thousand feet, and approaching the shores of Lake Ladoga, could see a large fire burning at Muolaa. We flew steadily on over Käkisalmi towards Taipale, and shortly afterwards spotted a formation of eight enemy bombers flying northwards at an altitude of about twenty thousand feet, white vapour trails streaming from the exhausts of each bomber. With engines turning at full revs we began climbing towards the Russians, but as we passed sixteen thousand feet the enemy formation made a full 180 degrees turn. For a moment this puzzled me, and then, glancing over my shoulder to ensure that the rest of the flight was keeping up, I saw that we too were leaving vapour trails.

These had evidently given the game away to the Russians who were now fleeing back over their own territory. Cursing the vapour trails, we continued to pursue the bombers for some minutes, but at the speed and altitude at which they were flying we had little hope of getting within firing range and, reluctantly, turned back without having accomplished our mission. At least we had the satisfaction of knowing that we had forced the Russians back over their own lines with their bombs still in their bomb bays. On the return flight, cruising above the shores of Lake Ladoga, near Käkisalmi, we once again encountered some of our old Bulldog fighters evidently sent up on the same mission as ourselves, though I could not help reflecting sadly on the chances of one of these ancient biplanes against a modern Russian SB-2.

During the final approach, I saw that our "breakfast truck" was awaiting us near the flight line, keeping our food from freezing in the bitterly cold weather. During spells of alert duty, when we were continually near our aircraft, hot meals were a rarity, sandwiches and vacuum flasks of coffee being brought to us on the flight line. The hours awaiting orders to take-off were spent marching up and down endeavouring to keep warm, and during the early afternoon one of the mechanics with particularly keen hearing picked up the sound of aero engines in the far distance. Immediately we were all listening intently and simultaneously scanning the sky in the direction of the sound. The roar grew steadily in volume until we picked out a formation of nine bombers approaching at an altitude of some six thousand feet.

There was no time to await orders and we were already climbing into the fighters. Within sixty seconds we were off the ground, but we were only at treetop level when I saw the bombs falling—luckily into the Immola Lake. Now began a

THE WEATHER WORSENS

long chase which, from the outset, offered few chances of success, for the enemy bombers were already steaming back towards their own territory, and our Fokkers had little speed advantage over an unladen SB-2. The Russians also enjoyed the added advantage of altitude, but although one or two of the first fighters off the ground managed to get in some long-range shots, these apparently had no effect. However, my deputy, Tatu, spotted one of the enemy bombers diving for lower altitudes to make his escape, and succeeded in catching the Russian to notch up his first kill. This meant that every member of my flight now had at least one kill to his credit.

. . . . .

The weather continued bitterly cold but bright, and the long night hours were moonlit—perfect for the enemy bombers. Air activity was quite lively on both sides, and early in the morning of December 23rd I received what was to me the very best of Christmas presents—a replacement Fokker! The aircraft, which carried the serial number FR-108, had been flown in to Immola from Tampere where it had been undergoing repairs following an accident, but I had no opportunity to inspect my new mount, take it up for a test hop, or even bore-sight its guns. At 09.30 hours the whole squadron was ordered into the air to cover the withdrawal of our forces on the Summa Front. Our task was to maintain air superiority over the area, and the full squadron of eighteen aircraft formed up over the Heinjoki in stepped echelon, the lowest step flying at seven thousand feet, this being my flight which had been designated the "strike element".

A thin veil of cloud hung over the front at about five thousand feet, and the formation dropped below this. I scanned the countryside in every direction, but it was hard to distinguish a moving aircraft against the dark forest background. Occasionally I saw vehicles moving along the roads and the muzzle flashes of artillery, but there was no sign of any Russian aerial activity until, at 10.15 hours, I saw a movement below and to port. It was an elderly Russian Polikarpov R-5 reconnaissance biplane flying on a northerly course.

I gave the order to attack and, peeling off in sections as

though on a perfectly executed demonstration, the flight tore down on the unsuspecting Russian machine. I began firing at a distance of a hundred yards, my tracers ripping savagely along the fuselage, and at fifty yards the R-5 exploded like a bursting hand grenade, burning fragments flashing past my Fokker, and the flaming engine twisting and turning, the airscrew still windmilling, to crash somewhere in the area of the Kämärä station. My second kill!

We formed up again and, thirty minutes later, my starboard wingman signalled that enemy aircraft were ahead. Almost simultaneously, I spotted three enemy bombers winging their way north over Muolaanjärvi. We closed with the trio and began our attack. Within a blink of an eyelid, a Fokker was fastened on the tail of each of the SB-2s, firing short bursts from close range. Inside two minutes, all three bombers were falling in flames. During this scrap, Tilli and I had become separated from the rest of the group and, just in time, I caught sight of ten stubby little I-16 fighter monoplanes bearing down on us. It is an old adage that the best form of defence is offence, and this is particularly true in aerial combat. We turned sharply to face the Russians, and I fired a short burst head on at the first I-16, banked vertically and was lined up with the second.

All four guns pumped a stream of bullets into the Russian fighter, and as it swept past I noted that a puff of grey smoke came from it and that it was swaying crazily as though the pilot was having difficulty in maintaining control, but I had no chance to follow his progress for I was now boxed in by tracers myself. I kicked my Fokker into a climbing turn, but one of the I-16s was still clinging to my tail, firing short bursts. I half-rolled into a vertical dive, pulling out just above the trees and, to my relief, found that I had shaken off my opponent. Unfortunately, I had also lost sight of the I-16 that I had been firing at and so could only consider it as a "probable". High above, the fourth flight was continuing the fight where Tilli and I had left off, but within minutes we had re-formed and were heading back to base to replenish our fuel and ammunition. We were soon once more over the Summa front, but no further enemy aircraft were encountered that day.

In the evening, we sat around in the "alert tent" in a jovial mood, swopping experiences of the day. Outside, our mechanics were busily patching our fighters, checking the guns and ensuring that the Fokkers would be ready for whatever the morrow brought. Myself, I was more than satisfied with my new mount. She had received her operational baptism without even having been check flown, and she had acquitted herself well.

. . . . .

On Christmas Eve we were breakfasting off sandwiches on a flat-bed truck when we received the following order: "The third flight will thwart any attempt by the enemy to reconnoitre the main road between Summa and Huumola between 13.00 and 14.00 hours. This overrules all other orders." Later, our six machines were criss-crossing backwards and forwards over the Summa–Huumola road, but we could see no sign of any movement below. Even the front line appeared strangely still, and so, without having had so much as a glimpse of an enemy aircraft, at 14.20 hours we arrived back at base and began preparations for our yuletide festivities.

By using co-operative manpower, we had succeeded in completing a fine new dugout to which all the "alert tent" equipment had been transferred, and to this we repaired, together with the ground personnel, for the first stage of our celebrations. Men on guard duties were relieved to join in the party, several of us taking over their duties by patrolling around the planes for two hours. I strolled around the Fokkers with Tatu, recalling memories of past Christmases and comparing them with this, which, unknown to us, was destined to be Tatu's last. Fortunately, neither of us had any premonition.

When the guards reappeared at 21.00 hours, we set off to the officers' mess for our dessert. Arriving at the mess I was promptly handed a Christmas present in the form of orders which read: "The third flight, reinforced by a section from the first flight, will be designated Osasto (Fighter Group) 'L'[1] and at first light tomorrow, December 25th, will proceed to Värtsilä airfield from where it will undertake support missions for General Paavo Talvela's Group and the Fourth

[1] The "L" indicating "Luukkanen", such independent fighter groups usually being designated by the first letter of their commander's surname.

Army for a period of two days. The main task of Osasto 'L' will be the prevention of any interruption of supply line, and attacks on supply dumps. All combat with superior enemy forces is to be strictly avoided. Further orders will be issued verbally."

4

TWO ENEMIES—WINTER AND RUSSIANS

At 07.00 hours on Christmas Day of 1939 the newly created Fighter Group "L" gathered for its first pre-flight briefing. Since midnight the ground staff had been busily gathering serving equipment and spares, and loading these aboard trucks which were to follow us to Värtsilä over some two hundred miles of snow-covered roads. Before our departure there were dozens of matters to be taken care of, and the minus 20 degrees C. temperature did not lighten the work load. Our Fokkers had been sitting through a long, cold night, and we had to crank the engines for a long time before they finally sprang into life, but at 09.00 hours precisely, all eight Mercuries were ticking over nicely and, after sweeping away the coating of newly fallen snow that covered the fighters, we took off in two-plane sections, forming up in impeccable style over the field before turning in the direction of Värtsilä.

The side windows of the cockpits could not be closed owing to the hoar frost that formed on the inside of the cockpit canopy, and we had to suffer the icy blast until the frost finally melted away, enabling us to enjoy the brightly sunlit and deceptively peaceful Christmas scene. Our course took us near to Sortavala, my home town, and I led the formation down low as a form of Christmas greeting. As we passed Sortavala, however, the weather began to deteriorate, so we had to continue our journey at low altitude and were soon ploughing through a driving snowstorm. Fortunately, I knew the area over which we were flying as well as the back of my hand, so there was little risk of getting lost, and, at 10.00 hours, we saw Värtsilä airfield through the murk.

After operating from Immola, the landing at Värtsilä came as something of a surprise. The field was covered by a layer of snow more than three feet in depth, and no sooner had the skis of our small but heavy fighters made contact than they buried themselves, bringing the Fokkers to an abrupt standstill. In order to taxi we found that we needed almost full power to keep the fighters moving. We finally reached the northern rim of the field, and I jumped from the wing to find myself waist deep in snow. The others waded across to me, and I instructed them to stay near their aircraft until I had reported to General Talvela. On my way to find the general I ran into Major Viherto, the Commanding Officer of TLeLv 16, the 16th Reconnaissance Squadron, who promptly offered me the loan of some of his mechanics until our own arrived from Immola. His squadron was normally based at Sortavala, and by this time possessed only two or three serviceable Blackburn Ripon IIs,[1] vintage biplanes that had long since deserved honourable retirement in some museum.

General Talvela welcomed me most effusively, obviously much relieved by the arrival of our fighters. I was soon to discover, however, that Värtsilä possessed no buildings and no telephone communications. What is more, there were no tents available. I comforted myself with the thought that the orders had said that we were to be based here for only two days, and we would obviously have to make the best of it. There were many preparations to make before we could consider ourselves operational and, despite the intense cold, we were soon perspiring from our exertions. We stuck a pole into the deep snow and rigged a field telephone, but it was impossible to erect any worthwhile shelters, and so we had to pass our "alert" periods beneath the bare, freezing sky, standing in the snowdrifts or sitting on the wings of our Fokkers. The snow, which had been falling almost continuously since our landing, finally stopped at 13.00 hours at the same time as we scrambled for our first interception, the two Fokkers from the first flight being despatched to the Tolvajärvi to take on a group of SB-2s.

---

[1] The Blackburn Ripon first appeared in 1926 with a 450-h.p. Napier Lion XI engine, this being followed in 1928 by the Ripon II with a 570-h.p. Lion XIA. The later variant, which was of mixed construction, entered production for the Royal Navy as the Ripon IIA and was adopted by the Finnish Air Force as the Ripon IIF. A manufacturing licence was acquired by the Finnish government, and the Government Aircraft Factory at Tampere produced twenty-six Ripon IIF aircraft between 1930 and 1934. These were subsequently used with wheels, floats and skis.

The Fokkers were flown by Topi Vuorimaa and Joppe Karhunen, and they succeeded in approaching the Russians unobserved, getting among the bombers before the enemy had realised that they no longer had the sky to themselves. The result was the prompt despatch of two of the SB-2s. Joppe, incidentally, was to suffer a never-to-be-forgotten experience a short while later when, returning to base in a swirling snowstorm, his aircraft was over-run by that of his wingman during the landing. The scimitar-like steel airscrew chewed up Joppe's D.XXI from the tail to a point just aft of the cockpit! Fortunately for Joppe, at this moment his wingman's Fokker swerved slightly so that the airscrew missed his head, crunching through the radio equipment on the starboard side of the cockpit before swerving back to chop into the aircraft once more just forward of Joppe's knees.

As the afternoon wore on we made several more interception scrambles, but it was soon obvious that our fighters needed the skilled attention of our mechanics who had still to reach Värtsilä. At dusk, after arranging for the aircraft to be guarded, we found our way to the Reconnaissance Squadron's quarters in the Värtsilä grammar school where we received a much-needed and well-earned meal, the first for more than twelve hours. The quarters were very modest by comparison with those at Immola, but there were hot stoves in abundance, so we had little to grumble about. At 21.00 hours my senior mechanic, Urpo Raunio, arrived at the school with the news that the ground personnel had completed their long and exhausting journey and, despite the darkness and cold, were already hard at work.

It was snowing heavily again the following day, forcing us to kick our heels on the ground, and we passed the day endeavouring to keep warm. That night I was awakened by a hammering on my door. I glanced at the luminous dial of my watch. It was 02.00 hours. The hammering continued and a muffled voice shouted something about a telephone. I struggled into my flying boots, threw a fur coat over my shoulders, and groped my way outside where the sky was a blaze of stars and the temperature was far lower than that of a refrigerator. I ran across the open schoolyard to the headquarters office where I discovered that the call was from Air Force Regimental Headquarters. I finally managed to decipher the brief message:

"Status Quo for one day." I assumed that this meant we had to stay at Värtsilä a third day!

The next morning we continued our open-air "alert" routine, and during the five hours of full daylight of the Finnish winter's day, we carried out eight interception sorties, but only one section actually made contact with the enemy. The two D.XXIs, flown by Vic and Napu Mannila, encountered several Polikarpov I-15 fighters over the Suojärvi-Tolvajärvi area, and found themselves in a brief but furious free-for-all with the nimble Russian fighters. Despite the vastly superior manœuvrability of the little biplanes, our pilots' sharper eyes and steadier hands brought two more kills to HLeLv 24.

With the first signs of the approach of evening, Illu Juutilainen and I took-off for a reconnaissance mission deep into enemy territory. Our task, undertaken at the request of the Fourth Army Headquarters, was to reconnoitre the Tulomajärvi area, and before taking-off we carefully emptied our pockets of all items that, in the event of our being forced down on the wrong side of the lines, might give the enemy some clue to the position of our base. We cruised at four thousand five hundred feet on a south-easterly course, Illu keeping his eyes peeled for enemy interceptors and I devoting all my attention to the ground below.

To starboard we could see vaguely the snow-covered, frozen Lake Ladoga, and as we flew closer to the frontline, the spotless white mantle of snow became increasingly pock-marked by fresh shell craters. Here and there among the forests could be seen bivouac fires, and motor vehicles and some horse-drawn carts were slowly crawling along a narrow, winding road. Occasionally, the more venturesome anti-aircraft battery would open up at us, its red-and-yellow 20-mm. tracers curving lazily up towards us before flashing furiously past, and I carefully noted the position of each flak unit that revealed itself on my map.

Further south, the terrain gradually opened out, and the map indicated that we were passing over Finland's former frontier, although the snow had obliterated all but the most prominent of landmarks. The scene appeared tranquil enough, with an occasional village or isolated house providing the highlights of an otherwise totally monotonous vista, but just before

The Fokker D.XXI was the most advanced fighter serving with the Finnish Air Force during the "Winter War". Seven were acquired direct from the Dutch manufacturer and a further thirty-five were built in 1939 by the State Aircraft Factory, HLeLv 24 being the first unit to equip with this type. The D.XXI was not devoid of temperament and, although its flying characteristics were normally excellent, abrupt, high-speed stalls with little or no warning could catch out the inexperienced. Landing characteristics also left something to be desired. (*Below*) One of HLeLv 24's D.XXIs after landing with a ski damaged by Russian fire during the "Winter War".

(Above) A Fokker D.XXI at Värtsilä early in 1940, the temperature being of the order of minus forty degrees centigrade! During the winter of 1939–40 Finland suffered some of the lowest temperatures ever recorded. Värtsilä possessed no buildings, and during their stay at this base, Fighter Group L's personnel had to live in tents, and all aircraft maintenance was undertaken in the open! *(Below)* The author in the cockpit of his Fokker D.XXI (FR-104) shortly after making his first kill on December 1, 1939—a Tupolev SB-2.

reaching Tulomajärvi, I spotted a sign of movement on the main road—a convoy of thirty trucks heading northward. The village of Tulomajärvi appeared peaceful, with thin columns of smoke rising from the chimneys of the little houses, but at that moment Illu flew alongside waggling the wings of his Fokker. I glanced around without seeing anything untoward, and then, turning my gaze downwards I immediately saw what had attracted Illu's attention—there were aircraft on the ice below!

Almost simultaneously, 40-mm. shells began exploding around us, our fighters pitching in their blast. I kicked my Fokker into a half-roll and, with Illu clinging tightly to my tail, screamed downwards. We flattened our dive, lining up with a row of six I-16 monoplanes. The first fighter appeared squarely in my sights and, with infinite satisfaction, I depressed the firing trigger and watched my tracers lick along the line of aircraft. I glanced over my shoulder in time to see Illu begin his strafing run and, without hanging around to evaluate the results of our attack, we turned for home, flak bursts filling the sky behind us.

The long homeward flight was made at treetop level, and the first stars had already appeared when we touched down at Värtsilä. I reported the results of our reconnaissance to the Army Command, and then dragged my stiff limbs over to the school building to thaw out. Thank goodness, I thought, we would be returning to Immola and its comforts the next day! A few hours later, though, this was to prove wishful thinking for, again at 02.00 hours punctually, I was once more aroused from my slumbers to take a telephone call. Again the message was the same: "Status quo for one day."

. . . . .

The weather appeared to be getting slightly milder, but day after day in the open air in these temperatures was becoming unendurable. I finally succeeded in locating a tent which we pitched on the fringe of the forest behind the fighters. At least we now had some sort of shelter, but we were facing other problems. Our supplies, originally intended for a two-day stay, were all but exhausted. We were short of compressed air for the guns and brakes, motor oil, ammunition links, and other items, and investigation revealed that the nearest supply of these was to be found at Joutseno, near Lappeenranta, a 435-mile round trip by road.

I telephoned the squadron to ascertain if they had any knowledge of our future instructions, but getting a negative reply I concluded that there was no alternative but to despatch a truck on the long and tedious journey to Joutseno, much of which had to be made over roads rendered near-impassable by the snow and ice. Even *with* the vitally necessary items that the truck would fetch I was not happy about the serviceability of our fighters. All engine maintenance and inspection had to be carried out at night, in sub-zero temperatures and in the open air with, of course, totally inadequate lighting. We were also short of skilled personnel to undertake this work. We could perhaps operate at full strength for a few days, but after that . . .

In an attempt to alleviate the servicing problem slightly, I decided to scour the area for an alternative base on one of the frozen lakes in the vicinity of Sortavala. Begging a lift in a car, I rode to Sortavala and was depressed to find the streets that I had known so well as a boy abandoned and silent. In view of the fact that the town was apparently deserted, I was greatly surprised to encounter my old headmaster. He evinced keen interest in our aerial activities and, after hearing my story, commented that I appeared to have made up somewhat for my lack of scholastic attainments under his tutelage. A careful examination of the surrounding lakes dispelled my hopes of being able to operate from one of them, for without exception I had found a layer of water between the hard ice and the top covering of snow.

As the car that had carried me into Sortavala had to stay in town until late that evening to pick up other personnel, I took the opportunity to visit my parents who lived only thirty minutes out of town. The car dropped me at my home, and I spent a cheerful hour swopping news and drinking coffee, gradually ridding myself of the acute depression that had descended upon me at the sight of wartime Sortavala. All too soon it was time to leave, and my parents accompanied me to the nearby railway station of Kuokkaniemi to catch the local train back to town.

The train eventually arrived, and I boarded this for my first and, fortunately, last railway journey of the "Winter War".

The train chugged along in fits and starts for five minutes, and then—air raid! The train ground to a halt and its passengers leaped from the compartments, stumbling through the snowdrifts into the nearby woods. Others clambered under the train for protection from the anticipated attack. Surprised by all this sudden activity, I stood alone on the steps of the carriage. It was bitterly cold and absolutely still. The minutes ticked by . . . fifteen . . . thirty. Eventually a whole hour had passed with still no sign of an air raid. Then, from the direction of Sortavala, we saw several bright flashes and, in the far distance, heard the steady drone of aero engines. A few more flashes and the raid was over! I felt highly relieved to transfer from this slow, unreliable and highly vulnerable means of transport at the Sortavala station to the waiting car, and one hour later I was back at Värtsilä.

.　　.　　.　　.　　.

New Year's Eve arrived without any sign of the transfer of Fighter Group "L" from Värtsilä. Four of us took-off that morning beneath a lowering sky which afforded us a ceiling of only some three hundred feet to patrol the Kollaanjoki-Syskyjärvi area. The wilderness below made a truly splendid scene. Snow-covered pines as far as the eye could see, and no sign of human habitation whatsoever. Quite suddenly a Russian I-16 appeared out of a cloud, its pilot obviously unaware of our proximity. Illu, flying on my starboard side, pounced on the unwary Russian like a hawk, aimed and fired, all in a matter of seconds. His first burst must have scored for the I-16 immediately fell away on one wing and ploughed into a snowdrift.

Once again we flew serenely on, but not for long for we, in turn, were bounced by six Russians. Tracers whipped around us, forcing immediate evasive action, and we were soon engaged in a wild dogfight, Finnish and Russian pilots alike firing quick bursts every time an opponent flashed fleetingly across their sights. One moment I had a Russian fighter squarely in my sights and the next I was frenziedly endeavouring to avoid their fire. Time and again the tables were turned in that whirling conflict, but the bursts were short as aiming was difficult under such conditions, the fight actually taking place right among the treetops. I fired from every conceivable angle, throwing my

Fokker around like a cork in a fast-moving stream. The Russians were like a swarm of angry hornets, and it was impossible to tell if any of them had suffered any damage. Then, as suddenly as they had arrived, the Russians disappeared into the cloud, and with relief we formed up again and headed for the safety of our own side of the lines.

It was during the return flight to Värtsilä that I began to ponder on the chances of survival for a pilot crash-landing in the wilderness below. These would be slim indeed were he to be injured in the landing, but if he had skis . . . Immediately after landing I put in a request for eight pairs of collapsible skis complete with light metal ski sticks. These could be stored in the fuselages of our Fokkers and, expert skiers as we all were, our chances of survival were certainly increased.

. . . . .

We were far too tired to celebrate the dawn of a new year, and so 1939 gave place to 1940 while we were soundly sleeping. Despite the intense cold—later I was to learn that it was one of the coldest winters ever recorded in Finland—New Year's Day started with a flurry of activity. As soon as it was light we were off on an interception sortie. One mission followed another throughout the day, and many air battles were fought. In fact, operations were so lively and continuous that it was difficult to ascertain the day's true score of kills. Later, however, we found the remains of three Russian bombers on our side of the line, these having been destroyed by Joppe Karhunen, Vic Pyötsiä, and Topi Vuorimaa.

By this time my worries concerning serviceability were mounting rapidly, for our Fokkers were showing serious signs of weariness from the continuous action under these appalling weather conditions. Owing to the strictly limited facilities offered by Värtsilä, battle damage could only receive temporary repair. One Fokker was awaiting an engine change, and another had had its airscrew punched full of holes when the gun synchronization mechanism malfunctioned. Our fighting strength was down to six machines, and I reported the state of affairs to Squadron Headquarters, requesting replacement aircraft from other flights to enable us to continue operating effectively. The Ladoga-Karelian air surveillance network was stretched extremely thinly. I had succeeded in keeping a patrol of four aircraft almost continuously in the air during the hours of daylight, but the serviceability situation was now deteriorating hourly!

For several days only two or three planes were serviceable, and it became obvious that unless replacement aircraft were soon forthcoming, Fighter Group "L" would cease to exist except on paper! The efforts of our personnel had been stretched to the limit. It was now the Twelfth Day of Christmas but, nevertheless, at 06.00 hours the callous alarm bell rang, and we stumbled from our quarters to be greeted by a blast of bitterly cold air. The fantastically low temperatures had already forced us to forgo our morning wash, and the thermometer was reading minus 42 degrees C. as we hurried across the field. Although we walked rapidly and were dressed in heavy flying furs and thick felt boots, our teeth were chattering like so many machine-guns by the time we reached our aircraft.

Muffled to the eyes, our mechanics were frantically working on the Fokkers, but the news that they gave us was anything but good—only two fighters were now serviceable! These were Tatu's and my own. With stiffened, half-frozen hands, I pulled myself on to the wing and into the cockpit. I ran an engine warm-up check—in this weather it took almost a full half-hour for the oil temperature and pressure gauges to reach their operating levels. The cockpit windows were iced over, and I recalled with ironic amusement our peacetime orders which forbade us flying in temperatures below minus 15 degrees C.! I checked the guns and then sat in the "alert tent" to await scramble orders. The telephone remained silent but, without any prior warning, seven Russian bombers appeared almost directly over the field. The formation was evidently not looking for us, however, for it disappeared to the north-east. Sergeant Tilli was in process of warming up Tatu's engine, so I ordered him up after the bombers and returned to the tent.

Fifteen minutes later the telephone rang and we were informed that an enemy formation over the Kitilä Bend had to be repelled. With my chute bumping against my legs, I ran out to my Fokker. A hurried engine check, and in little more than a minute I was making a climbing turn to starboard, heading south. After about ten minutes, the coating of ice melted from my windscreen, and by that time I had climbed to ten thousand feet, and Pitkäranta and Sortavala were both within my view. The radio chattered in my headphones, but I managed to make out a plain-language message informing me that fifteen enemy bombers were over Sortavala at ten thousand feet.

I changed course slightly to starboard, and within a couple of minutes the snow-buried town of Sortavala lay directly beneath me. Immediately, I saw a large formation of bombers about three thousand feet above. It was not possible to distinguish their national markings, but there could be no doubt that they were Russians. At full throttle I began climbing towards the bombers. As my Fokker closed with the formation I called up the base to inform them of the situation, swearing to myself over the fact that I was not leading a whole flight of fighters!

The port flank of the formation was now only a hundred yards away, and just a slight correction with the rudder pedals brought the nearest bomber swimming into my sights. I fired a long burst with all four guns, and the starboard engine and wing fuel tanks of the SB-2 erupted in flame, but now I found myself centred in the crossfire of three other SB-2s that had dropped back from the body of the formation to afford my victim some protection. This indicated rather better formation discipline and spirit than had characterized most Russian bomber formations that we had encountered at that time. I banked away sharply, noting with satisfaction that my SB-2 was completely engulfed by flames and had started its death plunge, turned towards the starboard side of the formation and lined my Fokker with another SB-2. I fired several short bursts into the bomber and oily smoke immediately streamed back from one of its engines, although there was no sign of fire. Three of the other SB-2s now had me boxed by crossfire. I kicked my rudder bar violently, tugging the stick across, and throwing my Fokker to starboard to escape the murderous hail of bullets, then pulled the nose up sharply, flicked over on my back and swept down on the rearmost bombers.

My second target was, by this time, tightly boxed in by his comrades, so I fired two long bursts into the bombers on the tail of the formation, but these had no apparent results, although the tracers seemed to be finding their targets, so, my ammunition exhausted, I broke off combat and allowed the fourteen survivors to head back to their base in a south-easterly direction, one of them trailing a long plume of black smoke.

I crossed the lines in a shallow dive, and within fifteen minutes my airscrew was raising snow flurries as I taxied across to where Tatu and my mechanic were waiting for me. In the excitement of my third kill all weariness and even the bitter cold were forgotten, and as we examined my Fokker we found three bullet holes in the fabric—it was a wonder that the D.XXI did not look like a sieve in view of the murderous crossfire thrown up by those bombers. My elation was doubled when I heard that Sergeant Tilli, who had taken off in Tatu's machine in pursuit of the bombers that had passed over the field, had succeeded in catching the formation and had destroyed one of the Russians.

That evening I received an invitation to visit the local pharmacist's home where I enjoyed a most effusive welcome. I told the pharmacist and his family of our operations from the field, and we all toasted the day's victories before, at 22.00 hours, I left to walk back to the field. The temperature was minus 40 degrees C. as I stumbled over the rutted, frozen snow. It was deathly quiet but, although there was not a glimmer of light to be seen in any direction, the skies were perfectly clear and ablaze with innumerable stars, and blinking like so many diamonds, they lit my way to my quarters in the school.

· · · · ·

The intense cold of early January which penetrated any protection gradually passed, and our operational strength improved. From the squadron we had received three replacement aircraft, while one of our damaged Fokkers had been repaired at Tampere, but the servicing situation had not changed. Our mechanics set about their prodigious task with amazing cheerfulness which even the persistently low temperatures had failed to quell. The conditions under which they worked were unbelievably harsh, and as during daylight hours the fighters were either in the air or on immediate standby, all servicing and repairs were effected at night with the aid of the stars, some flashlights and a few oil lanterns. An engine change demanded considerable skill, precision and care, usually being performed in a warm hangar under powerful lights, but at Värtsilä such conditions were mere memories of luxuries long since past. Watching these muffled figures working night after night in the bitter cold under the poor light cast by oil lamps, I began to wonder whose deeds demanded the greater courage, those of the pilot or of the mechanic? Kills are always credited to the pilot, but without such dedicated mechanics as these there could be no kills.

The skis that I had ordered for our use in the event of forced landings in far from friendly habitation duly arrived and were stowed aboard our fighters, and I began to consider other safety measures. Most of the enemy aircraft that we had encountered were well protected with armour plate, but our D.XXIs had no such luxuries, and aluminium sheet and fabric were poor protection against bullets or cannon shells.

Tatu and I discussed the problem many times and eventually decided to try out a little improvization. A considerable amount of armour plate had been stripped from the Russian aircraft that had fallen on our side of the lines, and forging some of this into some form of seat armour for our fighters did not appear to afford any insurmountable problems. All that was needed was the necessary permission to undertake this extemporization. I worked out the details and sent these to headquarters together with a request for immediate approval so that we could begin work. I soon discovered to my annoyance that I had been wasting my time, for my urgent letter received no response whatsoever. Admittedly, the increased weight would have knocked a little off our performance, but this would have been a small penalty to pay for the number of lives that I am sure this improvization would have saved, and the improved morale of our pilots enjoying some form of protection in that most dangerous "element-of-surprise" area behind their backs.

The lack of response to my letter did not encourage me to write further to headquarters and, in fact, apart from combat reports, this was to be the only written communication that I sent to headquarters throughout the "Winter War". We had no office staff assigned to us, and what letters had to be written were laboriously pounded out on the Reconnaissance Squadron's ancient typewriter.

In the middle of January the squadron's maintenance officer, Captain Jukka Schaumann, paid us a visit to acquaint himself with maintenance problems at Värtsilä. His visit was a welcome one as he brought with him a supply of American tobacco, a pleasant change indeed to the strong local tobacco that we had been smoking, and Vic's fetid old pipe emitted quite fragrant clouds of smoke for once, but the good captain could not make any suggestions as to how we could improve the lot of our mechanics.

About this time the temperature began to rise quite markedly, and we even experienced rain one day, although this quickly changed into an intense snowstorm so thick that it was not possible to see the end of one's outstretched arm. All flying activities on both sides were suspended for several days, and for a change from standing about and cursing the weather, we took the opportunity provided by this inactivity to visit Värtsilä's market square where captured enemy equipment had been gathered together for display.

News arrived that there was a plan afoot to transfer Fighter Group "L" from Värtsilä to the surface of the Suistamo Lake, some nineteen miles to the south-east. Operating from the ice of this lake we could cut four or five minutes from the flying time needed by our fighters to reach the front. I drove to the lake to discover for myself the local conditions, and I was not in too happy a frame of mind when I finally got back to Värtsilä. A layer of water between the snow and the firm ice covering the lake rendered take-offs and landings marginal in the extreme; servicing conditions would obviously be even more primitive than those we were enduring at Värtsilä, if such were possible, and, to make matters worse, the lake was within range of the heavy Russian artillery.

I reported my findings, stressing the difficulties that the lake would offer as a base, but, nevertheless, on January 19th orders came to transfer Fighter Group "L" to the Suistamo Lake. At 09.45 hours on that day we took-off to provide top cover for an unloading operation at the Leppäsyrjä railway station, proceeding directly from this assignment to the lake. I made the first landing on the snow-covered ice, and as my speed decreased, the skis of my Fokker broke through the snow crust, spraying water over the tail surfaces. The fighter slid across the lake, bumping over the uneven ice, and I eventually came to a standstill near the shore. By this time, the tail surfaces were locked solid with ice which we eventually had to melt away carefully with the aid of blow torches. The rest of our fighters landed in much the same fashion as my own, and we were still engaged in de-icing the tail surfaces when several Russian bombers appeared overhead. Only two of our fighters were ready to scramble in pursuit of the intruders.

Colonel Rekola, the Fourth Army's Air Commander, had been awaiting us at the lake and, fortunately, witnessed the difficulties that we encountered. It was immediately obvious to him that the extra few minutes that we would gain in flying from the Suistamo Lake would be far outweighed in value by the reduced serviceability that operation from the lake made inevitable, and we were promptly given permission to return to Värtsilä the next morning. We did not, therefore, even trouble to unload our servicing equipment from the trucks which had arrived in the meantime.

The next morning dawned bright and clear, although the temperature had again dropped. We took-off in two-plane sections at half-hourly intervals to patrol above the front line. A brief scuffle with some enemy fighters near Ruhtinamäki and we headed back towards Värtsilä. Near Suistamo the Russians had evidently attempted to cut the railway track, but although there were some forty large craters it appeared that not one bomb had actually hit the track. So much for Russian bombing accuracy.

After our twenty-four-hour jaunt to Suistamo Lake, we had little time to familiarize ourselves once again with the interior of our "alert tent" at Värtsilä, for that day the Russians were exceptionally lively. Throughout the day we were taking-off on interception missions, adding four bombers to our growing score, destroying two of them immediately over our base, but there was little rejoicing as, for the first time since our arrival at Värtsilä, the Grim Reaper had changed sides. Sergeant Pentii Teodor Tilli had been shot down over the Uomaa wilderness! The first casualty of Fighter Group "L", Tilli—who, at the age of four, had secretly climbed aboard his father's two-seater light plane to give his parent the greatest shock of his life when, in mid-air, he tapped his father on the back of his neck—had been leading a section of two Fokkers assigned to intercept a formation of five bombers returning from a raid into Central Finland. He had shot down one of the bombers

TWO ENEMIES—WINTER AND RUSSIANS 59

and was preparing to attack a second when he was bounced by six enemy fighters and shot down in flames.

. . . . .

The tremendously cold January of 1940 drew to a close, and our original two-day assignment at Värtsilä now entered its second month. To some extent we had become acclimatized to the harsh conditions at our "temporary" base, and I had to admit to myself that being responsible for the aerial protection of an area which included my home gave me much satisfaction. We flew patrols in the Matkaselkä-Kollaanjoki area, interception sorties over the Suistamo and Pitkäranta sectors, and reconnaissance flights to Lemetii and other points on the extensive front line.

During interception sorties we often had drawn to our attention forcibly the unpalatable fact that our fighters possessed an insufficient edge in speed over some of the faster Russian bombers, such as the Ilyushin DB-3. For instance, during a bombing attack on Sortavala on February 2nd, we were patrolling over the town at an altitude of thirteen thousand feet when we observed a large bomber formation at twenty thousand feet. We pursued the formation at full throttle as far as Pitkäranta without narrowing the gap in the least, and our impotent fury was increased when we flew through a batch of fluttering propaganda leaflets jettisoned by the departing bombers. Tatu enjoyed some success that day, however, as he pursued two enemy bombers for nearly two hundred and fifty miles, his patience finally being rewarded when he caught and destroyed one of the bombers near Pieksämäki, in Central Finland.

5

CATASTROPHE

As suddenly as we had been ordered to Värtsilä on Christmas Day, on February 4th we received instructions to leave for the Karelian Isthmus Front. Our six weeks at Värtsilä had taught us much. We had learned that fighters could continue to operate under conditions infinitely worse than would have grounded us in peacetime, and with facilities so limited that virtually every repair had to be a feat of improvization. We had acquired a tremendous respect for our servicing personnel whose tireless efforts alone had enabled us to maintain some operational strength throughout our stay. We now understood that kills were not individual victories but the victories of the members of the entire unit.

From the briskness with which the men packed our equipment, it was obvious that our transfer was extremely welcome. Within four hours the trucks were ready to start their journey. We bade farewell to our friends of the Reconnaissance Squadron who, during our sojourn at Värtsilä, had patiently awaited more modern equipment with which to carry out their tasks than their tired old Ripons, and in the early afternoon our Fokkers sped across the field for the last time, leaving a flurry of snow. We joined up in tight formation over the field, and then flew low over the little town where the news of our departure must have been common knowledge, for it seemed that the occupants of every house were standing in their yards or in the streets waving goodbye. We climbed steadily to eight thousand feet, spread out in search formation, and set a westerly course.

The blue sky and bright sunshine made our flight across Karelia a delight, and although we kept a wary eye open for any sign of intruders, apart from our own Fokkers the sky remained empty. As we traversed the continually changing, snow-shrouded terrain, we could see the ruins of the heavily bombed towns of Sortavala, Lahdenpohja, Elisenvaara, and

Hiitola, and in less than an hour, the familiar landscape of Vuoksenlaakso appeared before us. During our absence the rest of the squadron had been transferred to Joutseno, and we had been ordered to Ruokolahti, about twelve miles north of Immola. The sun was quite low on the horizon as we circled to land on the snow-covered ice of Lake Saimaa, selecting a long, narrow bay near the church.

So we began to familiarize ourselves with our new home. Our mess was located in the Pätilä estate, virtually on the lakeshore, our "alert" room being the estate's sauna. The sauna was ideally situated for this purpose as we could taxi our fighters alongside the building. We discovered that our Fokkers could now be serviced and repaired in the Lappeenranta workshops, a mere fifteen minutes' hop from the lake. In fact, we could not have wished for a more pleasant situation; a direct contrast to the hardships of Värtsilä.

Unfortunately, the weather now took a turn for the worse, and the forecasts predicted fog and snow. Therefore, I decided to make a three-day trip to Utti, Tampere, and Turku, and upon my return, Tatu, who had taken over command in my absence, reported that no operational sorties had been made owing to the adverse weather conditions. Soon after our arrival we received a welcome reinforcement in the shape of four Fokkers and their pilots from the squadron's second flight which had been operating from Turku, these bringing the total number of serviceable aircraft available to us to ten machines.

By mid-February the weather had again turned colder, the temperature sometimes falling as low as minus 32 degrees C., but the skies were clear and aerial activity began to increase. For nearly a week we carried out defensive patrols over the Hiitola-Viipuri railway junctions, and some interception missions were conducted as far south as the bloody Summa-Taipale sector. The landscape in the vicinity of the frontline had changed radically since we had last flown in these skies, and Taipale, continuously under enemy shellfire, looked like a ploughed field from the air. Enemy air activity was continuously increasing, and during one interception sortie on February 18th, we could, from an altitude of twenty-three thousand feet, see fires burning simultaneously in Viipuri, Tienhaara, Simola, Koivisto, Makslahti, Hamina, Käkisalmi, Antrea and Lapeenranta.

In fact, whatever the direction we could see columns of smoke ascending skywards. It formed a sobering picture!

We were now flying from early morning until late at night, from the treetops to altitudes above twenty thousand feet. Combat followed combat, but the enemy appeared inexhaustible, continually committing fresh formations to the battle. The situation in the air had indeed changed during the previous two months. Enemy fighters had begun to range over our bases, and so much had the Russians learned during the conflict that we seemed to be fighting an entirely different enemy. Of course, it was possible that our invaders had believed the conquest of little Finland to be so simple a task that they had committed only second-line units during the opening stages of the conflict.

We now found that our small-calibre machine-guns were ineffective from normal firing angles owing to the enemy's increasing use of armour plate, and we no longer continually sought combat—it found us! Russian numerical superiority was such that we frequently had to take violent evasive action to break off combat when our puny formations were beset by hordes of Russian fighters. We possessed no reserves of either fighters or pilots. Everything in our armoury had already been thrown into the struggle, and during each day every pilot logged between four and five hours in the air, most of this flying time at high altitudes and much in continuous combat. By the time darkness brought an end to the day's flying, we felt as though the last ounces of energy had been wrung from us, and could barely stagger to our bunks where we slept like the dead, not even the constant howling of the air-raid sirens disturbing us.

. . . . .

I had now been a lieutenant for five years, and received promotion to captain on February 15th. Fighter Group "L" continued to grow: eleven Gloster Gladiator II fighter biplanes newly arrived from England were flown in to Ruokolahti and, together with their pilots, were placed under my command. The Gladiator, which had been dubbed "Gelli" in Finnish service, was highly manœuvrable and possessed excellent flying characteristics, but it was hardly modern in concept and not very well suited for combat against modern Russian fighters, as the air war in which it participated was soon to reveal. The

Gladiator was too slow, lacked firepower, possessed no firewall or armour, and tended to burn easily, but needs must when the devil drives.

The pilots of the Gladiators included two Danish volunteers, Lieutenants Christensen and Kristensen, and the similarity of their names with their identical pronunciation presented an immediate problem, so we agreed to designate them "Kristensen" and "Kristensen-CH". The Danes proved to be excellent fellows who fitted in well with our group. First-rate pilots, extremely active and courageous if, perhaps, lacking something of the caution in combat that is only acquired with experience, they even proved themselves capable of withstanding the rigours of our sauna bath!

Our first joint operational sortie took place on February 25th, our mission being a fighting patrol over the Summa-Salmeneaida front. So accustomed had I become to leading a section of two or, at the most, four fighters, that it was quite overwhelming to find nine Fokkers and six Gladiators formating on me, and I found a feeling of security such as I had not experienced for many a long day.

As we approached the front, however, this sense of security burst like a bubble, for I could see at least a hundred Russian aircraft in the sky. I hardly knew which way to lead the formation, for wherever the eye strayed there were targets aplenty. Russian bombers, reconnaissance aircraft and fighters seemed to fill the sky over the front line. For the next thirty minutes we were engaged in a hectic battle. Tracers streaked backwards and forwards, and twisting, turning aircraft followed each other across the sky. While I was firing on a bomber, one of the Gladiators immediately above knocked down a reconnaissance aircraft which narrowly missed my Fokker, seemed to hang in the air, then fell away on one wing and plunged earthwards. From time to time an aircraft spiralled down, but until we broke off combat and formed up for the return flight, it was impossible to count heads. Two of our Gladiators were missing.

I was later to learn that one of the missing Gladiators, flown by Lieutenant Pentti Tevä, a particularly distinguished pre-war pilot, was hit by fire from the dorsal gun of the reconnaissance aircraft that he was attacking, his aircraft exploding at an altitude of less than seven hundred feet. The other Gladiator, flown by young Sergeant Sukanen, was hit several times after shooting down another reconnaissance aircraft, but succeeded in making a forced landing on our side of the front line, the pilot escaping uninjured.

By the time we landed back at base, the day's activities had died down, and we hurried to the mess for dinner. After the meal we gathered for the usual post-mortem that takes place in the pilots' mess of any air force after a particularly hectic battle. Kristensen's hands were executing graceful glides, dives and chandelles in his efforts to explain a particular incident when our discussion was abruptly cut short by the banshee-like wail of the air-raid siren.

Illu and I walked down to the shoreline where we could just discern the fighters' white-shrouded shapes against the black trees. The base was as silent as the grave, and as cold. A large, silvery orb of a moon had climbed high into the sky, its light projecting weird shadows from the surrounding trees. Two or three mechanics joined us, and we discussed the possibility of finding the raiders in this moonlit sky, concluding that it was worth while experimenting. Two of the fighters were readied for take-off, and just as we began our run across the lake, three flares blossomed in the sky to the south of us, hung seemingly motionless and then slowly descended. In no time at all we were flying over the flares which were illuminating our old base, the Immola airfield, and we could even see the bombs bursting beneath us, but no amount of peering revealed the Russian bombers and, as we had no means of judging the altitude of the enemy, we could only conclude that our attempted interception was abortive and return to base.

· · · · ·

Awakening in the darkness of the morning of February 28th, I had no idea that the day was to prove one of the most nerve-racking of my war. On the previous day there had been a strong southerly wind followed by drizzling rain and then some ground fog, and as I walked across to the "alert" room I saw a heavy layer of cloud, its base resting in the tops of the trees. "To-day," I thought to myself, "we will get a well-earned respite!" By dawn, however, the clouds had disappeared as though swept aside by a giant broom, and with first light we took-off on our

The antiquated Blackburn Ripon IIF was flown by TLeLv 16 which was operating out of Värtsilä during Fighter Group L's sojourn at that base. Seen above on skis and below, in "Continuation War" camouflage, on floats, the Ripon IIF had been built under licence by the State Aircraft Factory between 1930 and 1934 when twenty-six aircraft of this type were produced. Powered by a 570 h.p. Napier Lion XIA radial, the Ripon was truly a relic of a bygone age, and its crews needed tremendous courage to operate such machines which stood virtually no chance whatsoever when bounced by Russian fighters.

On February 15, 1940, Fighter Group L at Ruokolahti was reinforced by eleven Gloster Gladiator IIs newly arrived from England. The Gladiator (*above*), dubbed "Gelli" in Finnish service, enjoyed outstanding manoeuvrability but was too slow, lacked adequate fire-power and tended to burn easily. Thirty Gladiator IIs were sent to Finland, these serving primarily with HLeLv 26, but in the few weeks that they were operational they proved no match for the I-153 Tchaika and the I-16, and thirteen were lost. (*Left*) The author immediately after being promoted to the rank of captain, and (*below*) Fighter Group L at Värtsilä. The author is fifth from the right, Eino-Ilmari "Illu" Juutilainen is fifth from the left, and Joppe Karhunen and Tatu Huhanantti are third and seventh from the right respectively.

first interception sortie of the day. This sortie proved abortive, no enemy aircraft being encountered, but just as we approached our base, the Gladiators following in the wake of our Fokkers, a lone Russian fighter appeared like a wraith, shot down one of the Gladiators in flames, and was gone as suddenly as it had arrived.

After we had landed there was a lull until 12.00 hours when we received a message: "Twenty-one bombers heading towards Antrea from the south. Altitude, sixteen thousand five hundred feet." I immediately gave the order for the fighters to scramble for an attempted interception, and ran towards my Fokker. As I clambered on to the wing, my mechanic shouted to me that my starboard ski was loose and that he was in process of fixing it! It appeared that during an earlier mission a bullet had struck the ski, tearing off the sheet metal base which had come adrift during my last landing. Swearing under my breath, I jumped down and ran across to Tatu's aircraft which was already moving, shouting to him to take over for me.

Dejectedly, I watched the last of the fighters get airborne, and I was just turning back towards the "alert" room when, clearly above the roar of the departing engines, I heard the rattle of machine-gun fire. In the direction from which the sound came an unforgettable scene was being enacted. In a few seconds the sky had filled with twisting, cavorting aircraft. The control centre had evidently given us incorrect information regarding the course and strength of the enemy aircraft, or else they had been referring to an entirely different formation, for our fifteen Fokkers and Gladiators were just climbing out of the field when they found themselves the targets for thirty-six Russian fighters.

I was like a cat on hot bricks. I had never watched a dogfight from the ground and I didn't relish the experience. At that moment the squadron commander, Major Magnusson, arrived in his car, and together we watched the raging battle taking place above our heads. Even "Hell's Angels" had nothing on that breathtaking mêlée. Our D.XXIs, stubby I-16s, Gladiators and little I-153 Tchaika[1] biplanes were all engaged in whirling

---

[1] Tchaika (Gull) was the unofficial but widely used name given by the Russians to the I-153 owing to its gull-type upper wing. Although the name was not officially approved, to all Russian pilots Tchaika was synonymous with I-153, and this appellation was also used by the Finnish and German forces.

confusion. This was the first time, to my knowledge, that the Russians had used gaudily painted aircraft. All those that we had encountered previously had sported dirty, olive drab upper surfaces and pale blue-grey under surfaces, but some of these fighters were bedecked with large areas of red or yellow paint, perhaps indicating that they belonged to one of the crack Guards Fighter Brigades.

The fight raged from the treetops to about six thousand feet. Immelmanns, snap rolls, pull-ups, loops, spins, screaming dives, every combat manœuvre in the book was performed before our anxious eyes. No quarter was given and none asked, and every now and then an aircraft would plummet from the conflict and smash into the ground, smoke drifting above the trees from the pyre marking its last resting-place, and in almost every direction parachutes were blossoming. The fantastic cacophony of some fifty aero engines all screaming at full revs, and the intermittent, staccato chatter of perhaps four times as many machine-guns bears no description. It was such fantastic duels as this that must have been seen in the skies over France more than a score of years earlier. The battle lasted only some fifteen minutes, though it seemed an eternity to us viewing from the ground, and as the enemy withdrew, our fighters returned to base singly and in pairs.

The Reaper had certainly wielded that scythe without fear or favour in that quarter of an hour, for one Fokker and five Gladiators failed to return. Such a staggering loss could not have occurred had not our small force been caught in such disadvantageous circumstances. Lieutenants Tatu Huhanantti, Erkki Halme, and the Danish Lieutenant Kristensen gave their lives in the battle. The other Danish volunteer, Lieutenant Christensen, and Second Lieutenant Olavi Lilja had been saved by their parachutes, although the latter had suffered some injuries. Second Lieutenant Tolkki had a remarkable escape by falling into a snow bank when his fighter disintegrated just above the trees. Of all these losses, that of Tatu was the most bitter to me. An inspired pilot, an excellent marksman and possessing the largest score of kills of any pilot in the squadron, Tatu had been largely responsible for the early evaluation of the D.XXI, and I could never have wished for a more exemplary and fearless deputy flight leader. I learned that Tatu must have

CATASTROPHE

been badly wounded during the conflict but, during his last moments, succeeded in ramming one of his Russian opponents.

.   .   .   .   .

There was little time in which to lick our wounds or mourn our comrades for, during the afternoon, we had to carry out two defensive patrols, returning finally in the twilight of evening to a very subdued gathering in the mess. Even the news that the Russians had apparently lost eight of their number during the battle failed to raise the mantle of gloom. We had all begun to wonder how long we could hold out against the might of the Soviet Union. From the windows we could see an ominous glow over the Karelian "heel"; the dull crimson of raging fires. To the south and south-east vast columns of smoke were rising. Säiniä, Sommee, Laurimaki, Kauhala and many other towns were aflame. Some conflagrations were the result of enemy shelling and bombing, but most were a part of our scorched-earth policy as our troops were forced to retreat, step by step. Indeed, the red skies were fully in keeping with our mood.

Late that evening we received orders informing us that our fighters were to pull out from Lake Saimaa before daybreak the next morning, and fly to Lemi airfield, south-west of Ruokolahti. Although exhausted from the combat sorties undertaken during the day, it was past midnight before I fell into my bunk as I had first the sad task of gathering together the personal effects of my friend Tatu to send to his relatives. Although lacking the superstitions that seem commonplace among fighter pilots, I could not help feeling that Tatu had had some premonition of his fate on the previous day for, usually so cheerful and smiling, he had been singularly morose.

My eyes seemed to have only just closed when my orderly was shaking me violently, saying that it was already 04.00 hours. He told me that several times during the small hours enemy bombers had paid visits to our base, but we had suffered no casualties and our aircraft remained undamaged. I had been truly in the arms of Morpheus.

An hour before sunrise we were winging our way towards the new hideaway at Lemi. The Russians were evidently well aware of our operations from Lake Saimaa, and the base was obviously no longer tenable. We landed on the ice of the

Kivijärvi, and thus my two months of command drew to a close.

The need to be always ready to transfer from one base to another had certainly made us masters of mobility, and within a few hours of our arrival on the Kivijärvi we were ready to scramble. We had found quarters in the rear of the near-by post office building, and repairs to our fighters could be effected on the near-by Lemi airfield.

We had virtually forgotten what it was like to be at peace; to enjoy regular meals undisturbed; to have eight hours' continuous sleep. The world of comfortable living-rooms, fine linen and vacations had ceased to exist. Our world was the "alert" room, overheated and full of stale tobacco smoke, and the cockpit of the Fokker D.XXI, with its instruments, control column, throttle and gunsight. We had ceased to wonder when or how it would end, or what the future held. We were living from one hour to the next, and now that the war was entering its fourth month, we all felt as though we had aged at least ten years. Indeed, perhaps we had crammed a decade of experience into barely more than a dozen weeks. We had learned the true meanings of comradeship, fear and sorrow, but, most important, we now knew ourselves; our capabilities *and* our limitations.

6

THE END OF THE FIRST ROUND

The morning hours of March 4th passed quietly enough. Indeed, we had seen little action since our arrival on the ice of the Kivijärvi owing to the poor flying weather which had, apart from a few abortive patrols, kept us on the ground or, more accurately, the ice. The morning had dawned with a ten-tenths cloud cover, the ceiling being little more than six hundred feet, but although there seemed little likelihood of action, we remained ready for instant take-off, passing our time in the "alert" hut playing cards. Such periods of inactivity had become increasingly hard on the nerves. We were not an effusive lot. In fact, we would undoubtedly have been considered a quiet, moody bunch by those who didn't know us, and the war had, perhaps, made us a little introverted. It was only after dinner in the mess as we sat and smoked our pipes that conversation flowed easily and opinions were expressed freely. In the "alert" hut we always had one ear cocked for the telephone bell, the ring of which invariably meant a hurried take-off, and conversation was desultory.

As the odds had steadily mounted against us, I had begun to find myself thinking more of my diminishing chances of survival; of the possibility that the next flight might be my last. Uncertainty was predominant in all our minds, and at such times as these, when there was nothing to do but wait for the weather to clear, our nerves were strained to their limit and tempers became frayed. Once we were in our cockpits with the Mercury engines roaring in front of us, forebodings and tensions disappeared in a flash.

Shortly after 12.00 hours the telephone bell finally rang, jerking us from our lethargy. A coastal artillery battery had reported that the Russians were attempting a landing in force across the frozen gulf at Virolahti. Our task was to strafe the advancing columns. We had had little experience of ground strafing, and I was worried over the proximity of the Russian fighter base on Suursaari, so assigning four pilots to act as top cover, we took-off in sections and formed up at a thousand feet. The cloud had lifted somewhat and broken up a little, but now the weather began to deteriorate once more, and as we passed over Luumäki we were flying through intermittent snow showers. By the time we had reached Miehikkälä, the grey-black, snow-laden clouds had forced us down to treetop level, making flying both difficult and hazardous, but as we approached the shores of the Gulf, the cloud lifted once more, and we found it possible to climb back to an altitude of a thousand feet.

We did not have to search for our target for no sooner had we crossed the shoreline than we could see, about six miles away, a column of men and horses trudging across the ice. I judged that the column, which looked like a long black snake, was a reinforced battalion with about five hundred men, and from the air the troops appeared motionless. Suursaari was covered by fog, so we had little to fear from Russian fighters, and as we closed with our target our Fokkers lined up in single file for the strafing run. We could not have been offered a better target. The Russians were not even wearing white parkas as camouflage, and were sharply defined against the snow-covered ice. I gently eased the stick forward to commence my strafing run. I can only assume that the Russians had been expecting some form of air cover, for they made no attempt to break column at the noise of our engines. I levelled off at thirty feet, loosing a lethal stream of bullets into the column from all four guns.

Panic immediately overtook the Russians as I roared past their heads. Some dropped in their tracks, some endeavoured to hold the frightened horses, while others scattered in all directions, slipping and sliding on the ice. My undercarriage almost scraped their heads before I began my pull-up. As I banked round I could see the enormous effect of my strafing run, and now Illu was making his run followed closely by the others. I picked as my next target a four-barrel organ gun mounted on some sort of cart. Backwards and forwards we roamed across the remnants of the column, pouring some eight thousand rounds into the Russians from our thirty-two machine-guns.

THE END OF THE FIRST ROUND

That was one column of Russians that would certainly not attack Virolahti! When we landed a signal had been received from the artillery battery commander who had watched our "hunting expedition" stating that the column had lost half its men and all its vehicles, and that the survivors were making a forced-march back across the Gulf.

· · · · ·

That evening the sauna in the post office building was heated, and after a fine steam bath we rolled, in true Finnish style, naked in the snow, but our enjoyment was marred by the background of rumbling explosions coming from the direction of Luumäki-Viipuri.

The "Winter War" had now reached its most critical phase, with the Russians at the gates of Viipuri. The enemy had crossed the Viipuri Bay and were forcing their way on to the Vila Peninsula to threaten the key city of Viipuri from the west. The success of our initial ground-strafing foray had evidently not passed unnoticed at headquarters, for this was to remain our principal task until the end of the fighting.

The next morning I received orders to lead two flights on ground-strafing runs between Vilaniemi and Tuppura. I knew that this mission would not be the picnic of our initial strafing essay over the Gulf, for we would now have to fight our way through heavy flak and a strong fighter screen. The cloud base was a little above three thousand feet, so I decided to make our approach in the cloud and then let down for our attack in the south, behind the enemy, thus utilizing the element of surprise. It seemed unlikely that the Russians would anticipate an attack from that direction. I carefully briefed the fifteen pilots that were to accompany me, and we took-off, formed up in a loose, stepped formation, and set course for Johannes, directly south of Viipuri. We cruised steadily just above the cloud base, catching only occasional glimpses of the terrain below. A Russian formation passed beneath us, flying in the opposite direction. It formed a very tempting target, but we were not on an interception mission and had to allow them to pass unmolested.

The factory chimneys of Johannes showed briefly through a break in the cloud and, for the first time, I broke radio silence to order the formation out of the cloud. Approaching from behind them, the Russian anti-aircraft gunners assumed that we were friendly as I had hoped, and we flew steadily until I banked to port and entered a dive to begin my strafing run. There was certainly no shortage of targets, for the Tuppura-Vilaniemi area was teeming with columns of men, trucks, guns and armoured vehicles. Over Uuraa I could see a formation of I-16 fighters spiralling lazily, and a similar formation was to be seen over Ristiniemi, on our other side, but neither seemed to have spotted us. We had to hit hard and quickly, and then climb back into the cloud to avoid interception.

The distance to our first target was less than a half-mile when the air around us became alive with flak bursts, our aircraft bouncing around in the turbulence of their blast. These puff-balls of black, grey and white were obviously going to reveal our position to the patrolling Russian fighters, but we were quickly through the barrage of bursting shells, and streams of bullets from my quartet of guns were scything through a column of marching men which immediately broke up, the troops running helter-skelter in all directions. I then lined up with a pair of tanks, but my light machine-guns did no apparent damage, the bullets ricochetting from their armoured skins. Banking around at the end of my run, I glanced over my shoulder and noted that the other fifteen Fokkers were following in similar fashion.

Hugging the contours of the ground, we flew westward, then turned sharply north, just in case enemy fighters were chasing us. We did not want to reveal the whereabouts of our base. On landing, I discovered that we had lost one of our number, and later learned that a Russian fighter had managed to get on to the tail of the Fokker, the pilot, Sergeant Fräntilä, receiving a bullet in the chest. However, despite the severity of his wound and loss of blood, Fräntilä had succeeded in landing his fighter in "No Man's Land" on the ice near Vilaniemi, had crawled from his cockpit into the nearby woods, and been found by a Finnish patrol which quickly carried him to the nearest casualty station. Unfortunately, it was impossible to retrieve his Fokker which had to be destroyed.

For a week we undertook similar strafing sorties, averaging two missions per day, but these became increasingly hazardous

THE END OF THE FIRST ROUND

as the weather improved. Frequently there was little cloud to cover our approach or protect our retreat, and ever stronger fighter forces were covering the Russian hordes advancing over the ice. After each mission, shrapnel and bullet holes could be found in our planes, and every pilot wondered even more how much longer his luck could last out. These strafing sorties were undoubtedly the toughest missions we had been assigned, and we feared them. It would be naïve to deny this, but we were not frightened. Fear and fright are very different emotions. Fear breeds slowly and grows particularly during periods of helpless inactivity. It is contagious but it can be controlled. Fright is a sudden emotion; unpredictable and rendering clear-thinking impossible. There are several types of fear, and their effects differ from pilot to pilot. One type of fear blossoms gradually and paralyses, the pilot becoming panicky. Another type of fear is suppressed, although always present, stimulating courage, eliminating excitement and resulting in a calmness vital in a combat pilot if he is to survive. Fear is a natural emotion and not one to be ashamed of, and although none of us would have spoken of it, we were all experiencing fear. For some, the conquering of fear once airborne was easy; for others it was more difficult. But the combat pilot who was not afraid was already shaking hands with the Grim Reaper. In the heat of action fear seemed to evaporate; it rarely occurred to one that those tracers snaking past the windscreen betrayed a stream of bullets with lethal capabilities. Once tension was relaxed and the flight was over, then fear returned to stand like a shadow at one's shoulder.

. . . . .

In the early grey dawn of March 10th two enemy fighters flew low over our secret base at Lemi. We were not sure if their pilots had spotted our aircraft hidden among the birches along the shores of the frozen lake, but, to be on the safe side, for the following two days we operated from a frozen bay north of Lemi, a part of the Saimaa waters, near the village of Ristiina. At night, however, we returned to our quarters in Lemi.

On the evening of the 12th Vic, Illu and I loaded the parachutes of the entire flight on to a truck and took them to Immola for repacking. In peacetime the 'chutes had been repacked at least once every month, but now they had lain in various corners or outside in the frosty air without any attention for nearly four months. We strung them up on lines to dry out, spent a few hours in the mess, and then, during the early morning hours, repacked the 'chutes. We were just in process of loading them aboard the truck for the return journey to Lemi when somebody ran past shouting something about peace.

We hurried back to the mess and were just in time to hear the radio announcer say, "Today, March 13th, hostilities between Finland and the Soviet Union terminate. The cease-fire will be effective from 11.00 hours." Some references were made to the ceding of certain territory, particularly in Karelia where I was born, and other drastic conditions as being a part of the armistice terms, but we simply could not take it all in. We were stunned. We knew that we had been facing impossible odds; that our troops had been tenaciously clinging on, but an armistice on Russian terms!

We hardly noticed the flags flying at half-mast as we drove back to Lemi, lost in our thoughts. A perceptible cloud of gloom hung over the base. Even the fighters wrapped in their white covers had a mournful air. The men sat around with little to say, and all was strangely quiet now that the rumbling of the guns had ceased. What an anti-climax to these months of hectic activity.

It was a few days before we returned to reality. The combined efforts of the Finnish forces had ended. They had not suffered defeat but they could no longer continue to sustain themselves in the face of the immense numbers of the Russian forces. The armistice terms were harsh, but perhaps we had fought only the first round. The whole of Europe would soon be aflame, and who knew what that year or the year after might bring. Our fighters and their pilots had not been found wanting in battle. Their task had not been easy for, numerically, they had been outnumbered ten to one and, qualitatively, had frequently been opposed by superior machines. They had also been confronted by a second adversary—the weather. The winter had been one of the coldest ever recorded in Finland, and for days at a time the thermometer had remained in the vicinity of minus 40 degrees C.

THE END OF THE FIRST ROUND

The air war had changed radically during the conflict. For the first six weeks of the fighting our losses had been small. Russian intrusions over Finnish territory had been timid, and their flying personnel had evidently enjoyed only the lowest of training standards. Despite the strong defensive crossfire that could be put up by their bomber formations, they would often turn tail at the sight of two or three of our interceptors, using their superior speed to elude us. It was patently obvious that the Russians were flying by orders in which courage and audacity played no part. We were fighting over our homeland, and our fighting spirit came from the depths of our souls.

As the weeks had passed we had begun to realise that our opponents were becoming acclimatised. Their fighting ability was improving, and the addition of large fighter formations to their strength seemed to boost their morale and improve their fighting spirit. While we had relatively puny fighter forces from the outset which, without hope of replacements, dwindled with each passing day, Russian fighter strength increased by leaps and bounds. The only replacement fighters that we had succeeded in obtaining had been Gladiator II biplanes, which were not even able to compete with our own Fokker D.XXIs, themselves hardly the last word in fighter potency. Fiat G.50 fighters purchased in Italy had not reached us in time. But we surviving fighter pilots had learned infinitely more about aerial combat in those one hundred and five days of fighting than could ever have been learned in a decade of peacetime training. War is the best advanced training school for the combat pilot, and nothing can simulate it.

Nothing that I had experienced or witnessed during the fighting, however, moved me so deeply as the scenes along the roads from Karelia after that fateful March 13th. One-eighth of Finland's population had lost their homes, and were now trudging away from the areas ceded to the Soviet Union. The movable possessions of the refugees were on their backs or in hand- or horse-drawn carts. The men, both young and old, walked with their cattle, and the mothers, their young children, the aged and the sick, rode atop of the piled carts. These Karelians who were now forced to leave the homes of many generations to make a new start in other parts of Finland had strong faces, furrowed by years of toiling in the Ladoga winds in all weathers, and they displayed no outward signs of grief. Some appeared stunned by the tragic sequence of events that had deprived them of their homes, farms and villages, and others seemed puzzled, but their faces were brave and unconquerable; the faces of people who would rather starve than live under the rule of foreigners who had usurped their heritage.

7

LULL BETWEEN STORMS

Within a week of the cessation of hostilities, we flew our fighters off the ice of the Kivijärvi for the last time and, dipping our wings in salute to the little community of Lemi, turned northwards towards an airfield at Joroinen. Now began a tedious period of waiting upon the Army Headquarters to decide where our squadron was to be based. Our much-patched and war-weary Fokker D.XXIs could at last receive the thorough overhaul they had needed for so long, and their pilots, who had spent more hours in the air during the previous few months than they normally spent in more than a couple of years of peacetime flying, were happy to deliver their mounts into the hands of the ground staff for this well-deserved rest.

The icy grip of that most severe of winters began to lessen soon after our arrival at Joroinen, and that indescribable air of spring peculiar to northern latitudes sent the blood tingling through our veins, dispelling the numbness and lethargy that had followed the acceptance of Russian surrender terms. I took sandwiches and spent much time ski-ing over the frozen surface of a near-by lake. The sun rose fairly high by noon, and the immense snow banks sparkled like mounds of jewels in its rays. From time to time, I found a spot among the pines sheltered from the brisk wind, and soon had the beginnings of a sun tan, but this idyll was to be short-lived. After ten days I received orders to proceed to southern Sweden to begin the task of ferrying home new Brewster B-239 fighters which had arrived somewhat belatedly from America.

Vic Pyötsiä and I took the car to Lahti from where we could catch the express to Helsinki. It was now March 31st, and we both looked forward to our trip with pleasurable anticipation. We clambered aboard the Aero O/Y airliner at 15.00 hours, and two hours after taking-off from Malmi Airport we found ourselves approaching Bromma, having thoroughly enjoyed this strange experience of flying without continuously watching the flickering needles of a dozen instruments or anxiously peering around the sky for the Russian that might be warily stalking one.

From Bromma Airport we hurried into Stockholm, our intention being to continue our journey southward that same evening. We discovered that our train for Gothenburg did not leave until 23.00 hours, so, having purchased our tickets and deposited our flying-kit at the left-luggage office, we had several hours to spend in sight-seeing. After the strict blackout that had been observed in Finland, the lights of Stockholm were dazzling! Both Vic and I wandered along with our eyes opened as widely as those of little boys seeing their first Christmas tree. But an even greater contrast with war-torn Finland was provided by the citizens of Stockholm. Travelling across country to Helsinki, I had observed the sombre mien of the average Finn, still stunned by the armistice terms, and the wartime attire of most Finnish women, with their long, woollen trousers and heavy footwear, but here, in the Kungsgatan, the people were light-hearted and well-dressed. In fact, their mood was so infectious that we decided to have dinner at a large and fashionable restaurant. Vic and I were treated very well indeed, for the "David and Goliath" struggle against Russia had placed Finns in high esteem in the Swedish capital, and all too soon we had to leave to catch our train at the Union Station.

Our fellow-passengers watched us with undisguised curiosity, and the fact that Finns were aboard must have travelled the length of the train very quickly indeed for we were soon visited by the conductor's wife who spoke fluent Finnish and proved to be a native of Jällivaara. Our train reached Gothenburg early in the morning, and after a further spell of sight-seeing, we joined another train which carried us to our final destination, Tröllhättan, where we found accommodation in the City Hotel.

· · · · ·

Early next morning we walked to the near-by airfield in the clear, spring air, still cool from the night's frost. This far south the snow had already disappeared, and the only remaining vestiges of winter were a few small frozen puddles. The single-seat Brewster B-239 fighters that we were about to collect had been relinquished by the U.S. Navy, shipped to Sweden and assembled at Tröllhättan by Norwegian mechanics working under the directions of the Brewster company's representative, Ray Matthews, test pilot R. A. Winston, the well-known Finnish aviator, Wäinö Bremer, and his engineer, Berger. We reached the airfield and at last, in front of us, was a modern fighter which, although born about the same time as the Fokker, had all the contemporary developments that our old D.XXIs lacked, such as a retractable undercarriage and a controllable-pitch airscrew. A barrel-like mid-wing monoplane of all-metal construction with a flush-riveted metal stressed skin, the Brewster had hydraulically-operated split flaps, and its performance offered a substantial improvement over that of our Fokkers. I climbed into the cockpit and the purpose and function of each of the switches and levers were explained to me. After carefully familiarizing myself with the arrangement of the instruments, I took-off for a half-hour check flight.

One cannot become fully acquainted with a new aircraft during such a short indoctrination flight, especially when one is flying over unfamiliar terrain and must keep one eye on the airfield which tended to blend with its surroundings. In fact, I could do little more than check that all instruments and controls were functioning normally and, after this brief hop, had only the haziest idea of the fighter's flying characteristics. But the Brewsters had to be ferried back to Finland as quickly as possible before the thaw set in. We had now been joined by two other ferry pilots, and I decided that after they had made their check flights and before my courage failed me we would start the long return flight that same day!

The B-239 fighter that I elected to fly bore the Finnish serial number BW-375, and this machine was to become my personal aircraft for more than two years, carrying me safely over some sixty-two thousand miles. Our four Brewsters took-off from Tröllhättan shortly after midday, the first leg of our journey being the three hundred and ten plus miles to Stockholm where we planned to spend the night. Flying conditions were ideal, and we now had an excellent opportunity to acquaint ourselves with the peculiarities of the new machine.

Our course offered us a continuously superb panorama of southern Sweden, with its innumerable lakes and connecting rivers, and although we were not very conversant with the country over which we were flying and had few charts, there was little chance of losing ourselves as visibility was outstanding, and there were several excellent check points, such as Sweden's largest lakes, Vännern and Vettern. Cheerful dance music picked up over the plane's radio accompanied the deep-throated, steady drone of the Brewster's Wright Cyclone engine, and in slightly more than an hour we were over the waters of Mälar, and could see the smoke haze hanging over Stockholm.

Our four Brewsters circled Bromma once and were cleared for landing. The wind was coming from an unfavourable direction, forcing us to use the number eight runway—the worst offered by the airfield. With my cockpit canopy pushed back, I began my let down, and immediately my fighter's wheels touched the sloping asphalt runway the aircraft tried to ground loop. I used each toe brake alternately to keep the Brewster straight, my progress down the runway accompanied by awful screeching noises as the tortured tyres skidded on the hard surface, but finally I managed to bring the aircraft to a standstill. The second and third Brewsters made identical landings to mine, but the fourth got into trouble when the pilot overcorrected in his attempt to keep the aircraft straight on the runway, the starboard wingtip brushing the ground. Fortunately the damage was slight, and we tied the planes down and threw covers over them for the night.

Within the hour we were in the heart of Stockholm, but a chance meeting with one of Aero O/Y's pilots dampened our spirits, for he told us that the thaw had already started at Malmi, our destination of the morrow. The next morning I received instructions from our Air Force representative in Stockholm to leave immediately for Finland, despite the poor conditions at Malmi Airport, our hasty departure being necessitated by the imminent arrival at Bromma of a Russian airliner! It would have been somewhat embarrassing for our Swedish friends had a quartet of Finnish fighters been on hand to greet Ivan when he landed. We therefore hurriedly refuelled, settled our landing fees and, by noon, were already winging our way towards Finland. The weather was clear, and cruising at an altitude of six thousand five hundred feet, we were over Helsinki within an hour and a half, and luck was

Forty-four Brewster B-239 fighters were ferried to Finland in the spring of 1940, and (*at foot of page*) one is shown shortly after its arrival, experimentally fitted with skis. (*Above*) Ferry pilots at Trollhättan, April 1940. Left to right: Vic Pyötsiä, the author, Yrjö Turkka, Joppe Karhunen, and Jorma Sarvanto. In the background, to the left is Ray Matthews of the Brewster Aeronautical Corporation.

The Aero O Y Junkers Ju 52 3m airliner "Kaleva" (*above, right*) which was deliberately shot down by two Russian SB-2 bombers just off the Estonian coastline on June 14, 1940, while on the regular Tallinn-Helsinki route. Seven passengers and two crew members perished.

Immediately before hostilities between Russian and Finnish forces were resumed, the Brewster B-239 fighters (*above*) were camouflaged with an irregular pattern of black and forest green over the upper surfaces. The rudders were painted in various colours, a yellow band was painted around the rear fuselage, the undersurfaces of the wingtips were painted yellow, and, later, the engine cowlings were also painted yellow. (*Left*) Nils "Hard Luck" Katajainen who had more lives than a cat and survived the war with thirty-six kills. This photograph was taken at Lunkula in 1941. (*Below*) The "Lynx" emblem of HLeLv 24. This was painted in black on a white background.

LULL BETWEEN STORMS

indeed with us for we all landed safely on the slush-covered field.

. . . . .

Our stay in the capital was short, for the next morning we were again at Malmi, climbing aboard one of Aero O/Y's Junkers Ju 52/3M tri-motors named *Kaleva* for the return trip to Stockholm and another batch of Brewster fighters. Within twenty-four hours of our arrival at Tröllhättan, on April 9th, 1940, the radio informed us that German forces had invaded Norway. Early in the morning of the 10th, I took-off in one of the Brewsters for a look around since we were very close to the border. I climbed to thirteen thousand feet, and the Skagerrak on the Atlantic side was directly below, to the south-west was Denmark and to the north-west was Norway. I could pick out several vessels of a convoy headed north. There was also a formation of about twenty lumbering transport aircraft escorted by two large groups of fighters—probably more of the German invasion forces. I dared not venture across the Swedish border, however, and had to witness these historic events from a distance.

Shortly after landing back at Tröllhättan, a Swedish bomber squadron arrived at the field. The Swedes had evidently begun some sort of mobilization preparations. We combat veterans had difficulty in hiding our amusement. The personnel of the squadron were all impeccably dressed in parade-ground uniforms, white collars, brightly shining boots, et cetera. Their aircraft were not dispersed but left standing in the middle of the field, where they would have been sitting ducks in the event of a surprise attack, and their crews headed en masse for the town!

A solitary guard leaned on his rifle by a hangar and promptly accepted the cigarette which we proffered despite the large "No Smoking" sign immediately above him. We reflected that there are times when a small "stimulating" war can be of value. Our amusement soon turned to wrath, however, when the Swedes politely informed us that, since they now considered themselves to be on a wartime footing, they were impounding our remaining fighters.

Our Norwegian mechanics had already left to join in the

defence of their homeland, but, in any case, their task was almost complete, and what additional assembly work was required by the Brewsters could be undertaken by ourselves and the Brewster representatives. Our protests at the Swedes' high-handed action had been to no avail, but we constantly badgered the authorities in Stockholm by telephone throughout the day, meanwhile completing the work that still remained to be done on our fighters. Finally, on the 11th, the Swedes remarked, jocularly, "O.K. You can take-off if you can get the fuel!"

They knew full well that all fuel supplies at the airfield were carefully guarded. There and then we decided that he who laughed last. ... We telephoned the Shell distributor in Tröllhättan and arranged for him to send his tankers to the airfield while the Swedish personnel were lunching in their mess. Unaware of the situation, he complied with our wishes, and we quickly and quietly filled the tanks of the Brewsters. Later in the afternoon, after duty hours, we cranked up all four fighters simultaneously, shattering the stillness of the airfield with the powerful throaty bass of our four Cyclones. Without delaying for a complete warm-up, we took-off directly from the concrete apron, circled the field once, pretending not to understand the frantic signals of the Swedes who were now milling around below us, and we were on our way!

After flying steadily for thirty minutes, a heavy layer of cloud forced us down to a lower altitude. Visibility steadily worsened as the sky blackened, but suddenly I spotted a shaft of sunlight. I decided to climb above the cloud layer, and accompanied by my wingman, Flight-Master Turkka,[1] emerged from the clouds at nine thousand feet. Joppe Karhunen, the pilot leading the other section, had evidently misunderstood my intentions for he continued flying at the lower altitude. Beneath us now stretched an unbroken carpet of cloud, its surface as smooth as a layer of fresh snow. We flew strictly by compass readings

---

[1] Flight-Master Yrjö O. Turkka was later nicknamed "Pappa" as a result of an R/T conversation in June 1941. Sergeant Hemmi Lampi's Brewster was cornered by three Tchaikas, and Turkka, hurrying to his aid, called over the R/T, "Don't worry, boy ... Pappa's coming." The RCA radio equipment installed in the Brewster was exceptionally efficient, and all heard Turkka who, from that moment, was known as Pappa. Flight-Master, or Lentomestari, was the equivalent rank in the Finnish Air Force to that of Warrant Officer.

and the clock, and after nearly two hours had passed I estimated that we should be just about over Stockholm.

There was still no sign of a break in the clouds, and it was obvious that we would now have to go down through them. Turkka came in closer so that we would not lose contact with each other. The cloud layer soon proved to be thicker than I had anticipated, and we were down to less than a thousand feet when the ground hazily swam into view. The terrain was totally unfamiliar, although I knew that we were still over Sweden. The populated areas, lakes and rivers that swept past beneath us offered no clue, and owing to the fuel situation we could not afford to spend much time getting our bearings. More by instinct than judgment, I set a southerly course. Five minutes later we were over Stockholm! Before reaching the heart of the city, we set an easterly course, and just at that moment a couple of anti-aircraft shells burst some distance behind us; probably the Swedish way of bidding us farewell after our sly take-off from Tröllhättan.

· · · · ·

The coastline of Sweden and the outlying islands slipped beneath us, giving place to the turbulent waters of the Pohjanlahti, or Gulf of Bothnia, and after passing the islands of Ahvenanmaa, and then Turku, we were once again flying over our homeland, finally reaching Malmi at exactly the same time as Joppe's section. It could not have been timed more effectively had a rendezvous been arranged. The next day, together with Turkka, I flew back to Stockholm aboard ABA-Swedish Air Lines' airliner *Vikingaland* to collect two more Brewsters that had already been ferried from Tröllhättan to the Swedish capital. The following evening we were once more back in Helsinki, and the task of flying the fighters back to Finland was complete. The ferrying job had proved invigorating after our arduous weeks of fighting under the severest winter conditions, and I had found it absorbingly interesting. Two weeks had passed as though on wings. Indeed, a very large proportion of them *had* been spent on wings.

During my absence the squadron had relinquished its faithful old Fokkers and had been transferred to Helsinki where it was now to form a part of the capital's defences. In transferring the

D.XXIs from Joroinen to Tampere, where they were to be virtually rebuilt, an unfortunate accident had occurred, two of the fighters colliding in mid-air, resulting in the deaths of two of the squadron's most promising second lieutenants, Heikki Ilveskorpi and Eero Savonen, each of whom had survived the "Winter War" as a member of my flight.

The arrival of the Brewster B-239s gave a new zest to squadron life, and we set about discovering the capabilities of the American fighter under all the various combat situations that we had experienced during the fighting. We had to make ourselves thoroughly conversant with the nine-cylinder radial air-cooled Wright Cyclone R-1820-G5 engine which gave 1,000 h.p. for take-off and 850 h.p. at altitude, with the 0·5-in. calibre Colt-Browning machine-guns, the undercarriage retraction mechanism, the controllable-pitch airscrew, the radio and the many other features of the plane.

On June 14th, 1940, the Aero O/Y airliner on the regular Tallinn-Helsinki route was shot down by Russian bombers, and we were immediately ordered to take-off on an "alert"-type mission over the area in which the incident had taken place. However, the Gulf had already claimed its victims by the time we arrived on the scene, and all that remained to be seen was a widening patch of oil. We were ready for trouble but none came our way.

The Malmi Airport was hardly suitable for supporting the operations of a squadron of forty fighters and airline traffic simultaneously, and so, with the completion at the end of August of the new Vesivehmaa airfield at Lahti, north of Helsinki, the squadron was transferred there in its entirety. We were now once again surrounded by pleasantly quiet countryside, although we tended to disrupt this quiet with gunnery exercises. These exercises were eminently successful, auguring well for any future operations in which we might be involved. The Brewster proved to be an even better gun platform than the Fokker, and we often achieved nearly a hundred hits on a target out of a hundred rounds fired. Between training flights I now once again found time for athletics. Our billets were situated alongside the Vääsky Canal, and the situation was ideal for cross-country running and, later, ski-ing. We made mushroom-gathering trips which usually entailed hikes of between five and ten miles, and some hard rowing during fishing trips helped to keep us at the peak of physical fitness.

Life was pleasant but quiet. Too quiet, and my friend, Pate Berg, Pelle Sovelius, and I even discussed the possibility of obtaining some sort of leave from the squadron in order to enlist with the air force of one or other of the major warring powers to obtain experience in combat on modern fighters. However, a tentative approach resulted in a reprimand from our senior officers, and we could only work off our surplus energy and soothe our injured feelings by throwing ourselves even more energetically into athletic activities. Little did we know that not so many months would pass before this peaceful interlude at Vesivehmaa would have taken on a roseate glow of a pleasant memory. War clouds were once again gathering on the horizon. This was the lull between the storms and soon we would be seeing all the action that we could wish for.

8

AT WAR ONCE MORE

"HLeLv 24 is to maintain a state of combat readiness on a twenty-four-hour basis until further notice." Both winter and spring had passed, and the war in Europe raged on. We had had more than a year in which to recuperate from the wounds inflicted by the "Winter War", and it was now June 1941. At 16.00 hours on the sixteenth day of that month we received the order that could mean only one thing: our government expected a renewal of hostilities with the Russians.

In a frenzy of activity we dug revetments to protect our dispersed fighters; covered the light-grey finish of the Brewsters with dark forest-green paint splotched with black; carefully bore-sighted our guns, and thoroughly camouflaged the field. The summer days were long and beautiful, and we were on duty from 06.00 to 23.00 hours, readying ourselves for a renewal of the trial of strength. Reserves recalled to active duty began to arrive and were checked out in short, intensive refresher courses. Throughout the long daylight hours Brewsters were taking-off and landing at Vesivehmaa. A constant chatter of machine-guns could be heard on the firing-range, and there was the continuous roar of engines being run up by the mechanics. A noisy prelude to war indeed.

A week after we received our standby orders, on June 22nd, we heard the news that German forces had begun an attack on the Soviet Union that morning. We were all of the opinion that our participation could not be long delayed and, on the 25th, the flames of war once again licked Finnish soil, for Soviet aircraft attacked Finnish coastal batteries while Russian artillery on the Hango Peninsula opened fire on our territory. We were at war once more, but this time we were not alone. The exceptionally severe conditions of the "Winter War" were still fresh in our memories, but this new conflict, our "Continuation War", was beginning at a time when our northern climate was displaying its most delightful face, and we were not joining combat as beginners but as hardened veterans. What is more, our squadron at least had new, more modern equipment.

Aerial warfare was a reality from the very first day of the "Continuation War", and I was commanding the first flight of HLeLv 24 with eight Brewster B-239s. All that first day we flew offensive patrols and, in fact, we continued flying until 02.00 hours the next morning as there was little true night at that time of the year at such latitudes. We failed to make contact with the enemy, however, owing to the unfavourable situation of our base, which was too far behind the front line, and the slow telephone connections in our defence set-up which resulted in our arrival at a designated interception point after the Russians had departed! Elsewhere many contacts with the enemy had been made, other units knocking down some twenty Russian bombers during the day.

. . . . .

Being the senior flight leader, it was my task to take over the command of the squadron in the absence of the C.O., a job that was strictly against my personal taste as its responsibilities restricted the amount of flying time that I could get in, and I was on duty in the Command Post on the evening of June 30th when one of our coastal warning stations reported three bombers approaching us from the north. I promptly sent off Vic Pyötsiä and Napu Mannila, together with one of our new and untried pilots, Kurre Ginman, to intercept the intruders.

Just south of the city of Lahti the trio of Brewsters made a successful interception, each of the pilots destroying one of the SB-2s. The citizens of Lahti were so grateful to us for our efforts that they promptly sent us a magnificent box of candies for distribution among our pilots.

Four of the Brewsters of my flight were detached to protect the headquarters at Mikkeli, these being commanded by Lieutenant Mustonen, but by this time it had become patently obvious that Vesivehmaa offered us few opportunities to make contact with the enemy, and we therefore began to prepare for a move to Rantasalmi airfield, about one hundred and twenty-five miles away. On July 3rd we at last began our move, and the Fokker D.XXI veterans of the "Winter War", which had now taken on a new lease of life after having been completely rebuilt at Tampere, landed at Vesivehmaa to take over our duties. We stowed our kitbags aboard the Brewsters, whose capacious fuselages featured a substantial baggage compartment, enabling pilots to carry their personal kit from base to base, and we were soon at Rantasalmi where we immediately set off in search of quarters among the Pyyvilä farm buildings.

The morning after our arrival we acted as escort to some of our own Blenheim bombers assigned to targets in the Elisenvaara, Jaakkima, and Tyrjä sectors, and it gave me infinite satisfaction to once again cross the borders to which we had been forced to withdraw by the iniquitous armistice of the previous year. The border could be clearly seen from the air, for a wide area had been cleared, and this ran like a scar across terrain with which I was so familiar. At Illhalla our Blenheims found their target and scored direct hits on what I assumed to be an important Russian dump, for it immediately erupted in flame and smoke.

After escorting the bombers back across the border, there was still sufficient fuel in our tanks to permit an offensive patrol which would serve the dual purpose of acquainting the newer members of the flight with the terrain and, perhaps, flush up some enemy fighters. We flew across the Mensuvaara airfield which was still in Russian hands, but there was no sign of activity, and since my old home was less than six miles away, I led the flight in that direction. North-east of Sortavala we observed a new enemy airfield from which we received a weak greeting of flak. We found that another base had been constructed at Läskelä, and then we were in the vicinity of our old "Winter War" base of Värtsilä, which was also now in enemy territory. But despite this impressive network of operational fields, not a single enemy aircraft came up to contest our right of way, and so my anxiety to test the Brewster in combat had still to see fruition.

So far, the new conflict lacked much of the hectic pace of the "Winter War". Two new pilots, Kaius Metsola and Väiski Suhonen, joined the flight, and after a few familiarization trips were ready for their first combat missions. The days passed in offensive patrols and interception sorties, but enemy aircraft were few and far between. The bulk of their formations appeared to have been transferred farther south in an attempt to stem the German penetration of the Soviet Union which was making fantastic progress. In the evenings, after flying had stopped for the day, we sat around Kurre Ginman's portable radio, listening to the news bulletins and the dance music, drinking vast quantities of boiling hot, fresh coffee, and eating sizzling fried sausages. This type of living was luxury indeed by comparison with the rigours that we had endured during the earlier conflict.

. . . . .

We had risen by 02.30 hours on July the 8th and, after sipping coffee from our Thermos flasks, had strolled leisurely to our dew-coated fighters. All was so still that it was almost possible to hear the silence, but gradually the smaller birds began their chirruping to which the larger birds added their song. The small puddles remaining from the previous day's rain shimmered in the early morning light, and the fresh, clean air was exhilarating. We chatted by our aircraft for a few minutes and then, at exactly 03.00 hours, the birds were stunned into silence by the throaty roars of four powerful engines. After a short warm-up of the Cyclones, we climbed into our fighters, and soon, splashing through the puddles, we were gathering speed across the field. Airborne, we tucked up our undercarriages and climbed steadily towards the sun, a reddish-golden globe which had already turned the horizon a superb daffodil yellow merging, in smoky pink, with the aquamarine of the sky. Apart from some white wisps of cirrus, we had the early morning sky to ourselves, and the sun's rays, reflected from the Haukivesi, sparkled on the wings and fuselages of the Brewsters, and turned each dewdrop on the canopy perspex into a multicoloured jewel. No artist, however talented, could have captured this superb scene on canvas.

All appeared so peaceful that one had to force oneself to remember that even on so beautiful a morning some youngster from Kursk, Kiev or Kalinin might be lurking above, just awaiting a chance to pump you full of bullet holes! We had to exercise exceptional vigilance, for we were flying straight into the sun's glaring rays where, unbeknown to us, a gaggle of Ivans could be preparing to pounce. From time to time I pulled up the nose of my Brewster to blank out the sun, but we reached the front line from the south-west side of Parkkila without incident.

We began to patrol along the front line and, suddenly, to port and below, the sun glinted on perspex—no more than a hundred or so feet above the ground were a half-dozen Tchaikas flying in line abreast. At my signal we peeled off, each selecting a Tchaika as his personal target. I carefully lined up my Ivan in my sights, and crept up stealthily behind him until he was so close that I could see the Russian pilot's head and shoulders hunched over the controls. I depressed the firing trigger and my tracers raked the Tchaika from stem to stern. Oily black smoke spewed from the Russian fighter's engine cowling, pieces of metal panelling hurtled past my Brewster, and the Tchaika rolled on to its back and then dived vertically into the woods just below.

To my starboard and above were three other fighters flying in follow-my-leader fashion—first a Tchaika, then one of our Brewsters and, bringing up the rear, another Tchaika! I pulled up the nose of my aircraft in a fast climbing turn, jumping the rearmost machine from one side, but I had not judged the deflection very well, and my tracers missed the Russian who immediately broke hard to port. I pivoted the Brewster on a wingtip, following the Tchaika round, but this bird was obviously an old hand, and he kept his fighter in a tight turn, knowing that I could not hold him with my less-manœuvrable Brewster. I could only get in a couple of short bursts as he was only in my sights fleetingly. Burning with resentment, I held the Brewster in the tightest of shuddering vertical turns, but my guns were spraying empty sky, and suddenly he broke hard to starboard, put his nose down, and was gone.

By this time, I had wandered away from the main combat area. There was no sign of my opponent who, his camouflaged aircraft merging superbly with the heavily wooded country below, had made good his escape "on the deck", but as I turned back towards the pre-arranged rendezvous, I spied a lone Tchaika above and speeding on a southerly course. I turned towards the Russian fighter, climbing at full throttle.

The only way to destroy this superbly manœuvrable biplane was to take its pilot by surprise, and I rapidly overhauled the Tchaika, approaching from his most serious blindspot, to the rear and slightly below. To make sure that my first burst would tell, I closed with the Russian until I could make out clearly the individual details of the fighter; the bright red stars on the pale blue-grey under-surfaces of the wings, the small puffs of black smoke emitted by the exhaust stubs, the bracing wires and even the lines of the wheel-well doors. Ivan was still unaware of my proximity, for he did not deviate a fraction from his course. At fifty yards I opened up, my first burst striking the underside of the engine cowling and then raking along the belly of the fuselage. The Tchaika clawed into a vertical stall and then fell away on one wing, plummeting into a meadow below. I glanced at my wristwatch; it was only 04.32 hours. The day had hardly begun!

I called the flight together over the R/T, we rendezvoused over Parkkila, and just after 05.00 hours we were making our landing approach at Rantasalmi. Between us we had five kills, and our early morning foray had done much to strengthen our confidence in the capabilities of the Brewster—our "Sky Pearl", as we had already affectionately dubbed the portly little monoplane. We had coffee for the second time that morning, and after discussing the battle for an hour and preparing a combat report, I took over the morning duty in the Command Post.

. . . . .

The hot summer weather continued, an occasional light shower washing the dust from our fighters. The army's drive in the northern Ladoga area had begun on July 10th, and the ground forces had moved forward with lightning speed so that, by the 21st, the Fourth Army at Salmi had crossed the old borders. Our squadron's regular duties were interrupted by these thrusts, which necessitated maintaining aerial superiority over Ladoga-Karelia, and we spent most of our time providing top cover, but rarely did the enemy come up to challenge us. For over a week we would take-off before dawn every morning, racing the sun, with the final flights of the day terminating after sunset. The wilderness below became increasingly familiar as each of our air-cover missions added some two hours and about six hundred miles to our logs. During these missions we could see "revenge fires" started by the retreating Russians, and forest fires burned unchecked at Ilomantsi, Tolvajärvi, and Loimola; and at Läskelä as many as twenty conflagrations, many houses were afire in Impilahti, and the Pitkäranta factory and the surrounding area was one sea of flames. Although most fires had been started by the Russians, others were the result of artillery fire, and as far as the eye could see columns of smoke rose into the sky, the acrid fumes even penetrating the cockpits of our fighters.

We flew over the Kollaa battlefields of the "Winter War", where the havoc wrought among the forests was still plainly visible, the undergrowth valiantly endeavouring to hide the scars. The infrequent air battle and the occasional burst of flak, usually over the Sortavala-Ryty area, were all that relieved the sheer monotony of our continual two- and three-hour patrols. We were assigned the task of providing air cover for large-scale troop movements at the Heinävesi, Varkaus, Pieksämäki, and Mikkeli railway yards, but these missions were equally monotonous as the Russians were obviously unaware of these movements, and no enemy aircraft ventured over the area by chance.

Haymaking was in full swing in the Pyyvilä fields adjoining the airfield, and during off-duty hours we joined in the task, the sweet smell of new-mown hay offering a refreshing change to the odour of high-octane fuel and mineral oil that continuously assailed our nostrils when on duty. The sauna bath, normally heated every other day, now worked overtime, and every evening found us in its steam, ridding ourselves of the dried perspiration and dust of the haymaking. The bay adjacent to our quarters provided a delightful spot for swimming after the sauna, and we usually arose an hour earlier each morning to get in a swim before taking-off. The waters of the bay seemed tepid indeed by comparison with the cool early-morning air.

On the last day of July our army began its attack on the Karelian Heel, and day after day we roamed above the advancing troops, ensuring that no enemy aircraft succeeded in reconnoitring the area, and occasionally escorting formations of Blenheims to their targets. We had a true bird's-eye view of the advance, the muzzle-flashes of the guns revealing the latest position of the front line, and the burning homes in the little villages giving an indication of the areas from which the Russian forces were about to withdraw.

Our forces had paused at Pohjanlahti, on the northern shore of Ladoga, when, on August 13th, we attacked our first convoy on Lake Ladoga. We had been patrolling as usual and, apart from some intense flak from batteries in the vicinity of Elisenvaara and Kurkijoki, our flight had been uneventful. Then, across the glittering surface of Ladoga, far to the south, I spotted a sizeable enemy convoy. Immediately reporting the position of the convoy to headquarters, I was given permission to attack. We skirted the convoy at a distance, so that we could make our strafing runs from out of the sun, and then, in pairs, began our dive. Of the twenty ships below us eight were warships, two of which promptly began laying a smokescreen. An intense curtain of flak sailed up towards us, brilliant balls of fire searing past our aircraft and a cloud of foul smoke forming behind us. There was a sharp, hollow crack from somewhere in the rear fuselage of my Brewster which lurched violently, the control column being almost wrested from my grasp. My fighter righted itself and, as no serious damage appeared to have been suffered, I began my run at the first ship. My machineguns raked the deck from end to end, and as I flashed past I caught a glimpse of the crew scurrying in all directions. The next vessel appeared in my sights, and I poured a hail of lead into its decks. A glance over my shoulder confirmed that the other Brewsters had begun their strafing runs, and then we were skimming across the surface of the lake, with one of the ships belching flames behind us.

During the approach Kurre Ginman could not lock his undercarriage in position, a hydraulic line having been fractured during our attack on the convoy, and was forced to make a belly landing, smashing the airscrew. Apart from a few small holes from shell splinters, one of which must have caused the noise that I had heard just before starting my strafing run, my Brewster was none the worse for diving through the flak curtain.

After landing, I discovered that two new pilots, Vilppu Lakio and Lila Lilja, had been posted to the flight, and for once our pilot roster was over strength—a very welcome situation in view of the fact that we were frequently on duty for twenty hours at a stretch. Indeed, at this period leave was unheard of, but one evening in mid-August I did succeed in getting an evening's pass into Varkaus for the whole flight. We all piled into Kurre's B.M.W. saloon and, after buying a much-needed coffee mill and visiting the barber's shop, treated ourselves to an excellent crab dinner.

  . . . . .

The field armies had advanced far more rapidly than had been anticipated and, on August 16th, after a bitter struggle, Sortavala was recaptured. Along the Kannas other troops had reached the banks of the swift-flowing Vuoksi River, the crossing of which began on the morning of the 18th. The crossing of the Vuoksi was no simple matter, and its width rendered the forces engaged in the crossing extremely vulnerable to air attack. We were assigned the task of providing air cover for the operation, and by 05.00 hours we were already zig-zagging backwards and forwards over the crossing points. A few flat-bottomed boats were already making the crossing, these being followed by large rafts loaded with equipment. In the distance we could see the airfields of Heinjoki and Paakkola, which were still in enemy hands, but there was no sign of any activity at either base.

The minutes ticked past, and the crossing continued in an orderly fashion, and after an hour I had begun to think that the Russians would make no attempt to interfere with the operation, when, just below a clump of cloud, six black specks appeared, growing rapidly until I could make out the distinctive shape of the Tchaika. We turned in to attack the Russians and soon a tremendous dogfight was drifting and eddying backwards and forwards across the river. Every Finn had singled out his own Tchaika, and out of the corner of my eye I noticed one of the Russians spin smoking into the woods. Almost simultaneously I saw another Tchaika making a low-level run at two pontoon rafts in the middle of the river. The only possible way of stopping this attack was by diving head-on at the Russian. I pushed down the nose of my Brewster and in a fraction of a second we were roaring at each other at a closing speed of nearly 600 m.p.h., both firing madly. Just as collision seemed certain, the Tchaika suddenly lurched to one side, pulled up vertically as I swept past within two or three yards, and then stalled into the trees below.

The battle was over almost as quickly as it had begun, four of the Tchaikas having flown for the last time, and the two survivors scurrying away as fast as they could go. We could not chase them, as our primary task was the protection of the troops crossing the river below, but at least our two newcomers, Vilppu Lakio and Lila Lilja, had gained their first kills, as had also Kaius Metsola. We continued to fly backwards and forwards over the crossing points for another thirty minutes and were then relieved by another flight. On the return trip a tremendous pile of cumulus rose in front of us, forcing us to climb above the front, but we were soon back at Rantasalmi where the ground staff immediately began the task of refuelling and rearming the Brewsters ready for another spell over the Vuoksi River. We were delighted to learn that still another pilot was to be added to the flight, Veka Rimminen, a real "old fox" and a highly skilled Brewster pilot.

. . . . .

It had become increasingly obvious that our base of operations was now too far behind the various fronts, and so, on August 21st, the date on which Käkisalmi was recaptured, we stuffed our belongings into the Brewsters. After a patrol over the main road between Kaukola and Kiviniemi, we were to land at Immola where, an eternity since, we had begun our "Winter War" operations.

The further into Karelia we flew the more frequent were the signs of the conflict. The mighty Antrea railway bridge had collapsed into the bed of the river after being blown up by the retreating Russians, and fires were burning furiously in Sakkola, Kiviniemi, Pyhäjärvi, and Taipale, towns buried beneath billowing clouds of black smoke and sparks. It was a depressing sight, and my mood was by no means improved when a trio of MiG-3 fighters which suddenly appeared managed to escape us, their pilots piling on the coals and showing us clean pairs of heels.

After the mission we landed at Immola, where the four Brewsters from the flight that had been detached for duty at

Mikkeli rejoined us. Thus, the first flight was once again at full strength.

A little over a week passed uneventfully, carrying us to August 29th, the date of Viipuri's recapture. The day dawned with heavy cloud and some mist, but at 06.30 hours the weather had cleared a little, and the flight was ordered to reconnoitre the area south of Summa. Eight Brewsters were assigned to this mission, but the base of the cloud was only three hundred feet, and at Muolaanjärvi we were forced to turn back as the cloud dropped to the tops of the trees. I reported these conditions to the Command Post only to be told that the mission was vital, so I ordered four of the Brewsters back to base and led the others in an attempt to reach our assigned reconnaissance area by a circuitous route.

Just before reaching Viipuri we managed to get above the lower layer of cloud at about four thousand feet. We flew steadily southwards between the two layers of cloud, and just at the right moment, as though by providence, an opening appeared immediately over the area that we had been ordered to reconnoitre. I began spiralling down through the gap as though down the inside of a funnel. I caught a glimpse of some enemy fortifications, but while my attention was riveted on the scene below, I inadvertently allowed my aircraft to slip into the cloud. It was as though I had suddenly plunged into pea soup. I couldn't even see my wingtips. The artificial horizon began to act up and I tried to fly towards what seemed to be a patch of light but had the unpleasant sensation of being forced into one corner of the cockpit, and the altimeter began to unwind. I pulled back the throttle and tried to centralise the controls. The altimeter stopped unwinding momentarily and the airspeed fell off, and suddenly I was in a spin! After several turns of a spin the Brewster was undoubtedly dangerous even in clear sky, and now I was immersed in thick cloud over enemy territory.

Full opposite rudder, stick forward and centralise the controls—the standard formula for recovering from a spin—but try as I may I could not right the aircraft. The slack in the safety-belt allowed me to be thrown from side to side, and I decided that there was only one thing to do—jump! I thrust back the cockpit canopy and attempted to stand on the seat, but a tremendous blast of wind filled the cockpit. The maps

The Fiat G.50 (*above*), thirty-five examples of which were acquired from Italy, was definitely not intended for conflict under Arctic conditions. Operated by HLeLv 26, it possessed inadequate firepower, but Oiva Tuominen and Olli Puhakka did exceptionally well while flying the G.50.

(*Left*) Captain Lauri Pekuri, Major Olavi Ehrnrooth and the author are seen left to right. Major Ehrnrooth was the Commanding Officer of HLeLv 32 equipped with Curtiss Hawk 75A fighters, and briefly commanded HLeLv 34, the first Finnish unit to operate Bf 109Gs. His untimely death while performing low-level aerobatics in a Pyry trainer on March 27, 1943 resulted in the author taking command of HLeLv 34. (*Below*) A Hawk 75A-3 of HLeLv 32. Finland purchased forty-four captured Hawk 75As from Germany.

(*Above*) Soft snow resulted in severa ground loops being suffered by the Brewster B-239s, yet the use of skis was forbidden. (*Left*) Lieutenant Kossi Karhila was a member of HLeLv 32 prior to joining HLeLv 34, and gained ten kills while flying Hawk 75As and a further nineteen and a half flying Bf 109Gs. He is currently a Flight Captain with Finnair. (*Below*) The M.S.406 was operated by HLeLv 28 whose main tasks were escort and ground attack. Small groups of M.S.406s were often stationed at the same fields as Fighter Group L.

flew past me, my revolver swung up and hit my head with a bang which nearly knocked me unconscious, and all the dirt and dust from beneath the cockpit floor eddied around me. I could never jump clear of this madly gyrating fighter! I pulled myself back into my seat once more, planted my feet firmly on the pedals, and tried once more to regain control. It was a last desperate effort. The altimeter was still unwinding frantically, and had already dropped below the thousand-feet mark, and I had never been so scared in my life. I would willingly have traded my situation for a sky full of enemy fighters, but then, when all seemed lost, my guardian angel must have come to my aid for, with the altimeter showing less than five hundred feet and still no sign of the ground, I felt control being restored.

Relief flooded through me. I slammed the canopy shut, gave the engine full throttle and pulled up the nose of the Brewster, climbing steadily up through the cloud, breaking through into clear air at forty-five hundred feet. I felt as though I had been presented with another lease of life. I called up Veka Rimminen over the R/T, arranging a rendezvous over Juustila, and finally landed back at Immola, my clothes wet with perspiration.

• • • • •

The following afternoon, still somewhat chastened as a result of my frightening experience, I led the flight on a reconnaissance mission over Jäppilä airfield. We circled around eastern Karelia, crossing the ruins of Käkisalmi where only a few gaunt chimney stacks remained pointing skywards like accusing fingers. From there we set course south-west towards Seivästö, near to the airfield that we had been told to reconnoitre. I split the flight into two groups of four fighters, one group providing top cover while the other reconnoitred the field.

We crossed the field at about twenty-five hundred feet, and I spotted a MiG-3 and two Tchaikas parked on one side, together with a couple of refuelling bowsers. Some light flak opened up at us from a clump of trees as I gave the signal to strafe the field. I banked around sharply and kicked my fighter over in a dive with Kaius Metsola on one wing and Veka Rimminen on the other. I got the MiG-3 squarely in my sights and could see that its airscrew was now rotating, raising a cloud of dust. I loosed a burst at the fighter just as it began to move, and one of its undercarriage legs immediately collapsed, the aircraft flopping down on one wingtip and the pilot leaping from the cockpit. I was now daisy-cutting across the field, and aimed a burst at a truck from which two men flung themselves. I pulled up slightly to clear the trees on the perimeter, and caught a glimpse of trucks, tents and large pyramids of fuel drums covered by branches. As I made a climbing turn and looked back at the field, I saw that Kaius and Veka had written *finis* to the two Tchaikas, one of which was burning furiously.

We rejoined our top cover and started back for Immola. We flew past the old fortress of Viipuri, as majestic as ever and now proudly flying the Finnish flag from its flagstaff. Sweeping low across Suur Merijoki we saw that our former officers' club had been completely ruined. The roof had caved in and few walls were still standing. The sun was low on the western horizon as we landed back at base.

. . . . .

I obtained permission to take a car to Viipuri, and Kurre Ginman and I took turns at the wheel. Vaffe Vahvelainen had joined us to take a look at his old home. Once across the border to which we had retired after the "Winter War" the scene became most disagreeable, desolation and destruction everywhere one looked. Few buildings remained intact, the fields were full of weeds, the hay was uncut, and the roadsides were littered with abandoned equipment and dead horses. But the farther from the border we travelled the less destruction we saw, for it seemed that the Russian retreat had gained momentum so rapidly that Ivan had been unable to carry out his scorched-earth policy, and some of the smaller villages were intact, while attempts had even been made to harvest some of the crops, suggesting that the villagers had not all left their homes.

Closer to Viipuri the aftermath of battle was still fresh, and as all the bridges had been blown, we had to drive cautiously over temporary plank bridges which threatened to pitch us into the water at any moment. The familiar Papula overhead bridge had crashed down on the railway tracks, and we were forced to make many detours before reaching the heart of the old city. Although I had lived in Viipuri I could hardly recognise the city. The superb railway station designed by Eliel Saarinen and claimed to have been the most beautiful in the whole of northern Europe was now a pile of rubble, and few buildings stood unscathed. The glass windows of the shopfronts had been shattered, and on Suonio Street syrup had run through the windows of a six-storey confectionary factory, coating the pavements with a sticky slime. In the basement we discovered hundreds of barrels of jam and cases of dried fruit, and greatly regretted that we were not driving a decent-sized truck.

We wandered around among the ruins, climbing piles of rubble and peering into the buildings that remained standing, and throughout our sojourn in the city we saw no more than a dozen other people. Feeling thoroughly miserable, we continued on through Viipuri until we reached Sainio, where I had left much of my spare clothing and kit during the "Winter War". Near the badly damaged hospital the horrible odour of burned human flesh assailed our nostrils, and we hastily turned away in the direction of the Ristimäki Cemetery, where I planned to visit the grave of my small son who had been laid to rest here. But everywhere we looked five-pointed stars had been added between the surviving crosses and headstones, and search as we might, there was no longer any trace of my son's grave.

Sainio's railway station and the Terijoki highway areas were jammed by the shattered remains of tanks, armoured cars, tracked vehicles and trucks, and it was with difficulty that we managed to edge our way through the tangled wreckage. There was no sign of the house that we were endeavouring to find, but then all that was left in this area, apart from the foundations of a large store, were corpses, the bloated carcasses of horses, heaps of ashes and mounds of débris. We had seen more than enough and, turning the car around, we headed back in the direction from which we had come.

9

OVER THE BORDER

On September 2nd, almost exactly two years from the start of fighting in Europe, we were elated to receive the news for which we had all waited so long; Finnish forces had reached all our pre-war boundaries. Our homeland was once more free of invaders, except, of course, for those ever-increasing thousands of dejected Russians languishing behind the barbed wire of our prisoner-of-war compounds. Accompanying this news was the report that we were to be transferred to an area from which we could provide our advancing troops with more direct air cover.

Four more Brewsters were now added to my flight, which once more gained its independence as Fighter Group "L", my orders being to proceed to the airfield on Lunkula Island in Lake Ladoga, near Salmi. We were all given anti-typhoid injections and were vaccinated against smallpox, and that evening a convoy of five heavy lorries, carrying our spares, servicing equipment, ground personnel, and six extra pilots, left on the 190-mile journey to our new base close to the front line.

Shortly after 11.00 hours the next day, September 3rd, our twelve Brewsters formed up over the field, and then headed eastward. We were all somewhat stiff and sore as a result of the previous day's visit to the medical unit, and every movement of the stick or rudder pedals seemed to call for more than the usual amount of effort, but we were light-hearted at the thought that we would now really have a chance to spit in Stalin's eye.

As the Valamo islands came into view ahead, a trigger-happy Finnish anti-aircraft battery decided to get in a little target practice. We were the targets! Fortunately for us, their marksmanship was not all that we would have desired had a Russian formation been in our place, and the evil grey blossoms left by their shells fouled the sky some considerable distance behind our aircraft. The remainder of the flight passed without incident, and at 12.30 hours we were bumping and swaying across the uneven surface of the Lunkula airfield, our aircraft sending up clouds of spray. I had already been told that this field was frequently water-logged, and with the autumnal rains there were already large areas under several inches of water. This poured in rivulets from the wings and fuselages of the fighters as we taxied to our assigned parking area—the field was already occupied by Fiat G.50s and Morane-Saulnier M.S.406s—to discover this to be a narrow strip barely three hundred yards in length! This was totally inadequate if we were to disperse our dozen Brewsters most effectively to avoid damage in the event of a surprise attack by Ivan, and as a partial safeguard against such an eventuality I sent four of the fighters to a small field on near-by Mantsin Island.

What few buildings existed were already packed to capacity with the earlier arrivals and, despite the soaking ground, we were forced to use our tents, managing to pitch two of these before nightfall and packing ourselves into them like herrings in a barrel. Before I could turn in, however, some sort of solution had to be found to the question of the utterly hopeless telephone communications. We had no ground radio, and contacting the various warning and control centres was obviously destined to be a nightmare. At such a time as this, when everybody was busily preparing for the full-scale onslaught by our forces scheduled to be launched at 05.00 hours on the morrow, all and sundry were claiming priority in getting their calls through, and there were no fewer than *five* switchboards between our detachment and the rest of the squadron nine miles away at Mantsinsaari! By the time this matter of priorities had been argued out it was quicker to *walk* with a message. Finally, by dint of a combination of pleading and threatening, constantly stressing the vital need for a direct link between the squadron and Fighter Group "L", I persuaded the communications engineers to provide a line, and leaving the problems of heating, lighting, and spares shortages for the next day as it was already past midnight, I crawled into my sleeping-bag on the damp floor of one of the tents and, exhausted, fell into a dreamless sleep.

No more than an hour had passed when I was aroused by

what at first I took to be the world exploding around me. It was the thunder of our own artillery, the volume of which was such that the very ground beneath the tent trembled. This tremendous barrage, the combined efforts of more than two hundred guns, was the prelude to the big advance that was to carry our forces over the border, and had brought Fighter Group "L" to Lunkula. Our task was the provision of aerial top cover for the spearhead of the Fourth Army north-east of Lake Ladoga. The Fourth Army had reached Tuulosjoki, just across Finland's pre-war border, and the plan called for a thrust towards Syväri, deep within Russian Karelia, while simultaneously the Seventh Army was to advance on Petroskoi, north of Syväri. The firing positions of about sixteen batteries were so close to our airfield that, once the barrage had begun, only the deaf and the dead could have slept. Despite this disturbance of our much-needed rest, we gained no little satisfaction from the fantastic cacophony; the roar of much the same sort of barrage as we had received from Ivan during the "Winter War".

At 04.30 hours we were stumbling along the edge of the airfield towards our fighters. A cold wind was blowing off Lake Ladoga and scattered clusters of low cloud chased each other across the horizon over which the sun was just beginning to rise. Our eight Brewsters took-off on the first sortie of the day just a few minutes before the advance was due to begin. Our task was to maintain local aerial superiority, and at the same time ensure that a Fokker C.X spotting for the artillery performed its mission unhindered.

We flew in finger-four formation at about five thousand feet above the twisting, log-jammed Tuulosjoki, one section of four Brewsters some three hundred feet above the other. Between scanning the skies for enemy aircraft, we examined intently the terrain over which we were flying, this being our first sortie beyond the East Karelian frontier, but the whole area presented a monotonous vista of marshland and forest, relieved only by the occasional cluster of drab, unpainted wooden huts on the banks of the river. Below us must have been the Russian positions, but apart from the occasional muzzle-flash as the Russian guns awakened to the challenge of our barrage, the countryside might have been completely deserted.

We eventually reached the town of Aunus, a straggling cluster of featureless, single-storey wooden buildings, and followed the main road between Aunus and the town of Tuulosjoki, trying vainly to form some sort of picture of the situation on the ground. Apart from a few groups of our own cycle-equipped troops, and the occasional column of smoke meandering into the sky as the retreating Russians blew up and set fire to stores and buildings, there was nothing to see, and we were quite alone in the morning sky.

After being airborne for nearly an hour we spotted a group of eight or ten aircraft over the Nurmoila airfield, near Aunus. We turned in their direction, throttles wide open, and as we closed the distance I tried to make out what the aircraft were. They appeared to be fairly large fighters but the type was new to me. Whatever they were, there was no doubt of their nationality, so I gave the signal to attack, and as we peeled off we each picked our own target. I bracketed mine with bursts of machine-gun fire before its pilot awoke to the fact that I was bearing down on him, but he reacted quickly, wrenching his aircraft into a steep climbing turn and disappearing like a wraith into the thickening rainclouds. Another Russian appeared momentarily in my sights, but I had hardly time to loose a burst of fire at him before he, too, had slipped into the sanctuary of the clouds. The fight was over almost before it had begun, with no apparent damage suffered by either side, and as fuel was beginning to run low, we turned for home, accompanied by driving rain which was to last out the day.

．　．　．　．　．

As no more sorties were possible under the prevailing weather conditions, I took the opportunity to cross to Mantsin Island to inspect our detachment of four Brewsters and, simultaneously, avail myself of the sauna which was one of the few facilities offered by the little field. By the time I got back to Lunkula, the rain had petered out and the moon was showing her face from time to time between the racing clouds. In the direction of Aunus a dull red glow stained the night sky; evidently a reflection of large fires and a sign that the Russians were already preparing to pull out of the town. On the base everything seemed peaceful enough, the only sounds being the sighing of the wind through the trees, the muffled tread of the sentries, the subdued rumble of distant gunfire, and the occasional clink of metal on metal as some mechanic laboured over his charge under a canvas screen.

I groped my way to one of our tents and was soon rolled up on the floor, sleeping soundly. It seemed that my eyes had hardly closed, however, when I was aroused by several drumming explosions. In my half-stupor I presumed that our artillery was once more firing near by, but at the sound of an aero engine I was instantly fully awake. It dawned on me simultaneously that our artillery had moved forward in the wake of the advancing troops! At that moment, everything exploded about my ears. The telephone and our precious coffee mill leaped from the rough-and-ready shelf that we had made for them; some bomb splinters swished through the sides of the tent, and stones and earth rained down on its roof.

I leaped from my sleeping-bag, propelling myself through the tent opening, landing on all fours in the bright moonlight, just in time to see the brilliant flash of a bomb that appeared to have landed slap in the midst of our parked fighters. Several of us ran in the direction of the aircraft, fearful of what we might find, as two more explosions came from the far side of the field. By the time we reached the Brewsters, the sound of the intruder's engine was already fading in the distance.

To our amazement, everything seemed to be as we had left it. Then we almost stumbled into an impressive crater between two of the Brewsters, both of which were covered by thick coats of wet earth. A closer examination revealed a couple of small holes made by bomb splinters in one of the fighters but, apart from these, nothing. It seemed that the spongy ground had absorbed most of the blast of a 220-pounder, for had the ground been harder it was almost certain that our available fighter strength would have been reduced by two machines. Another 220-pounder had fallen within fifty yards of our tent.

・　・　・　・　・

Our troops were now pressing forward at a tremendous pace and within three days had advanced nearly fifty miles, reaching the Syväri River early on the morning of September 7th. On the following day German forces coming up from the south captured Pähkinälinna, and thus Leningrad was all but surrounded and could only be supplied by sea or air. Our task remained the provision of part of the aerial umbrella for both the advancing forces and the supply columns coming up from the rear, and on the eighth we were assigned the task of covering the crossing of the Syväri by the first waves of our assault troops.

Late that afternoon our eight Brewsters took-off from Lunkula, and soon the whole of the Aunus isthmus lay spread before us like an interminable wilderness. Rarely were there signs of cultivation. Corn still stood in the few small fields that appeared to have been carved literally from the virgin forest, and in the little town of Hoskila, at the mouth of the Aunus River, a timberyard burned intensely, ugly clouds of smoke billowing into the sky. To the south, Finnish infantry, artillery, cars, lorries, motor-cycles, and horse-drawn vehicles were crawling along the roads like so many columns of ants, and eventually the onion-shaped domes and white walls and towers of the famous Troitsa Pilgrimage Monastery came into view below. In recent years this old monastery had been used by the Russians as a prison, though in the heart of these vast forests it sat with serene beauty in the early evening light, revealing nothing of the untold suffering that must have taken place within its mighty walls.

A Finnish flag fluttered bravely from the highest building in Pisi, almost on the shores of Lake Ladoga, and at the mouth of the lower course of the Syväri, the boat-building yards and slipways, and the fuel storage tanks were an inferno of flame and smoke. On the lower bank of the Syväri lay Lotinapelto, the southernmost Karelian town which, in peacetime, had possessed a population of some eight thousand. Along its western fringes some of the houses were burning, and the main bridge over the Syväri had been dynamited. To the south of the town there was a sizeable airfield with four hangars, but we could see no sign of activity, and it seemed evident that the Russians had already withdrawn their aircraft.

Once more we seemed to have the skies to ourselves until, between Aunus and the Syväri, near Märkjärvi, a solitary twin-engined Ilyushin DB-3 appeared flying low over the main road, the last of the sun's rays twinkling on the perspex of its cockpit, its crew apparently intent on their reconnaissance mission and unaware of our presence. Leaving Veka Rimminen and his section as top cover, I led my section down after the DB-3. In single file we bore down on the Russian, and as I lined the aircraft in my sights, its dorsal gunner began pumping away at me, his tracers arching past my cockpit too closely for comfort. The Russian pilot, surprisingly, took no evasive action, and I fired a long burst into his port engine from which a thin streamer of smoke appeared. The DB-3 continued to fly steadily southeast, hugging the contours of the ground and keeping to the main road. I banked to starboard to allow the next Brewster to make a firing pass, watching the results from above with interest. The tracers simply bounced off the bomber's wings and fuselage. Apart from the thin stream of smoke from the port engine, the aircraft seemed completely unscathed, and flew on unfalteringly.

We made pass after pass at the Russian, and although the dorsal gun was no longer replying, the aircraft showed no sign of damage; it was apparently impervious to our bullets. I could only conclude that this particular DB-3 was specially armoured, and this made me the more determined to knock the Russian from the sky. For fifteen minutes and more than fifty miles we made pass after pass at the DB-3, and then, without any prior warning, it flicked over on its back, burst into flames and ploughed into the ground, flaming pieces of wreckage rocketing in every direction. All four of us had fired at the Russian at least a half-dozen times, expending virtually almost all our ammunition against the armoured skin of this lone intruder, but none of us had actually been firing when the bomber fell out of control, so we could only claim its destruction as a collective kill.

While we had been concentrating our efforts on the DB-3, Veka Rimminen's section had found easier game for themselves for, upon our return to base, we learned that our comrades had jumped a trio of SB-2s, and Veka, Kaius Metsola, and Vaffe Vahvelainen had each accounted for one of the enemy aircraft.

· · · · ·

The front line now stretched along the Syväri River, and we found ourselves expending far too much of our fuel flying to and from our assigned patrol area. Having, in the meantime, acquired a field radio, I contacted the C.O. and suggested that I move Fighter Group "L" forward to Aunus. The C.O. gave his consent readily, and Kaius Metsola, Urppo Raunio, Kurre Ginman and I piled into our little BMW for an inspection of the Nurmoila airfield north-east of Aunus. The day was beautiful, although there was now a noticeable bite in the air. We crossed the pre-war frontier, passed the Vitele airfield, following the road as it wound along the Ladoga shoreline. In places the road appeared to have been freshly hewn from the forest, in others flooding rendered it almost impassable. From time to time we passed pathetic little groups of refugees, mostly women and children, clutching bundles or pushing small handcarts piled with their few possessions, and now and again we crossed newly raised pontoon bridges which had taken the place of permanent bridges blown up by the Russians as they fell back.

We drove through Aunus, which before the war had possessed a population of some two thousand, and five miles along the Petroskoi Road we finally reached the Nurmoila airfield, which had reputedly been built by female prison labourers. The actual barrack blocks were situated a couple of miles from the field, and here we found indescribable disorder and filth. The floors and surrounding area were littered with dirty clothes, bloody bandages, and even human excrement, and I decided immediately that we would be far better off in our tents than here. Near the airfield was a small lake, the Lintujärvi, and it was on the shores of this beautiful stretch of water that I decided to make our encampment.

Our cursory inspection completed, we began our journey back to Lunkula Island. In the evening, after our return, there was an alert, but if there were any intruders they were not headed in our direction, and when it was really dark we spent a fascinating hour on the shore watching the most fabulous pyrotechnic display. Although Leningrad was some sixty miles distant, we could see clearly the flashes of bombs, the bright fingers of searchlights as they sought the German night bombers, and the multi-coloured sparks of bursting anti-aircraft shells.

10

NINE MONTHS AT NURMOILA

September 12th dawned bright but gusty and, after having operated out of Lunkula Island for more than a week, the course that we set for Nurmoila, destined to serve as our home for the next nine months, was already a familiar one. We landed on the dirt runway in a strong cross-wind, and taxied our Brewsters to the northern and eastern boundaries of the field which I had selected as our dispersal areas. The ground staff were delayed in their arrival until late that afternoon as the bombing of the Vitele airfield the previous night had rendered difficult the procurement of the necessary transport vehicles.

We immediately got down to the job of making our new base habitable, and this proved a major operation. After erecting our tents on the shores of the Lintujärvi, about twelve hundred yards from the field, we began the task of making Nurmoila operational. So recently had the field been captured that the aftermath of battle was to be seen everywhere. The bodies of several Russian soldiers had to be buried, and when I reported the arrival of Fighter Group "L" to the Aunus Military Headquarters, I was informed that there were still many Russians slinking about in the surrounding forests, this necessitating the posting of guards around the aircraft from our already inadequate personnel roster. Needless to say, when we turned in we slept with our revolvers under our pillows.

During the night the Army erected telephone lines for us, an auxiliary power-plant was procured for our ground radio facilities, this also furnishing lighting for our tents, and gradually we made the place habitable. A captured field kitchen was installed in a semi-completed log cabin, the only permanent building in our area, offering a welcome relief from the dry rations that had been sustaining us during our stay on Lunkula Island, and an abandoned skiff and several fishing nets enabled us to vary our diet still further. The arrival of an anti-aircraft

NINE MONTHS AT NURMOILA 109

battery and an airfield maintenance team brought our total personnel strength to some two hundred men, this being augmented by the arrival of four additional pilots, Jokeli Savonen, Hasse Wind, Kale Tervo, and Masa Pellinen. We also received three more Brewsters.

Our forces on the southern front rapidly gained their objectives, many crossings being made of the wide Syväri River, and we were now called upon to fly air-cover missions over the north-east sectors where General Laguk's forces were advancing from the south on Petroskoi, the capital of Russian Karelia.

On September 28th, two days and two weeks after our arrival at Nurmoila, eight of us took-off on an offensive sweep, flying over the seemingly endless forests of East Karelia. Near Säämäjärvi we flew over the Suojärvi-Petroskoi railway which was being repaired by our army engineers, and in the far distance we could see the shores of the Äänisjärvi, or Lake Onega as it is also known. Eventually we were approaching the town of Petroskoi; a town of single- and two-storey buildings spread out over an area of about four square miles and possessing some seventy-seven thousand inhabitants. The Äänisjärvi was now only ten miles away, and we could see clearly the hulk of a burned-out collier at the water's edge, the coal spilled from its hold still smoking. The number of vessels suggested that, to the Russians, the loss of Petroskoi was a foregone conclusion, and evacuation of the town was already in progress.

South of Petroskoi, near the Derevjannov airfield, we came upon eight Russian aircraft—four fighters and four reconnaissance-bombers. During the somewhat confused but brief mêlée we accounted for three of the reconnaissance-bombers and one of the fighters, Reiska Valli and Hasse Wind scoring their first kills during this action, but the Russians had little fight in them, and the survivors plunged into a near-by cloud bank. With our appetites whetted for more action, we formed up once more and flew south-west, following the Murmansk railway at an altitude of thirteen hundred feet. One of our tasks was to shoot up any trains that we found in this area, and almost immediately we saw a column of white smoke rising from some locomotive still hidden in the forest. As soon as the train came into view, we formed up in single file, roaring down with all guns blazing. As I flashed over our target I realised that this was no ordinary train. It was an armoured locomotive pulling three special wagons equipped with 20-mm. anti-aircraft cannon. Our first run had evidently taken Ivan by surprise, but as we swung round to make our second pass we were greeted by a hail of cannonfire. As I lined up the locomotive once again in my sights and depressed the firing trigger, it was almost as though I was engaged in a personal duel with those anti-aircraft cannon, their tracers appearing to converge with mine midway between us. My 12·7-mm. machine-gun bullets were ricochetting harmlessly from the armoured sides of the locomotive. My efforts were obviously as useless as those of a woodpecker pecking at an iron gate. Swearing under my breath, I aimed one last burst at a cylinder from which, surprisingly, steam immediately began to pour. As I swept past the train, one of the 20-mm. shells pierced my starboard wing, and as we were obviously helpless against this armoured monster, and only wasting our ammunition, I called the three other Brewsters to formate on me, and we headed back to base.

. . . . .

With the occupation of Petroskoi our sorties were markedly reduced. The days of the East Karelian autumn were becoming progressively greyer and shorter, and we began to suffer frequent downpours of rain which steamed up the tiny windows of our small tents, and beat a continuous cacophony on their roofs. There could have been no more depressing weather for a pilot and, cooped up in our tiny tents, our mood was soon as grey as the skies. The monotony became progressively less bearable, being relieved only by hurried excursions through the streaming rain to the mess for our meals. The temperatures dropped and the dampness seemed to find its way into our bones, but one bright interlude raised our spirits; the arrival of a well-known Finnish vocalist trio, the Harmony Sisters, whose delightful repertoire of songs made us forget for a couple of hours the miserable weather and our enforced inactivity.

Rain and wind were followed by more rain and more wind, and soon the rivers were overflowing and the fields had become lakes. The roads were rapidly becoming impassable, and as all flying was out of the question, Kurre Ginman and I decided to take the BMW and drive towards the front line. We stopped in Aunus to peer into one or two of the deserted houses, and everywhere we found incredible disorder. Filthy clothing, cigarette ends, empty bottles, and torn Russian newspapers lay everywhere in profusion. The Russian troops billeted in these houses must have lived like animals. Our next stop was at Troitsa Pilgrimage Monastery which we had seen from the air for the first time some weeks previously. Whatever spiritual atmosphere the monastery had once possessed it had certainly been dispelled by its years of use as a prison, yet, strangely, the superb paintings of the Saints of the Greek Orthodox Church remained undamaged, and as bright and fresh as they must have been when monks had inhabited this mighty structure.

Some distance south of the monastery was the Troitsa airfield with which we had also become familiar from the air. On the field we discovered a crashed Tchaika, and we welcomed the opportunity to examine closely this little fighter biplane by which we had found ourselves opposed so many times. We had acquired a healthy respect for the superlative powers of manœuvre possessed by this aircraft which was one of the very few fighter biplanes featuring a retractable undercarriage[1] to be built in quantity, and certainly the only one to see any really extensive wartime service. It was also probably the *last* fighter biplane to enter service with any nation, for it did not join the Soviet Air Forces until the late summer of 1939, the prototype having flown in the previous year at a time when the Russians, along with many others, believed that there was still a place for the fighter biplane in the modern air arm. The Tchaika, or I-153, was a progressive but markedly improved development of the I-15 which that old veteran of Russian aircraft designers, Nicolai Polikarpov, had produced in 1933, although it was not until many years later that I was to learn that another designer, A. J. Scherbakov, had actually been responsible for the tremendous amount of redesign that had resulted in the Tchaika. Most of the fabric had been stripped from the rear fuselage, and we could see that, although perhaps a little crude in finish, the structure was pretty sturdy.

[1] The only other biplanes with retractable undercarriages to be built in some numbers were the Curtiss F11C-3 (alias BF2C-1) and the generally similar Hawk III and IV, the two-seater Grumman FF-1 and single-seater F2F-1, F3F-1 and F3F-2, and the DI-6 two-seater designed by S. A. Kochoringine, a member of Polikarpov's design collective.

Driving along the southern perimeter of the field we found our way blocked by a couple of fallen trees. Climbing from the BMW we were struggling with the first of the trees when the air above our heads was suddenly alive with the whirring of bullets, and the clatter of machine-guns came from the near-by trees. We dropped our burden as though it had become red hot, turned tail, covering the distance to the car like Olympic champions, leaped in and reversed it in a flurry of spray. It was one thing being fired at in the air when you had a chance to retaliate, and quite another thing on the ground, and we had not the least intention of providing a couple of sitting ducks.

The heavy rainstorms continued until October 15th when blue skies could be seen once more, and flying could be resumed. The Twelfth Reconnaissance Squadron, TLeLv 12, was transferred to Nurmoila that morning, accompanying the Sixth Army Headquarters which had now moved into the vicinity, and either by chance or by accurate intelligence, two Russian bombers suddenly appeared over the field but, fortunately, accurate flak disrupted the aim of their bombardiers who laid their eggs in the forest, well away from our aircraft. In the afternoon six of our Brewsters were assigned to fly protective cover over Voznesenja, on the neck of the southern Syväri. As we flew towards the patrol area, we could see several herds of half-wild horses south of Vatsojärvi, these apparently having belonged originally to the Russians who had abandoned the beasts during their retreat.

Cruising steadily, we approached the fast-flowing upper Syväri and the southern section of the Stalin Canal, and just a couple of miles to the east spouts of water suddenly mushroomed up, and our anti-aircraft guns fired a few tracers to attract our attention to a trio of enemy bombers skipping between the clouds. As the distance between our Brewsters and the bombers was eaten up I could hardly believe my eyes—the Russian SB-2s were equipped with skis. I had not previously encountered a *twin*-engined aircraft fitted with skis, but what was *really* surprising was the fact that nowhere was any snow to be seen. Three of our Brewsters pounced on one of the bombers which almost immediately erupted in a ball of flame and fell into the forest south of Otsa. Almost simultaneously, Jokeli Savonen and Väiski Suhonen got another of the bombers.

(Above, left) Sergeant Eric "Erkki" Lyly who flew with the author in HLeLv 24. A very capable pilot, he survived the war with seventeen kills, and is currently a Renault dealer. *(Above, right)* Sergeant Paavo Tolonen who lost his life on October 30, 1942 in a fight between four B-239s and six Russian I-16s and two Spitfires. Tolonen learned to fly before the war with the Karhumäki brothers. *(Below)* Flight Master Jätti Lehtovaara, better known as the "Little Giant" owing to his small stature. Lehtovaara gained forty-four kills and was awarded the Mannerheim Cross. He died in 1953.

(*Above*) The snow-buried tents of Fighter Group L at Nurmoila. (*Below*) The author taxiing out from beneath the trees in his Brewster (BW-390) in April 1942, but a few days later this aircraft burned fiercely (*left*) as a victim of a Russian incendiary bomb. Despite frequent Russian bombing attacks on Nurmoila, Fighter Group L lost only one Brewster in this way.

The third SB-2 fled eastward, taking violent evasive action, with me in hot pursuit. I followed every twist and turn of the Russian like some fantastic circus act, closing the range to less than a hundred yards. Just as my tracers began arching towards the fuselage of the SB-2 I received another surprise. Something like a flaming ribbon seemed to reach out from the Russian bomber towards my fighter. I broke hard to port. This was something entirely new in my experience. Could this be some new Russian secret weapon? Kaius Metsola, who by this time had joined me in pursuit of the surviving SB-2, made a firing pass at the bomber, and I once again lined up for a fresh attack on the aircraft, one engine of which was now smoking. I awaited the reappearance of the mysterious ribbon of flame with bated breath, but whatever it was, it was not used a second time, and to this day I have no idea what caused the phenomenon. I sent a long burst into the starboard engine which, like the port engine, now began to smoke. Out of the corner of my eye I saw that we were now over the Russian airfield of Kedra. I closed to within fifty yards of the SB-2, and was preparing to rake the belly of the bomber from beneath when two bundles tumbled from the Russian aircraft, and I had to bank sharply to avoid them. Two parachutes blossomed behind, and my quarry, now pilotless, began to sway erratically, lost speed, stalled, fell away on one wing, and crashed into the Sulandozero Forest.

I joined up with Kaius, and together we flew westward, calling the others over the R/T to rendezvous over the southern end of the Äänis Lake. Shortly after we joined up with the rest of the group, we spotted two gunboats in the Stalin Canal, and I couldn't resist the temptation to use up the rest of our ammunition on these small vessels. There was no movement to be seen on their decks until I had opened fire at about six hundred yards' range. Then men burst through the hatches, ran to their cannon and, almost immediately, had me boxed in by their tracers. Everywhere I looked were green, red and yellow tracers which had I not been slap in their centre would undoubtedly have made a beautiful sight, but much to my surprise I came through the barrage unscathed, and only one other Brewster had completed its firing run when "Antti Risto"—the code name for our ground control radio—came through in plain language: "Ground fog coming in from Ladoga. Return to base immediately. Repeat, immediately."

It was to be a race against time. We had ninety miles to cover, and I knew that within less than twenty minutes Nurmoila would be beneath an impenetrable blanket of fog. It was obviously to be touch and go. At full throttle we tore back towards our base. There was no sense in endeavouring to conserve fuel now. Over Aunus it was plain that seconds counted. The western perimeter of the field was already immersed in the fog which looked like a towering white cliff ahead of us, and its progress across the field could be visibly measured. We barely succeeded in slipping on to the ground before that wall of cold, damp vapour covered us like a shroud, and before we had completed our landing roll visibility was down to less than two score yards.

. . . . .

Autumn now began to fade into winter. Our combined efforts of more than a month had produced a respectable sauna bath house, and after inaugurating this vital amenity, we still had a chance to take a dip in the cold waters of the lake before it froze over. Before the snow came we made a trip to the nearby village of Siltsho in between operational sorties, our purpose being to barter tea with the local inhabitants for fresh milk and eggs. The dialect spoken by these East Karelians was closely related to Finnish, and they greeted us in the friendliest fashion.

During late October an early winter began to get an icy grip on the area. The lakes froze over as the temperature fell, and once more snowstorms became an everyday occurrence. I returned to Lunkula Island to which the rest of the squadron had transferred when Fighter Group "L" moved forward to Nurmoila, and took over command for a week while Major Magnusson took his leave, but poor weather kept flying activities to a minimum. Nevertheless, my visit to the island was not devoid of all excitement as every evening I visited our regimental headquarters in the near-by village of Salmi, and successfully defended our unit's reputation over the card-table.

I was not in the least sorry to return to Nurmoila at the end of the week as I had become quite used to the place. It was obvious that we were to spend the winter there, so we partly submerged our tents in the ground, and prepared covered revetments for our aircraft and vehicles. The depth of the snow on the field was soon such that we had to borrow a captured roller from Petroskoi, using this to pack down the snow on the runways. At the same time I put in a request for skis for our Brewsters. We had tested these during the previous spring with excellent results.

During this period we received a visit from the "old man". Our Commanding Officer had returned from his leave to be promoted to Lieutenant-Colonel, and during his visit he handed me a gold wristlet watch inscribed: "To HLeLv 24's best pilot —a token from a grateful citizen." This was certainly something of an exaggeration of my capabilities, and I was astounded by the gift. It was not until some time later that I discovered the "grateful citizen" to be a certain Doctor Feiring of Rantasalmi, a total stranger to me!

On the morning of November 7th, a cloudless blue sky and a bright if wintry sun greeted us as we made our way to the field. The ground crews were already fussing around the fighters, but as we prepared for our first mission—a reconnaissance sortie with four Brewsters to the Olhavanjoki and New Ladoga—four bombers escorted by three fighters appeared without warning overhead. We ran to our Brewsters accompanied by the staccato bark of the anti-aircraft guns and the screech and roar of the first bombs. Fortunately, our engines had already been warmed up, and within sixty seconds, as the last stick of bombs exploded on the western fringe of the field, we were tucking up our undercarriages and climbing full throttle to intercept our uninvited visitors.

The early morning sun blinded us, causing us to momentarily lose sight of our quarry, but at about nine thousand feet altitude we spotted them. The bombers were well ahead of their escort and we had little chance of intercepting them, but there was just a chance that we might overhaul the fighters. Gradually we climbed above our intended victims, closing the distance, and then, stick over and well forward, I plummeted down, building up speed rapidly as my altimeter unwound, the three other Brewsters clinging to mine like leeches. The trio of Russian fighters continued steadily on their course, apparently unaware of their imminent danger. I picked the fighter to starboard as my target, Väiski Suhonen and Hasse Wind taking the others. Still diving, we were closing with our quarry rapidly, and I could see that the Russian fighters were new LaGG-3s which, in level flight, could have shown the Brewster a clean pair of heels at most altitudes.

My LaGG grew larger in my sights, and then, suddenly, my target broke hard to starboard just as I was about to fire. Momentarily I thought that I must be up against an Ivan who really knew the score, but, surprisingly, no violent evasive action followed and, although the LaGG was obviously accelerating, I still had much of the impetus of my dive in hand and, closing to fifty yards, began firing. He took a full burst before making any attempt to evade me, and by that time he was too late. His M-105—quite a sewing machine of a power plant under normal circumstances—emitted a few puffs of smoke, the airscrew faltered and then stopped turning, and the nose of the LaGG dropped, the pilot starting down in a steep glide.

We were now down to less than three thousand feet over the northern side of the lower Syväri, and out of curiosity, I followed my victim as he glided rapidly towards the shore of Lake Ladoga. As I formated on the LaGG, my starboard wingtip just three or four feet above and behind the Russian's port wingtip, I could clearly see the instrument panel and the muffled Russian pilot crouched in the cockpit. The olive drab finish of the LaGG was dirty and oil-stained, and I could only just pick out the red five-pointed stars on the upper wing surfaces. The Russian was well behind our lines and so I held my fire, although I am not at all sure that I could have brought myself to finish off such a lame duck, if I may use a not entirely appropriate metaphor, as his inexperienced flying suggested that my "duck" could have been hardly more than a *duckling*! The Russian made a pathetic attempt to belly land on the shore, a wing digging in as he touched down, and the aircraft cartwheeled, pieces breaking away and one wing sheering off. However, the pilot could not have been badly hurt as I saw him leap from the cockpit immediately the remains of his aircraft slewed to a standstill.

I called the others over the R T and was delighted to hear Viäski and Hasse report the successful disposal of their LaGGs. In many respects the LaGG-3 had the edge on our Brewster and would certainly not have proved such easy meat had the Russian pilot-training standards been higher. We could not possibly catch the LaGG unless we had the element of surprise and could take it in a dive. If the Russian pilot saw us coming he would pile on the steam and elude us easily, but courage, spirit, guts, whatever it is that makes a fighting pilot, few of the Russians that we had encountered to that time had possessed it.

We climbed back to nine thousand feet, formed up once more, and set course for the Olhavanjoki as we still had enough fuel in our tanks to undertake the reconnaissance sortie originally assigned us. We cruised along in the clear morning air. Visibility was virtually unlimited, and there was no sign of another aircraft in the sky. At Sjastroja a large factory of some kind seemed to be running at full blast, smoke belching from multiple chimney stacks. On the Ladoga, near the mouth of the Olhavanjoki, there were at least two score of transports and warships riding at anchor, some apparently having steam up, and between the Koltsanovo and Ojat railway stations there were a total of fifteen trains with no fewer than four hundred trucks, some of these being of the flat-bed type, the tanks that they were carrying plainly visible. Apart from some desultory bursts of inaccurate flak, our reconnaissance sortie continued peacefully enough, and when we neared the German lines we turned and flew back to our base across the menacing, battleship-grey waters of Lake Ladoga.

The bombing attack that had taken place just as we were readying ourselves for our mission was, in fact, the eighth on Nurmoila, and a total of ninety-one bombs had been dropped, but apart from killing one and wounding five Russian prisoners-of-war labouring in the barracks area, a few severed telephone lines had been the total extent of the damage. So much for the standard of Russian bomb aiming.

· · · · ·

Storms and blizzards sometimes lasting for days on end became increasingly commonplace, and the snow steadily deepened until there was three feet of snow *above* our tents, the tops of our stovepipes being the only indication of the existence of any living quarters. The lights had to be kept burning all day, of course, as none could penetrate to the tents from above, and the stoves had to be watched with extreme care as they had a tendency to overheat. One night I awoke from a nightmare in which I had been vainly endeavouring to extricate myself from the cockpit of a burning plane. As I opened my eyes I was terrified to find flames really within a yard of my face. I let out a piercing yell which startled out of their slumbers the five pilots with whom I was sharing the tent. Had I not been so horrified, I am sure that the comical expressions on their faces would have sent me into paroxysms of laughter, but there was nothing funny in finding oneself in a blazing tent in the small hours, and we all set to with a will, beating at the flames with anything that came to hand. The fire had been started by an overheated stovepipe which had burned a hole in the tent roof about a square yard in size, melting the snow above which poured into the tent, soaking everything. Needless to say, nobody got much more sleep that night, with an icy wind whistling around the wet interior of the tent, and the cold stars above visible through the roof.

December 1st was the second anniversary of our squadron's first kill, and we had every intention of celebrating the event. We sent greetings to the squadron's headquarters at Lunkula, and as the snow had stopped falling and the sky was relatively clear, we ourselves took-off in the hope of adding a few more kills to the squadron's already impressive scoreboard. As had happened to be the case two years earlier, Vic Pyötsiä was once again my wingman, but I could not help reflecting how very different was the terrain below and, for that matter, our Brewsters to the Mercury-engined Fokker D.XXIs that we had been flying then. We flew the whole breadth of the Syväri, from Kuutilahti to the neck of the river itself, but fate determined a total dearth of enemy aircraft that day, and so, dejectedly, we returned to base. A low-level surprise attack without result by two enemy fighters just as twilight was falling and our anniversary celebration in the mess was beginning provided the only excitement of the day.

· · · · ·

The main group of the squadron at Lunkula was, by now, far behind the front line, and a week later it was transferred to Kontupohja, just north of Petroskoi. At this time Britain and her Dominions declared war on Finland, but undoubtedly the most important event was the opening of hostilities between Japan and the United States, and the first large-scale engagements in the Pacific, although, to us on this little airfield near Aunus with our tents under several feet of snow, the fighting in the Pacific seemed remote indeed.

Late in the month I managed to take a week's leave at Vääsky, and on the 28th reported to Sortavala where the C.O., who was now off on leave himself, turned over temporary command of the squadron to me, together with the squadron's official car. Since the official chauffeur was also on leave, I was faced with the unpleasant task of driving more than three hundred miles by night through a deserted wilderness with the temperature down to minus 30 degrees C.! By the time I had managed to scrounge enough petrol for the trip to Kontupohja by way of Nurmoila, the evening was already gone. But the night was clear if bitterly cold, and I eventually got started, maintaining an average speed of 37 m.p.h. until I reached Koirinoja. It was between here and Pitkäranta that my trials and tribulations really began.

The long slopes were as slippery as ski-runs and, without chains, my capabilities as a driver were taxed to their limits as was also, at times, my ingenuity. Sometimes I slid down a hill crabwise or even backwards as my spinning wheels vainly endeavoured to get a grip on the surface of hard-packed, frozen snow. At other times I accelerated madly in a more often than not vain attempt to reach the top of some incline. In the biting cold I shovelled sand under my wheels, and it was with infinite relief that I finally left behind the hillier portion of my trip and found myself coasting over level ground.

By this time a bright, full moon had risen above the heavily frosted trees, turning the snow-covered terrain into an indescribable fairyland. The snow glistened and shimmered as though myriads of tiny jewels had been sown across its surface, and in such surroundings I could well imagine the creations of Hans Andersen taking substance. Nature could not have provided more breathtaking beauty, and I was still enraptured when I finally reached Nurmoila—the halfway point in my journey—at 02.00 hours. Within a few minutes of my arrival I was sitting in the Command Post with an immense mug of steaming hot tea, but I could only afford to luxuriate in front of the hot stove for a short time as I still had the worst part of my journey to face; some three hours of driving over a road that would better be described as a track, through rugged wilderness, the monotony of which would remain unbroken by even the tiniest wooden shack.

Within sixty minutes I was back behind the wheel of the car. I bumped, swayed and skidded along the rutted road, the moon gradually sinking behind my back, and my veiled headlights the only illuminations for many, many miles. At this time of the year this part of the world was best left to the wolves, bears and other denizens of the forest. Although I had changed into my beloved felt boots at Nurmoila, the intense cold seemed to eat into the very marrow of my bones, and I finally drove into the two-hundred-year-old town of Petroskoi at 06.00 hours with my teeth chattering and shivering uncontrollably. It was as black as pitch, the moon having set long since, but after asking directions of several muffled sentries, I finally reached regimental headquarters where I thawed out with the aid of several cups of strong, boiling tea.

As soon as it was light I began the last stretch of the journey. A blanket of freezing fog had blown inland from the Äänisjärvi, and no sight could have been calculated to depress me more than the grey, wooden shacks of Petroskoi; depressing even in bright sunshine but, deserted and shrouded in this cold, dank vapour, as cheering as a graveyard. My spirits, temporarily raised by the hot tea at headquarters, sank to their lowest ebb yet, and I roundly cursed the winter, the war, the Russians and, in particular, the idiots that had made such a poor job of ploughing the snow on the road leading out of Petroskoi!

By the time the airfield near Kontupohja appeared, I felt completely exhausted, but a hearty meal and an hour or two with my feet up did wonders, and I decided to familiarize myself with the base, and then visit the little town of Kontupohja itself. In the latter I found few structures remaining undamaged, and the chimneys of the gutted buildings reached up from their bed of snow into the fog. The large hydro-electric plant was wrecked beyond repair. Through the gaping walls I could see that much of the machinery had been removed, and a very thorough job had been made of smashing what remained. Perhaps the most singular feature of Kontupohja was its beautiful theatre which was completely untouched. Surely the Russians could not have been conscience-stricken when it came to destroying this sole manifestation of culture for miles around. Near by, one of the small houses was relatively undamaged and obviously inhabited, but its occupants spoke only Russian, and owing to my extremely limited knowledge of that language, I only managed to discover that the men of the family were "somewhere out there", and that Kontupohja was suffering a severe food shortage.

. . . . .

Almost immediately after my arrival a tremendous snowstorm closed in the base completely for days. It was light only between 10.00 hours and 15.00 hours, and we all suffered from chronic boredom; a monotonous period in which the year 1941 died and 1942 was born. By Epiphany, the Twelfth Day, the icy grip of the East Karelian winter relaxed slightly, and the snowstorm subsided. Much rolling put the field in good shape, and I took three others with me on a long-range reconnaissance sortie which provided an opportunity to familiarize ourselves with the surrounding terrain. We flew northwards over the town of Poventsa, following the tracks of the Murmansk railway. This railway had been built during the first world war by forced labour under the most appalling weather conditions, and thousands of prisoners-of-war had been frozen to death or, during the summer months, lost in the tundra or drowned in the fast-flowing East Karelian rivers. The local inhabitants did not exaggerate when they said that the railway had been built on human bones.

Only one small train appeared on the line, trundling northward, and some heavy anti-aircraft batteries at Sekehe and Vojatsun greeted us with a concentrated but hardly accurate barrage through which we flew completely unscathed. After reaching the Solovetski Islands in the Viena Sea, we turned at Soroka for the return flight to our base. Just as we were crossing the lines on the peninsula between the Sees and Uiku lakes, the sun slid from behind the clouds that had shrouded it for so many days and the snow-draped landscape below dazzled our eyes. We couldn't distinguish the battle positions beneath us, all of which were veiled by the white carpet scarred only by a few freshly made shell craters, the black-green stretches of forest and, occasionally, a burned-out, abandoned village. The city of Karhumäki was almost completely buried under the snow, and but for the shadows cast by one or two of the taller buildings would have slid beneath us unnoticed. Ten minutes later we were landing at our base. The Russians evidently did not intend to take advantage of the long-awaited flying weather.

That night, despite a temperature of minus 20 degrees C., the bright moonlight lured Hasse Wind and me out of our tents for some exercise. Under the brilliant, star-bedecked sky we alternately ran and walked some six miles along tracks in the vicinity of the base, only the squeaking of our boots in the snow breaking the silence. We worked up a fine sweat by the time we got back to the base, heading straight for the sauna bath house. Afterwards, with every pore tingling, we were convinced that we had never felt so fit.

Colonel Magnusson returned from his leave and, on January 10th, in the middle of a blizzard, I turned up at Nurmoila to relieve Olli Puhakka who had taken charge of Fighter Group "L" during my absence. Two fresh young pilots, Mikko Siren and Pate Tolonen, arrived at Nurmoila from the Central Flying School on the same day, and they were to have to complete their type familiarization on the Brewster and their combat training as and when the weather and, of course, the Russians permitted. To my intense surprise, my request for skis for our Brewsters had been turned down flat. Our earlier trials with skis had been so successful that I was at a loss to understand why our group should be forbidden them now. Fortunately, we still had two pairs of skis and with these attached to their Brewsters our fledgelings were able to make several familiarization flights from the snow covering the field. As theoretical combat training seemed a complete waste of time under such conditions, their advanced training was eventually carried out over the front line in company with the old hands.

Keeping our runway serviceable was a constant trial and tribulation. Our heavy rollers packed the snow down hard, but as the temperatures rose to around 0 degrees C., the surface softened, presenting a very real hazard. Lacking skis our Brewsters could easily turn over during a take-off or landing as their narrow tyres tended to break through the hard-packed snow crust. One freezing night we attempted to turn the runway into a solid block of ice by dousing it with water, using a pump borrowed from the local fire unit. After pouring more than two hundred thousand gallons of water on just a small strip of the runway we gave up in disgust. All that was left was to remove the layers of softened snow, but this was more easily said than done, for a two-and-a-half million cubic foot area had to be cleared.

A Canadian rotary plough, and the largest plough that our engineering battalion possessed could not tackle the job so, in sheer desperation, I contacted the Sixth Army Headquarters to see if there was some way in which they could help us out of our dilemma. Lieutenant-General Blick himself came along to size up our problem, and in no time at all three hundred Russian prisoners-of-war had arrived with shovels. I had rarely seen poorer-looking specimens. They were gaunt, stoop-shouldered and, in many cases, very ragged, but although their individual efforts were meagre, there were so many of them that, collectively, they achieved the desired effect. Tractor-drawn sledges carried the snow to the perimeter, and in no time we had a perfectly usable runway.

We steadily improved the facilities of our base and, towards the end of February, our covered servicing revetments were completed. At the same time we moved into warm, well-built dugouts to bring an end to the tent life that we all detested so heartily. The dugout built for use as the Command Post was dubbed the "Bungalow", although nobody seemed to know why, and its windows, which were just above ground level, gave an excellent view across the Lintujärvi, merely a few yards away. From Nurmoila our transport regularly shuttled backwards and forwards between Petroskoi, from where we obtained our gasoline, and, less frequently, to Alavoisi, from where we drew our rations such as they were, for, to a very great extent, we lived "off the land", much of the food that we ate being captured enemy stores, the bag from hunting and fishing, or the spoils of local foraging.

The Russians were presumably aware that we had made ourselves thoroughly comfortable at Nurmoila, for they began to pay increasing attention to the base, and bomber and fighter attacks became an everyday occurrence. On one day we were attacked three times, but despite the quantity of bombs dropped, few actually fell on the airfield itself. In addition to bombs, the Russian aircraft carried propaganda leaflets which they strewed liberally over the base, usefully supplementing our supplies of toilet paper. The Russians evidently presumed that Nurmoila was occupied by the Luftwaffe, for the leaflets were all printed in German. So much for their intelligence reports and aircraft recognition. It was while providing us with this unwanted literature that our anti-aircraft guns added a second Russian bomber to their score.

Each Russian intrusion was a surprise attack so far as we were concerned. Nurmoila was only twenty-five miles behind the front line at its nearest point—just five minutes' flying time. If we had any warning whatsoever of the approach of Russian bombers it was only of one minute or two at the most. When low-flying fighters strafed the field, the rattle of their machine-guns was usually our only warning.

. . . . .

To our surprise, the first signs of the approaching spring had come with February, and the snow melted with remarkable rapidity, quickly losing its sparklingly fresh appearance and becoming a dirty grey, its surface looking as though it had received a dusting of soot. The immense drifts and banks of snow dwindled almost before our eyes, and the water trickled merrily and then poured in a torrent along the ditches, but each night everything froze solidly once more. The air was really enervating, and it was a real pleasure to draw in deep, intoxicating draughts without feeling that one's lungs were turning into blocks of ice. Quite pleasant breezes blew each evening when we all strapped on our skis to take advantage of the last snow, but there was soon too little snow for these evening jaunts, and we took to visiting the army barracks to watch film shows which appeared also to be much appreciated by the local inhabitants.

At this time there was much discussion about Russian agents and saboteurs in the area. There certainly seemed to be a secret radio operating in Aunus, although every effort of the Finnish Army to route out the agents operating the radio proved fruitless. As we took-off from Nurmoila on interception missions the enemy bomber formations withdrew, but as we returned to base, most of our fuel exhausted, they reappeared. There could be no doubt whatsoever that the Russians were receiving a running commentary on our activities, placing us at a distinct disadvantage.

By chance, I happened to hear that the pilot of the LaGG-3 that I had shot down a few months earlier was in a near-by Mäkriä prisoner-of-war compound. Never having met one of my victims face-to-face and hoping to enliven what, for him, must have been a monotonous and dull existence, I requested that he be brought to our base. He proved to be a young Ukrainian lieutenant with hardly more than a hundred flying hours to his credit. Apparently he had been flying his second operational mission when I came upon him, and I could not help but think how much more limited in general knowledge and how much cruder in behaviour were Russian officers to Finns of comparable rank. At first our guest was surly, merely glowering at us and evidently most suspicious of our friendly overtures, but after a hearty meal, a drink or two, and several cigarettes, he became friendliness itself, exuding bonhomie. He told us of his life as a student in Russia and of what to us seemed a drastically limited flying training. Before returning to the compound under escort, Lieutenant Petre F—v made a short speech in which he thanked us for our hospitality and even wished our group success in combat!

· · · · ·

Throughout March and April the days lengthened and the weather improved, and in addition to reconnaissance sorties, protective patrols and interception missions, we often undertook escort duties. Sometimes we found ourselves escorting a Junkers W.34 ambulance aircraft out of Vorobjev, a Fokker C.X artillery spotter directing our batteries in the Batashevskaja-Enojärvi area, and, now and again, we would escort a lone Blenheim on a high-altitude photo-reconnaissance sortie, such penetrations sometimes extending from the southern end of Lake Ladoga to the eastern shores of the Äänisjärvi in width, and almost to Tihvinä in depth, usually being flown at altitudes of around twenty thousand feet, necessitating our flying for protracted periods on oxygen.

On the eve of May Day my adjutant and I called in at the officers' club in Aunus where a celebration was being held, but we returned to Nurmoila before nightfall, and after supper we sat around our dugouts enjoying the quiet and the sweet, cool air of the moonlit spring evening. We had still to finish our first cigarettes when our relaxation was disrupted by the drone of an aero engine approaching from the south. We didn't need to hear the bombs shrieking down to know that the Russians were giving us the benefit of another of their nocturnal nuisance raids which did little damage and were obviously intended more for psychological effect, acting more on our nerves than on the airfield itself.

The roar of the aero engine grew until it seemed to be almost overhead, then it cut out completely and we could hear the whistling of the slipstream in the bracing wires as, in the moonlight, we saw the silhouette of an old Polikarpov R-5 two-seater in a shallow dive. As we heard the whistling of many small bombs, tracers began to scorch upwards from several points along the airfield perimeter as the anti-aircraft defences swung into action, these converging on the R-5, but it sailed through the barrage, apparently unharmed, and over the far end of the field its pilot opened up the engine once more and its noise gradually faded into the night.

Fifteen minutes of peace and quiet and then a repeat performance. In all, there were seven sorties by solitary R-5s at intervals of fifteen or twenty minutes, and it was long past midnight before we had finally extinguished the many small fires that had been started in the surrounding forest and, disgruntled, made our way to our sleeping-bags. Early in the morning the communications unit was busily repairing about fifteen breaks in our telephone lines caused by some of the hundred or so small bombs dropped during the night, and the discovery that some of these missiles had been special contraptions the size and shape of cricket balls which burst into flame immediately the sunlight fell on them necessitated combing the whole area very carefully indeed.

Noon on May Day was scheduled for the grand opening of our new theatre building, and keeping in mind the possibility of a surprise attack from Ivan, we laid on an aerial umbrella of Brewsters. Once we flew directly over the theatre almost "on the deck", and we learned afterwards that we had buzzed the building just as our choir had begun to sing "Again the Skylarks are in the Sky", and the effect was really tremendous, for the Wright Cyclone had a healthy growl, and our arrival at that moment brought a spontaneous burst of cheering.

A few hours later, at 15.58 hours to be exact, seven Russian bombers coming in from the Ladoga with the sun behind them took us completely by surprise. They dropped their bombs from a fairly high altitude and made good their escape by diving in the direction from which they had come. The whole attack took place so quickly that we had no chance to scramble more than two aircraft, my own and Reiska Valli's machines. Some of the bombs had fallen among our dugouts causing little damage, but at the barracks fifteen were killed, including three Lottas,[1] a number were injured, three cars were destroyed, the telephone exchange received a direct hit, and two of the barrack blocks were set afire.

Once airborne we realised that we stood no chance whatsoever of catching the bombers, and so we decided to make an offensive patrol over the enemy's lines. After two hours in the air without a sign of a Russian aircraft, I suddenly spotted two Tchaikas slightly below and to starboard. Knowing only too well the capabilities of these barrel-like little biplanes, I knew that our best chance of success lay in using the element of surprise. Fortunately, the sun was behind us, and as the Tchaikas did not deviate from their course it was obvious that we were unobserved.

Stealthily stalking our game with the sun hiding our approach, we got behind and slightly above the unsuspecting Russians, and then, throttles wide open, we closed for the kill. Picking the leading Tchaika, which was flying slightly above its fellow, I began firing at a range of between seventy and eighty yards with immediate results. The tailplane of the Tchaika seemed to disintegrate under my hail of fire, and before the pilot could have known what had hit him, it had fallen away in a spin. I watched as the little biplane spun straight into the ground near Kuutilahti, immediately turning into a vicious flower with a glowing core and black, swirling edges. Just at that moment, Reiska

[1] Lottas—Auxiliary women's units known as Lotta Svard and comparable with the wartime Allied women's auxiliary services.

Valli told me over the R/T that he too had bagged a Tchaika, and so, somewhat mollified at having partly avenged ourselves on Ivan for the surprise bombing raid, we flew back to Nurmoila.

· · · · ·

May 8th was truly visitors' day at Nurmoila for, after the arrival of nearly a score of Swedish Air Force officers who had come to see at first hand our methods of operation and the conditions under which we were flying, Captain Heinilä, the Commanding Officer of HLeLv 32, Fighter Squadron 32, turned up to inspect what he referred to as his future base. This served to confirm the rumour that had been going around for some weeks to the effect that we were to be transferred farther north. In the evening a further visitor arrived, this time Colonel Reiska Artola, Commanding Officer of the Dornier Do 17Z bomber squadron, PLeLv 46,[1] who came to discuss the provision of a fighter escort for an attack to be made by his bombers the next morning. I promised to have six Brewsters in the air in time to rendezvous with his Do 17Zs at 06.10 hours.

The next day dawned without a cloud in the sky. I strolled across to the dispersal area where the rising sun was already sparkling on the cockpit canopies of the squat, camouflaged Brewsters, and the ground staff were making their final inspections and adjustments. I briefed the five pilots who were to accompany me on this escort mission as we smoked our first cigarettes of the day. We clambered into our cockpits, and one by one the Cyclones were run up, their throaty roaring coarsely disturbing the early morning stillness. We took-off in pairs and formed up in two Vics over the field as eleven of Artola's Dorniers, in superb formation, appeared from the north-west. Our sextet of Brewsters positioned itself slightly aft, to port and above its charges, and the whole formation swung east. This meant that we were facing directly into the sun and would have had no warning of the approach of enemy interceptors from that direction. Accordingly, I divided our fighters into two flights of three which flew well out to port and starboard of the Dorniers to increase our chances of spotting any Russian fighters before they could make a pass at them.

---

[1] PLeLv 46 had re-equipped with Do 17Z bombers from Blenheims in January 1942.

(*Above, left*) On the left, Colonel Riku Lorentz, the Commander of Air Regiment LeR 2, and, on the right, Lieut-Col. G. E. Magnusson. Colonel Lorentz virtually created Finland's fighter force, and had it not been for his tactical foresight Finnish successes in the air would undoubtedly have been drastically reduced. Colonel Magnusson took over the command of Air Regiment LeR 3 in May 1943, this comprising HLeLv 24, 26 and 34, and he set the example for his men by scoring a number of kills while flying Fokkers and Brewsters. (*Above, right*) The author photographed before his last flight in a Brewster. The beer bottle labels on the fin represented his score at that time. (*Below*) Handing over the Mensuvaara base in July 1942 to Leutnant Götz of I/J.G.54, the "Green Hearts". The author is on the left.

(*Above*) Korppu Paltila standing beside his I-153 Tchaika which was used for reconnaissance purposes by TLeLv 30. The M-63 engine of the Tchaika was supremely unreliable, and Paltila, who was the Leader of the Tchaika Flight, was drowned when his aircraft had to be ditched in the Gulf of Finland after an engine failure. (*Below*) Some of the pilots of TLeLv 30. Left to right, T. A. "Ture" Mattila, Petter Ahonius, the author, H. Himmanen and Otto Karme. Mattila joined the author in HLeLv 34, scoring four kills, and Sergeant Major Karme transferred from TLeLv 30 to HLeLv 26 which had converted from G.50s to worn-out Brewster B-239s.

As we crossed over Mäkiselkä at an altitude of about five thousand feet, along the Murmansk railway, we were fired upon by our own flak despite giving the pre-arranged recognition signal. Perhaps the gunners hadn't rubbed the sleep from their eyes, and a lone enemy fighter, obviously attracted by the anti-aircraft fire, beat a hasty retreat when its pilot saw the size of our formation. We flew on steadily, crossed the Äänisjärvi, and finally reached our objective, Olkava, at the mouth of the Äänis River. If we were to be bounced by enemy fighters this seemed to be the best time for such an attack, and we all kept our eyes peeled for an attempted interception. The targets for our Dorniers were a number of supply barges, and I watched with satisfaction as the sticks of bombs tumbled from the gaping bomb-bays, rapidly dwindled in size and, seconds later, erupted in columns of débris and water, several of the barges receiving direct hits, some turning turtle, and others, holed below the waterline, settling quickly. I metaphorically took my hat off to the bomber boys for their accuracy. With their bomb-doors now closed, the Dorniers began a wide turn towards home, and once we had escorted them back to the western bank of the Äänisjärvi, a weight had been lifted from my shoulders and, having plenty of fuel remaining in our tanks, I decided to skirt the southern shores of the big lake in an attempt to flush up some enemy fighters.

During the previous few days we had flown several cover missions for the ground forces in the battle area south of the Syväri at Bulajeva, and I thought that the distinctive outline of the Brewster fighter would have been known to every artilleryman for miles around, but we soon learned that such was not the case. As we approached the familiar area at an altitude of about two thousand feet a stream of what seemed to be brightly-coloured golf balls hurtled past the cockpit, and in the wink of an eye we were flying through one of the most vicious flak barrages that I had ever had the misfortune to experience. What was most disconcerting was the fact that the shells being hurled at us were Finnish.

I hastily gave the recognition signal, but the barrage was only intensified, and as two holes suddenly appeared in the starboard wing of my aircraft, I decided to head for safer altitudes at full throttle. Dame Fortune must certainly have smiled upon us for, apart from the two rents in my starboard wing, so far as I could see our aircraft appeared to have flown through the concentrated barrage undamaged. With no further thought of flushing up some Russians, and thoroughly sobered by our unpleasant experience, we flew back to Nurmoila, landing there as the hands of the clock pointed to 08.00 hours.

I hurried to the Command Post telephone to complain heatedly to Army Headquarters that their flak batteries not only failed to recognise friendly aircraft; they couldn't even remember the signal for the day! With my temper somewhat assauged after letting off steam, I headed for the mess and a hearty breakfast. Later that day I was told that an anti-aircraft unit commander newly arrived from Central Finland had given the order to fire which had, automatically, gone out to all batteries in the area. His abject apologies were duly accepted, and afterwards we laughed at the thought of his embarrassment when he learned that he had wasted all that ammunition on friendly fighters.

11

A NOMAD'S LIFE

While I was on leave Fighter Group "L" received orders to move from Nurmoila to Hirvas, where we were to rejoin the rest of the squadron. I returned to Nurmoila from my leave on May 30th, and was saddened to learn that, on the previous day, while the boys had been busily readying everything for the move, we had received a visit from Russian bombers, and one of our Brewsters, BW-390, had been set ablaze. In the nine months that we had been at Nurmoila we had been attacked forty-seven times and had been on the receiving end of eleven hundred bombs, yet we had not lost one man or major item of equipment. Now, at the very last moment, we had lost one of our precious fighters.

I had reached Nurmoila in the small hours, and decided to leave for the new base in the BMW on the same morning. So, loading my kit into the car, and bidding farewell to the so-familiar "Bungalow", I drove leisurely in the direction of Petroskoi. I stopped at the radio station, which was managed by an old friend of mine, Pekka Tiilikainen, and, after coffee, strolled around the streets of the town, most of which were cobbled with wooden sidewalks. Only one had an asphalt surface, the so-called Karl Marx Street, and I was amused to see that all the original Finnish signposts had had Russian directions added. I drove on some sixty miles, passing through the town of Kontopohja, but during the last forty miles the only sign of civilization in this wild area was the village of Mundjärvi, after which I found myself on the peninsula between the Pällä lakes, finally reaching Hirvas airfield which really was in the middle of nowhere.

There could be no doubt, however, that Hirvas was surrounded by far more than its share of natural beauty. Alongside the field was a fast-flowing, turbulent river running through a steep-sided gorge, and the wild terrain, totally unspoiled by power lines, telegraph poles or other signs of the twentieth century, had remained unchanged for hundreds of years. War seemed remote among the spruces and pines of this spot, and nothing sounded as unnatural as the roar of powerful aero engines.

The sun shone continuously throughout the long summer days, and we could not have wished for better flying weather. We flew many missions, and on June 4th had the honour of providing the fighter escort for our much-loved Marshal Mannerheim on the occasion of his seventy-fifth birthday. Adolf Hitler himself flew to Immola to offer the marshal his personal greetings, and it was announced that henceforth our great leader was to be known as the Marshal of Finland. In the excitement I almost forgot that the day was also my thirty-third birthday.

The next day found us back at Hirvas, and as the whole squadron was now based here, we all had more free time than what we had become accustomed to, and I spent much of this wandering in the near-by countryside, fishing in the lakes and streams. These abounded with fish, and the best of tall fishing stories could be capped by the actual catches that we made. Two or three hours' fishing found the angler with as many fish as he could carry away.

The well-known Finnish accordionist Toivo Manninen and his troupe of artistes, Lili Menz-Nifontova, Liisa Rope and Olavi Tilli, arrived at Hirvas to provide us with an evening's entertainment which was attended by our regimental commander, Colonel Lorentz, and as the C.O. was away, the task of organizing the special dinner for our guests descended upon me. The repast of freshly smoked fish and roast venison was simple fare perhaps, but eaten in the twilight on the bank of the river it became a memorable occasion.

Our idyll in this unspoiled spot was to be short-lived, however, for the rumour already circulating around the squadron that our aircraft were needed elsewhere became fact on June 9th, when the order was received that one flight was to be despatched immediately to the Suulajärvi airfield, near Perkjärvi, some three hundred and seventy miles away. As my flight possessed the most combat experience, it was decided that this should be the flight to be transferred, so Fighter Group "L" resumed its existence, but as the C.O. was still away I had to stay behind at Hirvas to hand over command on his return.

A week later my ten-plane flight was instructed to take over the Mensuvaara airfield in addition to Suulajärvi in order to provide interceptor cover for the northern end of Ladoga. Mensuvaara was just north-west of Sortavala and, with the return of the C.O., I decided to drive there first, planning to take my time over the journey, making the trip via Aunus and taking the opportunity to check and confirm the locations of some of our probable kills. According to the map, the total distance by road was some six hundred and twenty miles, and from Aunus I travelled to the Kuutilahti front where, plagued by mosquitoes and crawling through woodland under the crossfire of Finnish and Russian artillery, I found the last of the victims that we had recorded previously as probable kills.

I drove continuously for some four hundred and thirty miles until I finally reached Mensuvaara airfield, where five of our Brewsters had been flown in the day before. The airfield didn't possess a sauna bath house, so I drove the six miles to my former home for a sauna to sweat the road dust from my pores. By this time I had had my fill of driving over bad roads in the little BMW, so leaving the car at Mensuvaara, I took one of the Brewsters, landed at Immola to get a briefing from Lieutenant-Colonel Nuotio at regimental headquarters, and then flew on to the circular Russian-built airfield at Suulajärvi.

All available quarters had already been commandeered by another squadron, so once again we were forced to erect our own "nests", although we had progressed somewhat from the crude tents in which we had spent so many uncomfortable nights—we now erected small pasteboard huts which we placed along the fringes of a near-by forest. During this period of the midnight sun we were all on duty twenty-four hours a day, and as my group had been split in half, I frequently took part in an interception mission from Mensuvaara and, after completing the mission, landed back at Suulajärvi. My existence was thus quite nomadic, but in this way I kept in close touch with both components of Fighter Group "L". At the former base some log cabins had been built in the near-by woods, making living conditions quite tolerable. In fact, we could almost taxi our fighters to the doorsteps of our cabins, and if we had to take-off quickly on an emergency mission during the "night", we could put our flying jackets over our pyjamas, stepping almost straight from our bunks into our cockpits, and vice versa. Fortunately, none of us had to make a forced landing in pyjamas!

Early in July a number of Luftwaffe Messerschmitt Bf 109F fighters from the 1st Gruppe of Jagdgeschwader 54, the "Green Hearts", arrived at Mensuvaara. I/JG 54 was led by a very well-known German fighter pilot, Hauptmann Hans Philips,[1] and the Bf 109Fs of this detachment operated alongside our Brewsters for several days, and during the evenings we enjoyed the hospitality of our German comrades under the wings of their Junkers Ju 52/3m transport. The Luftwaffe fighters were led by Oberleutnant Götz to whom I handed over the base on July 8th, returning to Suulajärvi where the rest of the squadron had now arrived to participate in the Somer occupation air battles. Once again attached to the squadron, we all managed to get some free time once more, and took the opportunity to visit Viipuri in a vain attempt to recapture some of our pre-war memories of the city. But Viipuri had suffered severely, and no matter in which direction we looked we found depressing evidence of the ravages of war, so we took to finding our recreation nearer at hand. The Karelian isthmus was extremely beautiful at this time of the year. The summer flowers were all in full bloom, and all along the narrow roads a profusion of bright red wild roses gave off a heady perfume.

. . . . .

At 03.00 hours on the sultry night of July 20th we were hurriedly aroused on a standby alert. There was evidently an unusual amount of enemy air activity over the Gulf. We ran up our engines, made the usual cockpit checks, switched off, and stood around our aircraft, smoking and talking. Shortly before 04.30 hours orders came through to send four fighters on a patrol, and a few minutes later we were in the air and heading south, with the sun rising on our port side. Despite the earliness of the hour, an artillery duel was in progress between

[1] Oberleutnant Hans Philips, a Staffelkapitän of JG 54 (Green Hearts), was promoted to Hauptmann and Gruppenkommandeur early in 1942. He lost his life on the Western Front on October 8, 1943, by which time he had been promoted to Oberstleutnant and had become Kommodore of JG 1.

the Ino coastal batteries and Russian batteries across the Gulf. Farther to the west we could see the island of Seiskari, and some fifteen or twenty ships could be seen moving in its vicinity. Our early-warning radio station was now located at Seivästö, and was using the code name "Tarhapöllö" (Yard Owl). Tarhapöllö came on the air at that moment to inform us that they could hear the noise of aero engines to the west. I scanned the sky ahead carefully, and I eventually saw a tiny speck against the cloudless blue. Gradually the speck took on the shape of a Petlyakov Pe-2; a sleek and fast light reconnaissance-bomber. Following it were four enemy fighters. I selected the Pe-2 as my personal target, ordering the others to take on its fighter escort.

The Pe-2 was flying east, evidently returning to its base from an early-morning long-range reconnaissance mission. We were above the Russians but, flying into the sun, were partly blinded. The Pe-2, which appeared to have pale-grey upper surfaces, banked sharply to starboard and then put its nose down as I drew within range, exposing its sky-blue belly. I was surprised to see what appeared to be a torpedo hanging beneath the aircraft, but the pilot hurriedly jettisoned this burden in order to increase his speed. I clung tightly to the Russian's tail, loosing short bursts into the empennage and rear fuselage, quickly silencing the dorsal gunner. I then concentrated on his engines, and we were tearing past the Kronstadt Fortress at low level when, without warning, the Pe-2's starboard wing burst into flame. I immediately pulled up the nose of my Brewster and watched two crew members jump from my victim, their 'chutes hanging lazily in the sky as the Russian aircraft splashed into the sea near Pietarhov, the outer harbour of Leningrad.

This, my tenth kill, had carried me over the outskirts of this city of a million inhabitants built at the mouth of the Neva River, but I had no time for sight-seeing for my intrusion had aroused the heavy flak batteries, and I had no desire to run the gauntlet of their barrage. I carefully circumnavigated the area covered by the Kronstadt anti-aircraft defences, and met up with Mikko Siren and Erkki Lyly over Ino. It transpired that they had taken care of two of the Russian fighters, and it was a pleasure to awaken everybody at the base so early in the morning with our three low-level victory rolls. But the day hadn't really started and, as we enjoyed breakfast, the armourers were replenishing our ammunition, the fuel tanks were being topped up, and the mechanics were busily checking over our aircraft.

In the meantime, our ally, Germany, had suffered a serious reverse. The drive to the east had bogged down in the ruins of Stalingrad,[1] and the conflict on the Eastern Front had become static. For the time being it was stalemate. So far as we were concerned, enemy air activity was largely restricted to the Gulf of Finland and Finnish coastal areas, so, early in August, we were transferred to the Römpötti airfield, near the town of Makslahti, this base offering us better hunting than Suulajärvi in Central Karelia. Our operations now covered the area bounded by Lugalahti, Seiskari, Lavansaari, and Suursaari, to the southern shores of Finland. The Russian fighters were based on the two islands Lavansaari and Seiskari, and above these bases we were to fight some of our most violent air battles, but although Ivan proved to be full of fight when over his home base, we managed to destroy a number of the Russians without loss to ourselves.

To increase effective control of our fighters, several additional ground radio stations were established along the shoreline of the Kannas, or Karelian Heel, as well as in the area of the front line itself. During an inspection of one of these radio stations, the C.O. and I called on General Pajari's headquarters. This straddled the pre-war frontier, on the shore of a small lake, the Kaukijärvi, in the midst of beautiful pine and spruce forests. The whole area was incredibly neat, with a beautifully trimmed lawn, sand-covered paths, and delightful flower and vegetable gardens. After enjoying a fine meal, we went right up to the front line and Mainila, the exact spot where the infamous artillery rounds were alleged by the Russians to have been fired by Finnish frontier guards, killing a Russian N.C.O. and several troops, and providing the excuse to attack our country. After a visit to the general's sauna and a swim in the Kaukijärvi, we made our way back to our base.

· · · · ·

In Eastern Karelia, and particularly north of Karhumäki, the enemy began to step up his aerial activities early in September,

[1] Now known as Volgagrad.

and on the 16th of that month the order came for ten of our fighters to return to Hirvas. With barely an hour's notice, we were loading our gear aboard two transport aircraft and, after a hurried breakfast, were airborne and heading north-east. Within three hours of the receipt of our orders and three hundred miles away from the base that we had left that morning, we were once more ready for operations.

A week later, on September 23rd, all operational flying was cancelled as the clouds were hanging in the treetops and a fine drizzle of rain was falling, but by noon the ceiling had risen to about four hundred feet and, as it was necessary for me to visit squadron headquarters at Makslahti, I decided to take a chance. Hedge-hopping gives a pilot an exhilarating feeling of speed which disappears with altitude, and without any qualms, I set a rule-of-thumb course for my four-hundred-mile low-level flight, much of which was to be made over totally uninhabited areas of East Karelia where weather reports were unknown. I memorized the various check-points and took-off.

Flying just below the cloud base, I succeeded in maintaining an altitude of three hundred feet as far as Suojärvi, but over the Karelian Ladoga the cloud base dropped, forcing me to treetop level. Even the smaller hills were shrouded in mist, and, although instinct told me to turn back before it was too late, sheer obstinacy drove me on and, frequently changing course to avoid obstacles that loomed in my path, I was soon hopelessly lost! I tried to follow the occasional road, but one junction looked much like another, and I dared not drag my eyes away from the windscreen for a moment to glance at the map for fear that I would hit a hillock or a clump of trees on high ground. The compass was useless as my frequent deviations caused it to spin like a top, and I never kept one heading long enough for it to settle down.

I believed that I was somewhere over the north-east Ladoga sector, and hopefully peered around for a familiar landmark. Narrowly avoiding some high-tension cables, I suddenly found a railway line which I began to follow blindly in what seemed to be the opposite direction to that in which I had been travelling. I almost shouted with relief when, after ten minutes, the familiar outskirts of Sortavala appeared through the murk.

From Sortavala I followed the tracks to Viipuri from where I expected to continue following the tracks to Makslahti. The belly of my Brewster was barely clearing the telegraph poles alongside the railway tracks, and as I was flying at 250 m.p.h., it was a miracle how I avoided some obstacles which I failed to see at all until they flashed past to port or starboard.

From Jaakkimaa the situation became progressively worse. A thick pall of fog rose from the forests like the smoke from a thousand fires until, even at tree-top height, I could no longer see the terrain over which I was passing. I knew that Mensuvaara airfield was somewhere hereabouts, and under normal conditions I knew this countryside like the back of my hand. I made a 180-degrees turn with my tongue in my cheek, and a hundred-to-one chance came off. Through a slight gap in the veil of fog I got my bearings which told me that I was already on the approach to the main runway. There was not even time to lower my flaps, and the undercarriage had only just locked down when the wheels struck the ground. The Brewster bounded into the air, and then settled, and I taxied to the perimeter of the field, profoundly relieved that my nerve-racking experience was at an end.

The following morning the weather had improved sufficiently for me to continue my flight to the Römpötti airfield, near Makslahti, and twenty-four hours later I was once more on my way back to Hirvas. The weather by now was excellent, and my Cyclone engine sang sweetly as I cruised along at an altitude of ten thousand feet. Lake Ladoga lay before me, almost to the horizon, calm and as smooth as glass under the autumn sky, and I am not sure if something had subconsciously attracted my attention or if it was a desire to fly across my old home on the northern shore that lured me off my course.

As I crossed the town of Lahdenpohja I saw some puffs of anti-aircraft shells over the upper shores of Ladoga. I couldn't see what the gunners were firing at but it seemed possible that they were trying to give me a bearing on some intruding Russian. As I stared I thought I caught a momentary reflection of sunlight from a perspex surface, and turning in that direction I soon picked out a lone aircraft. As the distance between us narrowed I could see that it was a Pe-2. My approach had not gone unobserved, for the dorsal gun was flashing like a neon sign. I closed to within fifty yards of the Russian, my Brewster bouncing around in its slipstream. My first burst of fire shattered the perspex of the dorsal turret and, ten seconds later, my second burst knocked out the port engine which immediately spewed flame. The Pe-2 fell away on one wing and then went into a vertical dive, leaving a long black column of smoke which terminated in a tremendous flash on the island of Puutsalo.

I flew on over Pitkäjärvi, Kuokkajärvi, and Kuikkalampi, spots which brought back vivid memories of peaceful fishing, hunting, canoeing, and swimming excursions of my boyhood days, and although I kept a weather eye open, I was lost in reverie until I found myself in the landing circuit at Hirvas.

. . . . .

Erratic weather now kept us on the ground frequently, but our life was not without its diversifications as, during one of these periods when operational flying was impossible, a carefully organised search of the near-by forest as a result of a fix from radio direction-finders enabled us to locate an enemy agent, together with his radio apparatus, who had been faithfully reporting to the Russians every movement that we made. On another occasion a huge bear suddenly emerged from the forest on the edge of the field, and a tremendous hue and cry took place with all of us participating in the hunt, but without tracking dogs we soon lost our quarry in the dense undergrowth.

When we could get into the air again we undertook a number of escort and interception missions over the Merimaanselkä, Poventsa, and Krivi areas, and some extremely fierce dogfights took place. Our enemy was now flying substantial numbers of Hawker Hurricanes[1] and Curtiss P-40s[1] as well as other British and American types, and in raids on our field the Russians began to drop a new type of bomb which exploded

[1] More than a fifth of the Hurricanes built in the United Kingdom were shipped to the Soviet Union. The Hurricane IIBs of No. 151 Squadron R.A.F., which had operated from Vaenga airfield, Murmansk, had been handed over to the 72nd Regiment of the VVS-VMF (Air Forces of the Military Marine Fleet), and a total of 2,952 Hurricanes was eventually supplied to Russia, including 210 Mk. IIAs, 1,557 Mk. IIBs, 1,009 Mk. IICs, 60 Mk. IIDs, and 30 Mk. IVs. A total of 2,097 Curtiss P-40s was supplied to Russia, including 24 P-40Bs and 146 P-40Cs re-shipped from the United Kingdom. Variants supplied to the Soviet Air Forces included the P-40B, C, E, F, K, M and N.

just before striking the ground. However, the splinters had little effect on either personnel or equipment.

On October 1st, the first anniversary of our occupation of Petroskoi, we were ordered to provide protective cover for a celebration parade. Pive Ervi's flight, a detachment of our squadron based far to the north of Tiiksjärvi, paid us a visit, but in the midst of the celebrations I received a telegram from headquarters ordering Fighter Group "L" to rejoin the squadron immediately. Soon after lunch the wheels of my Brewster lifted from that East Karelian field of Hirvas for the last time and, not without some nostalgia for the many good times that we had enjoyed there, we formed up in a tight nine-plane formation, buzzed the field once, and set course for Römpötti and the main force of the squadron.

The weather was poor for some time after our return to Römpötti, low cloud, rain and dank mist keeping us grounded much of the time, and all of us anxiously awaited the arrival of decent flying weather. Finally, on October 30th, the ceiling lifted, and we took-off on an offensive patrol with five planes into a grey dawn. Reiska Valli's oil pump began to give trouble soon after the take-off, so he was forced to abort, leaving four of us to continue southward. The horizon was indistinct and visibility was not too good, but Vaffe Vahvelainen, one of our flight-sergeants who was taking a turn of duty at the Seivästö radio warning station, called us over the radio, directing us toward an enemy formation that had been spotted south of the station. I scanned the sky thoroughly and above the Inkeri shoreline, near Oranienbaum on the Russian side, and well above our altitude I counted eight tiny black specks. I called my companions, Kaius Metsola, Vilppu Lakio, and Pate Tolonen, pointing out the Russians above us, and suggesting that we might take on two each!

We began climbing towards the enemy formation, the needle of the altimeter slowly winding, eight . . . nine . . . ten . . . eleven thousand feet. At this altitude we could see that six of the Russians were I-16s, but the other two fighters were not so readily identifiable. Twelve . . . thirteen thousand feet, and it was obvious that the Russians had spotted us. There was no longer any chance of bouncing them so, with throttles wide open, we tore into the Ivans, each selecting a target. I fired one short burst at an I-16 and pulled up into an Immelmann. The sky was immediately a fantastic mêlée of frantically twisting and turning aircraft. The intercom was a babble of excited voices, oaths, warnings, and counter-warnings. The third flight was operating on the same wavelength and had evidently taken on a large gaggle of Russians somewhere near Seiskari. Everyone was shouting at the same time. Above me, an I-16 clawed into a vertical stall, stood on its tail for a fraction of a second, and then fell away into the forest below. Almost at the same moment tracers flickered past my cockpit. Instinctively, with throttle wide open, I pulled the Brewster into the tightest of shuddering vertical turns, and the I-16 that had managed to get on my tail flashed past and was gone.

Out of the corner of my eye I spotted one of our Brewsters far below with a Spitfire[1] on his tail. So that was what the two unidentified fighters had been—Spitfires. There was no mistaking the curved wings of the graceful British fighter, and this was the first time that we had encountered the type in Russian hands. I yawed the tail of my Brewster to make sure that no Ivan was stealing up on me, and then, stick over and well forward, I plunged down in a near-vertical dive. The pilot of the Spitfire was so intent on clobbering Pate that he didn't see me plummeting down on him. I fired one long burst into the cockpit of the Spitfire which immediately flicked over on its back and dived straight into the sea near the village of Karavalda, on the Gulf.

The vicious battle had been drifting and eddying all over the sky, but no sooner had I noted the destruction of the Spitfire than I realised that I was well away from the main battle and was about to be attacked by Russian reinforcements. For a moment I could hardly believe my eyes! As if conjured up by magic, everywhere I looked was an enemy fighter! Two . . . five . . . nine, no, twelve Tchaikas and I-16s all out for my blood!

In the twinkling of an eye they had formed a Spanish ring[2] around me, and I knew that it was too late to beat a retreat.

---

[1] One hundred and forty-three Spitfire Mk. VB fighters were shipped to Russia in 1942–43, many of these being conversions of Mk. IIBs. In 1944 a total of 1,186 Spitfire Mk. IXs was delivered to the U.S.S.R.
[2] A manœuvre evolved by the Russians during the Spanish Civil War.

My heart felt as though it was revving faster than the Cyclone engine, and I knew that I should be lucky indeed to get away with this one. My timing would have to be split-second, and I only hoped that I could keep my nerve and not do something foolish in the heat of the moment. There was no time to hesitate, and without giving the Russians the first opening, I picked the nearest I-16 which, foolishly, swung across my sights at that moment. I fired a good burst into him from the rear portside, but I had no time to evaluate the damage that I had inflicted, for two Tchaikas had jumped me and their tracers were flashing past my wings. I evaded them by breaking hard to port, simultaneously firing at an I-16 that flashed past momentarily.

Russians seemed to be milling about in every direction. Stall turns, snap rolls, split-S's, I put the Brewster through every manœuvre in the book. Streams of tracers were being hurled at me from every direction. Several of the enemy fighters were even equipped with what were to me entirely new devices—rocket missiles.[1] I now had my first experience of dodging these! I knew that one mistake, one moment of inattention, and I should be heading for the grey, undulating waters below. At least I had one consolation. I did not have to worry about the identity of the aircraft around me. They were *all* Russian, and I fired automatically whenever anything appeared in my sights.

I knew that my ammunition was beginning to run low, and I wondered how many more passes I could survive when a bullet seared through my cockpit canopy, showering me with splinters, and a dark shadow covered my Brewster. I glanced upwards and there, only a few feet above me, was the sooty black belly of an I-16. Evidently its pilot had miscalculated his speed build-up and had overshot me. And now he became *my* victim for, squarely in my sights at a range of only some forty yards, I pumped the last of my ammunition into him. There was a blinding flash, a swirling cloud of smoke, and I was flying through his débris.

Momentarily the Russians seemed to hesitate and I seized

---

[1] The RS-82 rocket missile had a velocity of eight hundred feet per second and was intended primarily for dispersing tight formations of aircraft. It was first used by I-15bis fighters in the fighting around the Khalkhiin Gol on the Manchukuoan-Mongolian frontier in 1939.

my chance. Out of ammunition, desperate measures were called for. I was now over the Kovash Church, near the Inkeri shoreline, and about a hundred and forty miles from the nearest Finnish airfield. Only cunning could get me out of my fix. I flicked the Brewster on to her back and pulled the stick into the pit of my stomach. Every sinew protested as the speed built up, but I held her in the dive, hoping that the Russians would believe that one of their number had delivered the coup de grâce and that I was diving uncontrollably into the ground. I was almost digging sandcastles on the shores of the Gulf when I eased the protesting fighter out of the dive, turning northwards with throttle wide open, thanking the heavens that the Brewster's engineers had designed my mount as a naval fighter and had built in all the rugged strength demanded by shipboard operations.

My ruse had worked for there was no sign of any pursuit, and although I was still soaked by perspiration and an icy blast was whistling through the hole in my canopy, I was highly elated as I performed two victory rolls over the base. My elation was soon turned to sorrow, however, when, on landing, I learned that Sergeant Paavo "Pate" Tolonen had failed to return, and had presumably been taken by an enemy fighter. Perhaps the Spitfire that I had picked from his back had already done its work. Vilppu and Kaius had bagged one of the enemy fighters each, but we were all silent and thoughtful in the mess.

This twelve-to-one fracas proved to be my last mission in the good old Brewster as, four days later, I was promoted to the rank of Major and ordered to take over the command of TLeLv 30, the 30th Reconnaissance Squadron. I handed command of my flight to Hasse Wind, feeling as though the bottom had dropped from my world. I had fought and lived with that flight continuously for two years, and it broke my heart to bid farewell to so many good friends and faithful comrades.

12

AU REVOIR TO FIGHTERS

Lowering clouds darkened the sky and wet snow fell to give the first real signs of winter on November 7th as I flew to Suulajärvi to take over command of TLeLv 30. The squadron comprised some four hundred personnel, and in an attempt to raise my spirits, I immediately began checking out on the types operated by the unit, the Twin Wasp Junior-engined Fokker D.XXI and the I-153 Tchaika. Both were, in fact, single-seater fighters, although their relatively low performances and inadequate armament rendered them obsolescent, and I felt a tremendous surge of nostalgia for my old Brewster.

With its Twin Wasp Junior the D.XXI was heavier than the Mercury-powered model on which I had fought throughout the "Winter War", and the installation of the American Pratt and Whitney engine had benefited neither performance nor manœuvrability, but the Tchaika was *extremely* interesting, being a Russian type captured by German forces in some numbers during their advance into the Soviet Union, and subsequently sold to us.

TLeLv 30 was a part of the Fifth Air Regiment, or LeR 5, commanded by Lieutenant-Colonel K. E. Ilanko, with headquarters in Helsinki to which I now had to report for my instructions. In all honesty, I did not relish the additional responsibilities that were now to be mine. Fighter Group "L" had been one thing, but a full squadron operating obsolescent aircraft was another. Colonel Ilanko merely outlined what was required of me, and it seemed that methods of operation and the assignment of aircraft were to be mine alone. Our principal task was reconnaissance of the eastern end of the Gulf of Finland and the Russian-held islands of Seiskari and Luvansaari, both of which sported enemy fighter fields, but as our base at Suulajärvi was a considerable distance from the area over which we were supposed to operate, I succeeded in arranging a trade

(*Above*) A Yak-7A shot down at Pitkäranta on the North-East shore of Lake Ladoga on February 12, 1943. The Yak-7A was one of the better Russian fighters that began to appear in numbers during 1943. It was a refined version of Yakovlev's first fighter, the Yak-1.

(*Right*) One Tupolev SB-2bis that would make no further attacks on Finnish towns. During the "Winter War" Finnish pilots flying the Fokker D.XXI experienced considerable difficulty in catching the SB-2bis as the fighter enjoyed only a narrow margin in speed over the Russian bomber. The SB-2bis had largely supplanted the earlier and less powerful SB-2 by the time the "Continuation War" began, and was used in very large numbers.

(*Below*) The Douglas DC-2 "Hanssin Jukka" as it appeared in 1942. This transport had an amazing career and its exploits were almost legendary. It was finally retired in 1955 and is today a coffee bar at the resort town of Hämeenlinna in southern central Finland.

(*Above*) The author's first Messerschmitt Bf 109G-2 (MT-201) in which he logged a total of forty-two hours. The author's log book shows that he flew no less than nineteen different Bf 109G-2s and G-6s at one time or another, logging a total of 462 flying hours in them. Finland purchased thirty Bf 109G-2s and one hundred and thirty-two Bf 109G-6s from Germany. (*Left*) Cranking a Bf 109G fighter in sub-zero temperatures. The DB 605A engine was frequently reluctant to start under these conditions. (*Below*) The Finnish Air Force received a small number of Dornier Do 17Z-2 bombers from the Luftwaffe late in 1941, and PLeLv 46 converted from Blenheims to this type on January 1942. Occasionally, Fighter Group L provided an escort for the Dornier bombers.

of bases with my old unit, HLeLv 24, and we took over Römpötti, thus placing us virtually on the shores of the Gulf itself, while they flew in to Suulajärvi.

We were soon fully operational after our arrival at Römpötti, and each day the Tchaika-equipped flight led by Korppu Paltila swapped missions with Petter Ahonius's D.XXI flight. I flew with both aircraft types, endeavouring to adapt myself psychologically to the new circumstances in which I found myself, and I soon learned that the entirely different tactics demanded by our reconnaissance sorties were a little less wearing on the nerves than fighter operations but, to counterbalance this advantage, the aircraft that we were operating were, for the most part, somewhat old and unreliable, and sending out anyone in such aircraft over large areas of water, especially when the risk of encountering far more potent enemy fighters was great, was by no means a pleasant duty. It was some time before I could compare the Pratt and Whitney-engined D.XXI with, for instance, a Brewster without having a bitter taste in my mouth, but I tried hard to forget the portly old "Sky Pearl", immersing myself in the activities of my new squadron, flying one day in a D.XXI accompanied by Ture Mattila, Kolta Lappalainen, and Oke Karme, and the next in a Tchaika with Korppu Paltila and Hanski Niemeier.

As Christmas neared and the days grew progressively shorter, the weather naturally became less predictable, somewhat curbing our activities, but on days when the clouds were moving fast at low altitude, we still undertook reconnaissance sorties, such weather which usually kept the enemy fighters grounded favouring us in our obsolescent planes.

On a typical reconnaissance mission in mid-December, I led a section of D.XXIs, taking-off just as the sky began to lighten. Everywhere was shrouded in a mantle of snow, but the Gulf was still largely free of ice. East of the island of Seiskari we spotted two ships, and their anti-aircraft fire followed us as we flew on past Peninsaari. The object of our reconnaissance was Lavansaari, and as we arrived over our destination we kept to the fringe of the clouds, noting a force of four destroyers and nine gunboats riding at anchor before their anti-aircraft fire forced us to plunge into the concealing vapour. We had a long over-water flight back to base, and the cloud forced us lower and lower so that our usual island checkpoints were invisible to us, necessitating reliance on our compasses, with the tops of the angry waves seemingly reaching out for our low-flying machines. From time to time we glanced at our fuel gauges as they flickered nearer and nearer to the "empty" mark, and then, suddenly, as though from the waves themselves, the spruces of the Tiurinsaari appeared, and we were home once more.

. . . . .

The year 1943 saw birth in a dull grey and bitterly cold day, and the first week of January passed uneventfully, but on the afternoon of Friday the 8th we were to have the fact dramatically underlined that, because of the old equipment we were forced to operate, each day could well be our last. We were returning from a sea-reconnaissance mission with three Tchaikas, and just as we were nearing the end of the long over-water flight and were nearing Tiurinsaari, Korppu Paltila's engine seized without warning. The Tchaika glided down and landed on the thin ice of the Gulf, just a couple of miles west of the island. The ice broke immediately the aircraft slowed down. Korppu released his safety-belt and sat on the edge of the cockpit waving to us before, a few moments later, he sank with the aircraft to his death. Korppu wore the standard Mae West-type flotation jacket, but he knew that swimming was useless as, in the Arctic temperatures of the Gulf, death would result in a matter of minutes.

Shocked by this appalling incident, we hurriedly landed back at base in an effort to get rescue launches to the spot as quickly as possible, although we knew that their search would be fruitless. In Korppu, who had just been promoted to the rank of captain, the Gulf had claimed one of the squadron's finest and bravest airmen. The cause of the accident was, of course, obvious: the seizure of the Tchaika's engine. It was the third such incident in which the Tchaika's supremely unreliable M-63 radial had seized for no apparent reason, and we now distrusted this Russian aircraft more than ever. It was certainly unnerving to have to fly long distances over water in winter time with land-based aircraft that one knew to be unsafe.

We certainly suffered no shortage of free time in TLeLv 30,

but the lack of variety in our diet became ever more monotonous. I sometimes drove to Viipuri of an evening, stopping in at the Posses or Pamaus clubs for a decent meal, but before long I found myself running short of cash, and was forced to ration strictly such pleasurable visits. Not very far from our base was a group of Koivisto fishermen, and sometimes we landed our two-seater de Havilland Moth that we had for liaison purposes on the ice among them, bargaining with them for their catch of sprats. We were already adept at smoking fish, and these delightful golden-grey smoked sprats made a welcome addition to our rations. To keep fit we spent much time ski-ing, and even organized ski-ing championships.

I had to give up some of our D.XXIs to another reconnaissance squadron early in February when a rumour began to circulate that we were to get new equipment from Germany; once again they were to be captured aircraft, but this time fast MiG-3 fighters. Our base was obviously unsuited for the operation of such types, and I visited Lapeenranta to discover if we should prepare to transfer to a more suitable field, but I was told in no uncertain terms that we were staying at Römpötti. So our rumoured MiG-3s did not exist! Our only consolation was the reappearance of the sun, although clear skies were hardly what *we* needed for our operations if we were to continue flying these obsolescent, extremely vulnerable machines.

In the frosty haze of the dawn of February 14th we made preparations for a reconnaissance sortie with four D.XXIs. By the time the first rays of the sun touched our aircraft we were high above Koivisto. The Gulf was still almost entirely covered by ice, and our mission was the reconnoitring of the open channels for sea traffic and Russia's island bases. Our altitude of twenty thousand feet gave us a wide range of vision over the vast icefield. To starboard we could vaguely see the shoreline, and south-east of us the Heel of Karelia, but ahead was only the glittering ice. Occasionally I glanced above and behind, but most of my time was spent in reflecting on the events of the previous two years; two years in which virtually the whole of the world had become embroiled in this vast conflict. I had spent hundreds of hours in the air, shooting and being shot at, and seeing my friends killed or injured; undergoing continual changes of altitude and high-G manœuvres in rarefied air. The continual nervous strain had to have some effect on even the best of physiques and dulled the senses, yet I didn't feel any overstrain. Life before the war seemed remote indeed, as though it had existed only in a novel. My world was confined to the tight little cockpit of an aircraft and I could no longer envisage any other life.

The flak from Lavansaari suddenly jerked me back to reality. I eased my throttle open slightly and put the nose of the D.XXI in a shallow dive, weaving from side to side, and noting the numbers of the ice-bound ships that were firing madly at me, and the aircraft like tiny black crosses dispersed around the airfield. We were soon out of range of the flak, and as I was about to land at Römpötti, I was told over the R/T that a truck had been seen travelling across the ice west of Shepelevski at about 25 m.p.h. Together with Hage Krohn I headed northwest over the seemingly endless ice field and, far off, spotted a tiny speck apparently motionless on the ice. We buzzed low over the truck to ascertain its contents and saw about ten drums, presumably containing fuel, and eight or ten men in white parkas seated on crates. As far as I could see, there was no sign of any enemy fighters, but as the truck was now only twelve miles from Seiskari, we had to destroy it quickly and retreat before fighters could take-off from the island.

I lined up the vehicle in my sights, and it came to a standstill as soon as I opened fire, the men leaping from the truck and crawling beneath it. But this was only a temporary refuge for, on our third run, the fuel drums burst into flame, scattering blazing petroleum all round the truck. We turned for home, leaving a column of smoke rising into the sky, and some badly singed Russians. The truck had not been important, but we had cocked a snoot right under Ivan's nose, and it cheered us to think of their annoyance.

    .   .   .   .   .

The days followed one after another without a further opportunity for a sortie arising until March 27th. We had been operating strictly with Tchaikas since the attack on the truck in the Gulf, and we now used these in the ground-attack role at Shepelevski. The Russians must really have been confused to find themselves the targets of an attack from the familiar

Tchaika. After the attack I called in at headquarters to pick up any mail, and I immediately saw that Olli Puhakka had news for me as his face revealed suppressed excitement. He handed me a teletype message from the Air Defence Commander. I was to take over the command of the newly-formed 34th Fighter Squadron, HLeLv 34.

13

FIGHTERS ONCE AGAIN

HLeLv 34 had been officially established on March 13th when our best fighter pilots ferried in sixteen brand-new Messerschmitt Bf 109G-2s from Wiener-Neustadt, Vienna, to Malmi, Helsinki. The squadron was to be based at Utti, on the mainland, to where the majority of the Bf 109Gs were promptly transferred, one flight remaining at Malmi to assist in the aerial defence of Helsinki. Probably none was better qualified to command this youngest of our squadrons than Major Erkki Olavi Ehnrooth, but death strikes when least expected, and before Ehnrooth could get HLeLv 34 operational, he met his death when the Pyry[1] trainer in which he was performing low-level aerobatics crashed into the woods surrounding Utti. Thus, my first duty on reaching Utti was to pay my last respects to my good friend as he was laid to rest in the Hietaniemi cemetery.

The April sunshine soon melted the snow and dried out Utti's long runway, and I spent as much time as I could familiarizing myself with the Mersu, as we dubbed the Bf 109G. This aircraft was, in our opinion, then the best fighter in the world, and my personal Mersu bore the serial number MT-201. It was a case of love at first sight. The sleek, powerful lines of the Messerschmitt were in such marked contrast to the portly contours of the Brewster that I could hardly conceal my excitement as I swung myself into the cockpit for the first time. The Bf 109G had a 1,475-h.p. Daimler-Benz DB 605A twelve-cylinder inverted-Vee liquid-cooled engine beneath its cowling, and after having made the usual cockpit check, tightened my seat straps, and signalled the mechanic to slam shut the hinging canopy, I started this power plant which roared like thunder, vibrating the whole fighter. Bluish flames alternating with black smoke

---

[1] The Pyry tandem two-seater advanced trainer was of Finnish design, and forty-one aircraft of this type were produced by the State Aircraft Factory at Tampere during 1939–41, the last being withdrawn from service on August 14, 1962.

darted back from the exhaust stacks, and in no time the temperature gauges told me that the engine was warm enough, so I motioned to the mechanic to pull out the chocks from beneath the wheels, and began taxi-ing around the perimeter track rapidly, carefully ensuring that I didn't overheat the engine. A quick check . . . canopy locked . . . airscrew pitch . . . intercoolers . . . flaps . . . trim . . . clearance for take-off, and I eased open the throttle gingerly, the Mersu gathering speed down the runway extremely rapidly. The acceleration pushed me back against the armoured seat—yes, armour at last—and without a bump I was airborne and the airfield boundary had flashed past beneath me.

Undercarriage up, flaps retracted, airscrew in correct pitch, and radiator flaps closed, I throttled back and began to get the feel of my new mount. It was extremely sensitive on the controls and climbed like a rocket. I was completely captivated by the Mersu's tremendous speed and power. What price the old "Sky Pearl" now! I eased the stick forward and in ten seconds the speedometer was clocking 435 m.p.h., the ground approaching rapidly. I began my pull-out and found that I needed to exert all my strength on the stick, and the G-forces were so tremendous that at one moment I feared that I might be pushed through the bottom of the plane. There was a buzzing in my ears and the instrument panel blurred—the beginnings of a black-out.

I rocketed back into the sky and found that an Immelmann at 310 m.p.h. took eighteen seconds and added more than three thousand feet to the altitude, while a loop at the same speed had a diameter of some three thousand feet and took twenty-six seconds. A 180-degree turn required ten seconds and a full turn was accomplished in eighteen seconds. Now came the problem of getting the speed down below 180 m.p.h. to lower the undercarriage. I opened the radiator flaps but it seemed an age before I finally lowered the flaps and undercarriage and changed the airscrew pitch to idling, and the Mersu was still sweeping down at 155 m.p.h. I hurriedly glanced at the instruments and checked that I had not forgotten anything as the fighter and its shadow racing along the ground came to meet, and the kiss of the Mersu's wheels on the runway was as sweet as I could possibly have wished. I had heard many rumours that the flying characteristics of the Messerschmitt were bad, but I had certainly not found them so. It possessed its shortcomings, but what fighter did not. Its narrow-tyred, narrow-track undercarriage was perhaps not ideally suited for some of the bases that the Mersu was to operate from in Finland, but stories that it had to be flown at full throttle in the landing circuit with flaps and undercarriage down had no basis in fact, at least, so far as the Bf 109G-2 version was concerned. No, the Mersu was a thoroughbred, and like all thoroughbreds it was mettlesome.

. . . . .

By mid-April Illu Juutilainen had begun to add kills to the squadron's tally board, as had also Pampsa Myllylä, Reiska Valli, Olli Puhakka, and Ami Euramo, and several additional pilots were selected and added to our personnel, among these being the familiar faces of Kössi Karhila, Ture Mattila, Pege Saalasti, and good old Pappa Turkka.

Only about half the Messerschmitts that we had purchased had actually reached Finland, and since things were rather quiet, the Air Defence Commander gave instructions for us to ferry the remaining fighters from Erding, in Bavaria, appointing me director of the ferrying operation. Thus, on May 6th, I joined thirteen other pilots and two mechanics in Helsinki, and after receiving our travel orders and changing some money for Reichsmarks, the next morning found us at Malmi, climbing aboard the famous Douglas DC-2 *Hanssin Jukka*.[1]

The *Hanssin Jukka* had been purchased privately from ABA-Swedish Air Lines by Count Carl Gustav von Rosen and presented to the Finnish government during the "Winter War". It was flown to Joroinen where its Swedish registration, SE-AXE, was painted out, and the Finnish serial "DC-1" and our blue swastikas painted on. A hole was cut in the cabin roof for a machine-gun on a swivelling mount, and bomb-racks were attached to the wing centre section. Von Rosen had volunteered for service with the Finnish Air Force, and together with

[1] This aircraft, the 115th DC-2 built, was flown on January 5, 1935, and was one of a batch of fourteen transports of this type ordered by the Dutch airline Koninklijke Luctvaart Maatschappij, or K.L.M. Registered PH-AKH and christened *De Haan* (The Cock), it was sold to ABA-Swedish Air Lines shortly after the beginning of the second world war.

another Swede as co-pilot, R. Windquist, he loaded *Hanssin Jukka* with two dozen 25-lb. bombs and made a night attack on a Russian airfield. All went well until, just after dropping its bomb load, *Hanssin Jukka* suffered an engine failure, one of its Cyclones freezing solid. Somehow von Rosen succeeded in keeping the converted transport airborne and regained his base, but *Hanssin Jukka* had to sit out the remainder of the "Winter War" awaiting a replacement engine.

A replacement engine was eventually acquired and, as a transport once more, *Hanssin Jukka* flew here, there and everywhere, but its resemblance to the Ilyushin DB-3 from certain angles attracted plenty of flak from Finnish and German gunners, yet this venerable old bird, already a legend in its lifetime, sailed serenely on. As one pair of engines wore out they were replaced, and at one time or another its Cyclones were supplanted by Bristol Mercurys and even captured Russian M-62B engines. Throughout its "Continuation War" career, *Hanssin Jukka* retained the same pilot, Flight-Master Fritu Väänänen, and he now carried us to Erding. Three hours after taking-off from Malmi we reached Königsberg, landing at the Devan airfield. After breakfast, complete with weak beer, in the airport restaurant, we were once more on our way, but poor visibility and strong headwinds forced the *Hanssin Jukka* down to about three hundred feet at which we enjoyed a wonderful view of the countryside over which we were passing.

Soon we were flying over multi-coloured orchards, and the farther we flew the more summery the terrain appeared. There was certainly a marked difference in the Finnish spring and what we could see here. Crossing the Oder River we saw for the first time the splendid German autobahns and highways, and full of wonder we eventually landed at Landsdorf airfield, Berlin. Here we were met by our Air Force representative, Major Helenius, who provided us with the flight maps for our return trip, and after a quick visit to the local officers' club, to sample the dark German beer, we began the last lap of our journey. Everywhere we looked were blossoming cherry trees and red-tiled roofs which added colour to the refreshingly green countryside, and the vast numbers of black-and-white Frisian cattle seemed strange to our Finnish eyes. We crossed the Elbe west of Dresden where the terrain began to undulate, and we were soon approaching superb mountains. At Regensburg the sun was still reflected by the cathedral spires, and at 17.25 hours we finally touched down at Erding, having flown more than twelve hundred miles since our take-off from Malmi that morning.

Dinner in the magnificent officers' club was superb, and this club, like all other Luftwaffe officers' clubs, really took our breath away with its immense size and extreme luxury. The walls of every one of the ten large rooms were decorated with delightful murals, and each room appeared to have been furnished without thought for cost. Quarters had been found for us in the Münchener Hof, a small hostelry typical of Bavaria, with a beer cellar downstairs and poultry in the yard.

The next morning *Hanssin Jukka* took-off for Switzerland where it was to collect Marshal Mannerheim, who had been spending a short leave in that tranquil country. With our mechanics, we carefully examined the Messerschmitt Bf 109G-2s that were awaiting us at the field, and discovered that they all needed a number of minor adjustments. Although relatively unimportant, these adjustments were time-consuming, and we were left with several days on our hands.

We took the opportunity to acquaint ourselves with the quiet and pretty town of Erding, so typical of many South German towns. The carefully tended lawns and vine-covered, gabled buildings were a delight, and in one day we seemed to have been transported from a cool Finnish spring to the very heart of summer. Late that afternoon we boarded a crowded and dirty train for Munich, and the next day met the Messerschmitt representative, Engineer Kull, for lunch in a beer cellar. Herr Kull took us on a guided tour of this large city, and we spent several hours roaming the vast halls of the fantastic Deutsches Museum. The innumerable exhibits left us speechless, ranging as they did from full-size aircraft and submarines to all types of motor vehicles and locomotives. The complete tour of the museum was like a six-mile route march, and after bidding farewell to our most considerate guide, we groped our way through the blackout, tired and hungry, to the Deutscher Hof and its splendid restaurant.

At 06.00 hours the next day, after one and a half memorable days in Munich, we were at the railway station awaiting the train that was to carry us back to Erding. Although the streets of the city had been empty at that early hour, the station was as busy as a beehive, and a trainload of troops had just arrived from the south. Their sand-coloured uniforms revealed the fact that they were members of Rommel's Afrika Korps, and some of them were staggering under immense baskets of tropical fruit. We finally reached Erding, checked out the fourteen Bf 109G fighters, and were soon taking-off in pairs from the circular, grass-covered field.

Although we had had little chance to make mental notes of landmarks during our flight in *Hanssin Jukka*, we did not stand much risk of losing ourselves as visibility was perfect, and climbing to six thousand feet, we had a superlative view. It was as though we could have touched the Garmisch Partenkirchen Alps and the Innsbruck ski slopes merely by stretching out our hands, and to the north-west the Bodensee gleamed like a sapphire in the sunlight. Landing once more at Erding, we were just in time to see ten Messerschmitts flown by youngsters fresh out of operational flying schools take-off for the Tunisian front. While strolling back to the Münchener Hof, a freight train passed us loaded with forty or fifty Bf 109s that had been badly damaged either in combat or as a result of bombing.

We returned to the field that afternoon and were still there when, early that evening, an Fw 190 fighter landed on its way back from the African theatre. It was as full of holes as a colander, and had obviously seen much combat. We took the pilot, a pleasant young lieutenant, with us to the officers' club where, over a glass of vodka, he told us of the near-impossible situation that the Luftwaffe was experiencing in Africa. Because of the Allies' overwhelming numerical superiority, it seemed that the Luftwaffe had been forced to lash bomb racks to its best fighters as these had the only chance of getting through to their targets. Conditions, he said, were deteriorating rapidly, and he had already lost the majority of his comrades in the fighting. We could well imagine his relief at obtaining a few days respite, but little did we know then that, as far as the Tunisian fighting was concerned, he had been extremely lucky. A few days later the Afrika Korps gave up and the war in the desert was over.

On the 11th we were ready to commence our long flight back to Finland, and local weather conditions looked promising, but the peaks of the Böhmerwald on our route were shrouded in fog, so our flight clearance was cancelled. So back to Erding we went, wandering around the shops which, apart from foodstuffs, were devoid of goods. The next day the mountains were clear, and our *Hanssin Jukka* arrived to pick up our mechanics and personal belongings, but the Germans continued to delay us with what we considered to be superfluous inspections of the fighters, and it was not until 17.00 hours that our fourteen Mersus took-off for Prague.

Flying on a north-easterly course, we traversed the Bavarian mountains, the mighty Böhmerwald looming ahead of us, but our powerful Daimler-Benz engines lifted us effortlessly above the peaks. We traversed the broad valley of the Danube, fascinated by the ever-changing scene below, and the Czechoslovak border slipped past beneath us unnoticed. In less than an hour we were over the Moldau, a tributary of the Elbe, along which the picturesque capital of Bohemia spreads itself on both banks. We searched among the veritable maze of airfields surrounding Prague until we found Rusini where we were supposed to land, and as I made my approach I carefully avoided the line of glass domes protecting the lights used to illuminate the runway for night flying. One of our pilots did not notice the domes until the last moment, however, and swerved his aircraft violently just after touching down, digging in a wingtip and damaging the Mersu extensively.

By this time dusk was falling, so we all climbed aboard a tram which ran near the airfield and were soon in the centre of the lovely Paris-like city where our consul, Koistinen, greeted us. The next morning was hot and sultry, and by chance, during a visit to our consulate, I met one of the veterans of the famous Richthofen Squadron of the first world war. After talking flying for a while, my new-found acquaintance suggested driving me around Prague as there was some time to spare before our scheduled take-off. I accepted with alacrity, and spent the morning sight-seeing and learning that Prague is all too appropriately named "The Golden City". By the time we reached Rusini, the heat of the day was almost unbearable. The temperature exceeded 30 degrees C., and heat-waves shimmered from every surface. I bade goodbye to my guide and was soon preparing for take-off. We had been forced to turn the damaged

Mersu over to the Luftwaffe for repairs, its shamefaced pilot having to await the arrival of the *Hanssin Jukka*, and I thought to myself as I roared down the runway that it was fortunate that few of us were superstitious for the time was 13.00 hours, it was the thirteenth day of the month, and thirteen fighters were about to head for Breslau!

This leg of the journey was probably the most scenic, crossing innumerable mountain peaks and gorges, but gradually the terrain flattened out, and by means of the Oder River, we soon located Breslau on its southern shore, and the small training field of Schöngarten, our destination. Of some three hundred training aircraft based there at least a half-dozen were constantly in the landing pattern, and it was soon obvious that no special consideration was being afforded visitors. We were forced to exercise all our skill to get into the tight pattern with the trainers and, eventually, land our powerful fighters on the short runway. Finally, we were all down, and the commander of the base, a Colonel Schulze, invited us to be his guests at the officers' club.

The intense heat of the day was already diminishing, and by the time we had enjoyed a delicious dinner and had taken drinks on to the terrace, the cool of the evening and the scent of the lilac trees that abounded around the club combined to provide us with a delightfully relaxed atmosphere, and in view of the fact that we planned an early take-off the next morning, we sat as late as we dare over numerous bottles of Sekt, enjoying the conversation of our host.

Early the next morning the weather looked promising, and we were soon once more heading north, our flight plan calling for two fuelling stops before Riga. Flying steadily across the Polish countryside which was partly obscured by the early morning haze, we arrived at Schönwald airfield on the bank of the Weiksel River. We were quickly refuelled and, forty minutes later, we were once again airborne, passing over the swamps and agricultural areas to northern Poland, the sun beating down on our cockpit canopies until the cockpit was hotter than the interior of a sauna bath house. South of Danzig it became steadily cooler, and a pleasant breeze blew from the Baltic through the cockpit side panel, and we soon found ourselves in the approach pattern at Jesau, near Königsberg.

From this point there was a chance of meeting enemy aircraft, so in addition to taking on fuel at Jesau, we took on ammunition. A late breakfast and the *Hanssin Jukka* arrived with our mechanics, but while they were servicing the Mersus they discovered that the engine of Ami Euramo's fighter was defective and needed replacing, so that afternoon we took-off on the last lap of our flight to Riga with only twelve machines. A haze now stretched up to some ten or twelve thousand feet, and it became increasingly difficult to pinpoint our position but, fortunately, we succeeded in picking up Tilsit on the Memel River, and, to our relief, discovered that we were bang on course. We flew by compass across Lithuania, checked our position at Mitau, found the Väinä River and, at its mouth, the city of Riga, and finally landed at the Spliv airfield. The runway was still covered by slush, and as we taxied in, one of our Mersus tangled with a Junkers Ju 88 fighter about to take-off. One wingtip of the Junkers was badly damaged, and we were subjected to a lengthy tirade from its pilot, the Commanding Officer of a night-fighter unit, who unleashed an admirable selection of the lesser-known German expletives, following these with disparaging references to our ancestry. Our Mersu, fortunately, needed only an airscrew change, and this was quickly effected.

We got a lift into Riga, had an early dinner in the officers' club of Luftflotte 1, and then made for our beds. The next morning, to our annoyance, we were forbidden take-off clearance owing to a strong crosswind that was blowing across Spliv, and so we spent a leisurely day exploring Riga, much of which had been completely destroyed during the German assault prior to the capture of the city. Nevertheless, what remained intact revealed the remarkable character of Riga, and what particularly surprised us was the fact that so many different nationalities were represented in the streets, especially noticeable being the large numbers of Spaniards. The evening was passed in the Riga Offizerheim, a fine three-storey building with a magnificent dining-room enjoying the services of a fine orchestra.

May 16th dawned fine with favourable winds, but there were a number of formalities to complete, and it was not until 12.00 hours that we finally took-off, following the Riga Bay shoreline until we ran into a vicious rainstorm near Pärnu. We flew on through the rain, Estonia's monotonous terrain being barely visible below, but every minute carried us five miles nearer to Finland. Tallin appeared through the murk beneath us, and seven minutes later we were over our Air Force Headquarters in Munkkiniemi, just outside Helsinki.

One by one we landed at Malmi, having flown halfway across Europe. Our tanks replenished, we were soon in the air again, running in front of a thunderstorm to Utti where our light-blue swastikas were painted over the German crosses. Our Mersus were now ready to fight under Finnish colours.

14

A HECTIC PACE

The squadron was now at full strength, with twenty-eight Messerschmitt Bf 109Gs and a full complement of qualified personnel. We had already discovered that our new mounts fully merited every praise, and I felt sure that they could not have had better pilots handling their controls. Apart from the three flight commanders, Pive Ervi, Kuije Lahtela and Olli Puhakka, who were outstanding pilots by any standard and skilful warriors, our pilots were all courageous and technically proficient and, what is more, they had inherited the hunter's instincts from their ancestors. They had thus found their true métier behind the controls of a fighter. As individualists they were remarkable; as a team they were superb, and I could have wished for no greater honour than that of being Commanding Officer of these men. As the youngest squadron commander in the Finnish Air Force, I knew that the fates had been more than kind to me.

From the moment HLeLv 34 attained full strength life ran at a hectic pace. Our capabilities were evidently rated very highly for we were severely over-extended from the moment of joining operations. Our interception area covered a 250-mile stretch embodying the entire shoreline of the Gulf of Finland and including all towns from Hango in the west to the Karelian Peninsula. We were thus forced to spread ourselves thinly over a number of airfields and, consequently, could rarely give battle with numerical superiority on our side. This did not matter overmuch when we were called upon to tackle marauding fighter formations, for such actions normally became a series of widely scattered individual combats, but when our task was the interception of a bombing force, our numbers were invariably inadequate to tie up any escorting fighters. Thus, we had to hope that luck would serve as our top cover while we waded into the bombers.

(*Above*) Flight Master Oippa Tuominen with his Messerschmitt Bf 109G. Tuominen was the first Finnish pilot to be awarded the Mannerheim Cross, receiving this highly coveted decoration on August 17, 1941 while flying Fiat G.50s. He gained forty-three kills, eight of which were recorded during the "Winter War". On June 2, 1943, Tuominen was forced to ditch his Bf 109G-2 in the water near the island of Somer, fragments from a Russian bomber that he had been attacking having damaged his fighter. The aircraft was later raised from some five fathoms. (*Below*) Lieutenant Mikko Pasila in his Bf 109G-2. Pasila, who, for a time, was the author's adjutant, scored a total of seventeen kills, and is now a doctor of medicine in Lahti.

(*Above, left*) Sergeant Pentti Tilli, the son of Flight Master Teodor Tilli. This young pilot was shot down in flames on January 20, 1940 when he was surprised by six enemy fighters shortly after gaining his fifth kill. (*Above, right*) Flight Master Eino Ilmari Juutilainen, Finland's Rene Fonck. His aircraft never seemed to be hit by enemy fire, and with ninety-four kills he was the leading Finnish ace. (*Below*) Joppe Karhunen (left) and Hasse Wind (right) who scored thirty-one and seventy-eight kills respectively, both receiving the Mannerheim Cross. Karhunen eventually became Commanding Officer of HLeLv 24, and is today a successful writer.

A HECTIC PACE

The major part of the squadron, the headquarters and the second and third flights were directly under my command at Utti, covering the area from the Karelian Kannus to Porvoo, with Kotka as the centre point, and the first flight led by Pive Ervi was detached to Malmi where it provided the centrepiece of the capital's aerial defences.

. . . . .

Within a few days of our arrival back in Finland, Ivan began stepping up his aerial activity far beyond anything to that time. Spring had given place to summer, and the nights were merely a few hours of twilight, necessitating the maintenance of twenty-hour alerts. At 03.00 hours, even before the birds had begun their chorus, we were readying our Mersus among the pines along the edge of the field, and it was not until 22.00 hours that we could tumble wearily into our bunks. Even these few hours passed with "one eye open" for, despite innumerable requests to regimental headquarters, our base was totally devoid of anti-aircraft defences. If Ivan had only known of our vulnerability, a low-level sneak attack in the twilight would have caught us with our pants down, and he would have stood an excellent chance of wiping us out on the ground. Throughout each day some of our number could be found cat-napping in our cockpits, ready for an instant scramble.

During the first three days of the Russian aerial offensive, May 19th–21st, we participated in a score or more of furious battles over the Gulf, and the squadron built up its score of kills rapidly. I personally added three kills to this score, including one of the newer Lavochkin La-5s that were now being encountered in increasing numbers. The La-5 had first appeared during the Stalingrad operations of the previous autumn, and although its airframe was basically similar to that of the LaGG-3, the introduction of a two-row fourteen-cylinder radial engine, the M-82F, had resulted in a truly sprightly performance and a worthy antagonist. Fast climbing and highly manœuvrable, the La-5 was a low-altitude fighter rarely encountered much above fifteen thousand feet, and we soon learned that there was little point in following it in a tight turn.

On each of the three days we reconnoitred the enemy naval units in the vicinity of Lavansaari, but the Russian gunners always misjudged our speed and, fortunately for us, the tremendous barrage of flak that they threw up as soon as we made our appearance was always well aft of our rapidly moving Mersus. On May 21st alone the squadron knocked down ten Ilyushin Il-2s, LaGG-3s and Tchaikas, but we also suffered our first losses. On the previous day Lieutenant Esko Ruotsila was on his way back from a mission over Seiskari, and his Mersu, which was seen to be leaving a trail of smoke, gradually lost altitude until, near Äljysaari, something tore loose from the fighter, which by that time was only about a hundred and fifty feet above the surface of the water, and the aircraft dived straight in, carrying Esko with it. The following afternoon at 15.28 hours, during a tremendous dogfight with a mixed gaggle of Russian fighters, Lieutenant Tauno "Pege" Saalasti rammed a Tchaika, both the Mersu and the Ivan fluttering down into the water west of Lavansaari.

On May 31st we had a visit from the Air Defence Commander, Lieutenant-General J. F. Lundquist, who had come to acquaint himself with our methods of operating. During his visit he told me that Lieutenant-Colonel Magnusson, my old Commanding Officer, was taking over the duties of regimental commander from Lieutenant-Colonel Nuotio, and this change meant a number of transfers from HLeLv 34. Pive Ervi relinquished the command of the first flight to join regimental headquarters, his place being taken by Lasse Lehtonen, and our intelligence officer and my adjutant, the latter a tall youngster with the abilities of a commercial counsellor and the tact of a diplomat, also left for headquarters.

One outcome of the commander's visit was the arrival of a flak unit, and to provide the anti-aircraft gunners with a better field of fire against low-flying intruders and, simultaneously, allow our Mersus to make use of the cross runway, I gave our service chief orders to have cut down several hundred valuable smooth-barked trees. I felt as though I was committing some sort of vandalism, but if by so doing I was giving us a better chance of survival, then I was more than justified. At this time, the third flight was despatched to Malmi on rotation and the first flight returned to Utti. It was during this transfer, on June 2nd, that Lasse Lehtonen, leading Poke Pokela, Manu Fräntilä and Oippa Tuominen, waded into a large formation of Ivans south of Kotka, shooting down no less than six of the enemy aircraft. Oippa's Mersu was damaged, however, when it flew through the débris of the Pe-2 that it had been attacking, forcing its pilot to ditch near the shore of the Someri Island. Oippa, who had been the first Finnish pilot to be awarded the Mannerheim Cross, had to swim for it. Later his fighter was raised from some thirty feet of water and, eventually, returned to flying condition.

. . . . .

The interception of the high-flying Russian twin-engined reconnaissance aircraft was presenting us with ever-increasing problems. These Pe-2s and Douglas A-20s[1] were usually active long before sunrise, and our warning stations could rarely provide us with sufficient advance warning to enable us to scramble and reach the altitude of the intruders in time. Such an intrusion occurred on June 17th. It was a clear, absolutely cloudless morning and the hands of the clock had not reached 03.00 hours when the Lahti warning station reported a single bomber flying east at an altitude of thirty thousand feet. Almost as we received the message we picked out the aircraft as a minute speck nearly directly over the base. We had been in process of running-up and checking our engines, and Sergeant Major Lauri Jutila immediately took-off to give chase.

Near Jääski, some ninety miles from the base, Lauri's Mersu finally caught up with the Russian at about twenty-six thousand feet. The action was followed through glasses by one of the warning stations, and the Russian aircraft was soon tumbling from the sky, leaving a ragged trail of black smoke. But the enemy had evidently fought tenaciously to the last, for Lauri's Mersu came screaming down vertically, crashing in a small clearing among spruce trees and scattering the remains of both pilot and aircraft over a wide area.

Although Utti was only thirty miles from the Gulf this added five minutes to our arrival for an interception, five minutes that could make all the difference between success and failure, and

[1] The Douglas A-20, known as the Boston in the R.A.F., was supplied in very large numbers to the Soviet Union, the Russians receiving almost half the total production of this type. In all, 2,908 examples of the A-20B, C, G, H and K were delivered.

so a new airstrip was built near to the outskirts of the town of Kotka, in the Kymi backwoods. From time to time I dropped in to see what progress was being made with the strip, and it seemed probable that we would be able to start operations from it at the beginning of August. Our transfer could not take place soon enough, for it had become impossible to defend the eastern section of the Gulf from Utti, and we had already despatched the first flight to Suulajärvi, leaving only the second flight at our main base.

The serious spares shortage and the acute lack of servicing equipment was now beginning to hamper our operations. We had originally received only one set of the principal repair tools, and with the squadron operating from three bases our overworked mechanics found the situation impossible. For instance, we had only one spanner wrench for airscrew hub removals, and being needed at Suulajärvi, it might well have to be collected from Malmi, one hundred and eighty-six miles to the west, and then be flown back to Utti! There were times when some of our Bf 109G fighters were grounded for long periods owing to the lack of a few small but vital parts. Finally, after repeated applications to the German Supply Depot in Pori, we succeeded in obtaining some of the needed items, but others we had to fabricate ourselves.

Our aircraft inspector and senior mechanic had both attended servicing courses in Germany, but they were faced with almost impossible tasks, and it was only by working the clock around, together with two Luftwaffe mechanics, Dörr and Kaiser, who had been assigned to us, that they maintained a reasonable operational strength. We had received no ground radio equipment for use with the FuG VII sets of the Mersus, incidentally, and were forced to use captured Russian RSB stations, the reliability of which was questionable and the audibility decidedly limited. The fighters themselves, while splendid from the performance viewpoint, now began to reveal the defects of hurried wartime manufacture, and there were two occasions when, while cruising on patrol, the DB 605 engines of two of the Messerschmitts inexplicably burst into flames, forcing their pilots to bale out!

We were almost constantly in the cockpits of our Mersus, either in the air or awaiting orders to scramble, and the short summer passed almost unnoticed. We had learned to make do with extremely little sleep, and on August 2nd we had finally flown our aircraft into the new strip near Kotka. The strip itself was about one and a quarter miles in length but very narrow and surrounded by tall trees. The Command Post and our sleeping quarters were still under construction, but the control tower, the mess and the sauna bath house, and servicing shelters for our aircraft were ready, and we were not sorry to give up the garrison life at Utti.

The three flights of the squadron were still spread among three bases, and we normally flew in two or, at the most, four-plane sections so that we never possessed numerical advantage over any enemy formations that we might encounter. Nevertheless, the squadron's score of kills continued to grow steadily. On August 20th, Kuije Lahtela, who had just transferred his flight on rotation from Suulajärvi to Malmi, shot down an Il-2, Ivan's much-vaunted Ilyusha or Shturmovik, while his wingman, Oippa, also bagged an Il-2; simultaneously, the first flight operating from Suulajärvi also got two, while our second flight flying from our new airstrip raised the score by no less than nine. We, in turn, suffered one loss: Lieutenant Tervo, a courageous pilot of the first flight with several kills, who was shot down near Lavansaari.

September 11th was the most notable day for the squadron, however, for Erik Lyly and Ture Mattila both shot down enemy fighters and Jösse Lönnfors nailed a bomber to give us our hundredth kill during our five months of operations as a squadron. The occasion gave us an excuse for a wild celebration party in which everybody joined, and for a short while, over our glasses of German rum, we forgot the unpleasant aspects of war and revelled in good comradeship. But next morning, despite thick heads, we started on our second "hundred" by knocking down a high-flying Douglas A-20 reconnaissance-bomber.

· · · ·

Once again it was autumn. The foliage began to look bedraggled, grey clouds hung for days over the Gulf, and the unsettled weather markedly reduced the aerial activities of both sides. Occasionally, between the usual interception missions, we were assigned the task of escorting a low-flying and lumbering Junkers Ju 52/3m which, fitted with an immense dural hoop energized by an auxiliary motor, was engaged in mine-sweeping the Orrengrund channels. The inclement weather at last allowed us to catch up on the sleep that we had lost during the summer months and, to keep fit, we did much cross-country running, and spent hours tramping through the undergrowth in search of mushrooms with which to vary our rather tedious diet.

When the weather was favourable, in addition to our usual activities over the Gulf, we made wide sweeps over the wilderness to the south, but our flying was progressively curtailed as the days shortened. On moonlit nights the air-raid warning sirens in Kotka, less than six miles away, aroused us, and as we watched the searchlights like so many probing fingers sweeping the night sky and the anti-aircraft shells bursting above, the ground beneath our feet trembling as bombs rained down on the town, we experienced an awful feeling of impotence, but like so many other unpleasant aspects of war, we soon became used to these nightly incursions and, as often as not, slept soundly through the heaviest raids.

The autumn winds blew themselves out, and winter's grip closed in on us inexorably. Further combat added to our score of kills but we suffered a perturbing and puzzling loss ourselves. On the afternoon of November 16th we had just disengaged after a battle with a number of enemy fighters and were heading back towards our base when, west of Lavansaari, over the open sea, one of our Mersus piloted by Flight-Sergeant Erkinheimo, a veteran of much combat and an extremely competent pilot, left the formation and began to spiral down towards the water below. His aircraft appeared to be under perfect control and we called him over the R/T without answer. It was quite inexplicable. His aircraft appeared undamaged and his engine was running smoothly, and the aircraft could not be flying itself, yet all we could do was to watch helplessly as the Messerschmitt spiralled closer and closer to the undulating, black water. The pilot made no attempt to jettison his cockpit canopy and, with its undercarriage still up, it skipped across the wave-tops between the islands of Suursaari and Tytärsaari, rapidly slowing down—a perfect ditching. Yet, the pilot made no attempt to extricate himself from the cockpit, and finally, the tail of the

Mersu slowly swung upwards and the fighter slipped beneath the waves with not so much as a ripple. I called up a rescue launch cruising some twelve miles away, but we all knew that a search would be fruitless.

The weeks passed, the temperatures dropping steadily. The Gulf froze over, and 1944 was born in a raging blizzard. Our little Sisu trucks were not suited for pushing snow-ploughs, so we attached these to the squadron's bus and to some Latil gun-tractors that we borrowed from the nearby anti-aircraft batteries and, working hard during our off-duty hours and the night, we succeeded in keeping the runway open. Despite the extreme cold, our Mersus were at constant readiness. We had learned much from the previous winters, and an electric lead was connected up to the sump of each engine to keep the oil fluid. In addition, we had adopted the German technique of "cold starts", adding some fifteen per cent benzine to the oil just before starting, this permitting us to run the engine up to full revs within a minute! This minute was consumed by taxiing the Mersu to the end of the runway, and we could thus begin operations immediately at a given signal, doing away with the time-consuming warm-up. Of course, taking-off with a cold engine running at full power was by no means pleasant. The aircraft vibrated so badly that you tended to wonder if you would be shaken through the cockpit canopy, but once the engine attained its normal operating temperatures the vibration disappeared.

· · · · ·

We had now been operating nearly six months from our strip in the Kymi backwoods, and we had a pretty good idea of our operational capabilities. The picture was anything but comforting. Our early-warning system was all but valueless. Ivan had the vast expanse of the Gulf over which to make his approach, and the enemy carefully avoided the islands of Someri and Suursaari so that we would receive little or no advance warning. What warnings we did receive were unreliable, and the use of sound-locators was hopeless as, so frequently, a warning stemming from their use resulted in the "enemy formation" turning out to be some Luftwaffe aircraft or even motor-torpedo boats! Numerical information and estimated altitudes were invariably inaccurate, yet for a really effective interception it was vital that we scrambled as the Russian fighters left their bases on Lavansaari. The Russian bomber formations usually flew to Lavansaari to pick up their fighter escort, and from there ninety per cent would fly along the Suursaari-Tytärsaari line to attack the Estonian front-line positions or German convoys operating in the Gulf of Finland, the remaining ten per cent usually attacking Kotka.

We did not possess enough fighters to keep standing patrols. The largest available number of Mersus for the defence of Kotka was ten, and frequently some of these were grounded for servicing or repairs. Somehow, therefore, we had to try to anticipate the direction from which attacks on Kotka would come and, more important still, when they would come. We had to ensure that we were not in the landing circuit low on fuel and ammunition, or on the ground being refuelled or rearmed when the attack came. But in some respects our defences could be compared with the attempts of a blind boxer to strike his opponent. Most of the time we were unaware of the approach of the enemy until their appearance over Kotka was heralded by the wail of sirens and the barking of the flak.

Despite the strongest protests from me, Kuije Lahtela, the commander of the second flight and one of my most highly valued pilots, was transferred to the Curtiss Hawk 75A-equipped squadron, HLeLv 32, and on February 12th he handed over command. A week previously, on the 6th, Helsinki, which city had suffered no daylight attacks for some time, was the target for one of the heaviest Russian nocturnal raids to that time. Equally heavy night raids were made on the capital on the 16th and 26th, about a thousand aircraft being used in the three raids, and several hundred civilians being killed and injured. The morning following the last of these attacks, I flew in to Malmi to make an inspection of the second flight and, at the same time, see the medical officer, Lieutenant-Colonel Leiri, to get some relief for the severe headcold that I seemed unable to shake off. My sinuses were blocked but I refused to submit to the drastic treatment that the doctor recommended and, ignoring his order grounding me, flew back to our base the same evening. A week later I was to succeed in clearing my blocked sinuses in a far more dramatic fashion than that recommended by the good doctor.

· · · ·

March 6th was the twenty-sixth anniversary of the creation of the Finnish Air Force, and after a bitterly cold night the sun climbed above the horizon to herald an exceptionally fine day. At noon we scrambled on an abortive interception, but just as we completed refuelling I became aware from radio exchanges that a large formation of Russians was forming up over Lavansaari. Five of the Mersus were ready for take-off, and we roared down the runway, heading south beyond Kotka to intercept the incoming raid well out over the Gulf. For once we were in good time, and as we passed the Hovinsaari anti-aircraft batteries, the Command Post informed us that thirty-nine enemy aircraft were approaching north of Suursaari at an altitude of sixteen thousand feet.

I flicked on the gunsight reflector lamp, clipped on my oxygen mask, and climbed steadily towards our point of interception. Visibility was superb and we easily spotted twenty-seven silver bombers, their polished surfaces reflecting the bright sunlight. Above the bombers we could make out the twelve fighters acting as their escort. The whole formation had now entered a shallow dive towards Kotka, and time and our small numbers necessitated disregarding the escort fighters and concentrating on the bombers.

Kössi Karhila was flying at my starboard wingtip with Onni Paronen to port, Pampsa Myllylä and Antti Tani bringing up the rear. We had now positioned ourselves between the sun and the enemy formation and, full throttle, we roared towards the intruders. Flicking off the safety-catch over the cannon trigger, I called over the R/T, "Leader here, I'm taking the third Ivan to the left!" Growing in my sights was a brand-new Pe-2. At two hundred yards the dorsal gunner began blasting away at me, but I held my fire until only a hundred yards separated the Russian and my Mersu and my 20-mm. cannon and pair of 7·9-mm. machine-guns were slamming shells and bullets into the fuselage and engine nacelles of my victim. As I swept past the Pe-2's starboard engine began to smoke and one undercarriage leg dropped suddenly, the aircraft rolling over on its back and diving straight down to crash north-west of Haapasaari.

Out of the corner of my eye I saw four bombers falling in flames or tumbling out of control, trailing smoke, and several parachutes had blossomed in the afternoon sunlight. The other Pe-2s had now completed a 180-degree turn and were diving in the direction from which they had come, but the escorting La-5s were now on our backs, and I took violent evasive action as cannon shells hurtled past my cockpit. I pivoted the Mersu on one wingtip, two vortices streaming back from the wing as I tightened the turn. Momentarily, one of the La-5s was in my sights and my cannon shells ripped through him from nose to tail, pieces of the Russian fighter whirling past as I broke to avoid collision.

Individual duels were now taking place over a wide area, and near Someri I spotted a lone La-5. I yawed the tail of my Mersu for a quick glance behind and saw another La-5, but it was quite a distance away and I was sure that I had enough time to pick off the unsuspecting La-5 ahead before the other could get on my tail. A few seconds later the Russian fighter was lined up in my sights, and my cannon was belching shells into its port wing from a distance of only fifty yards. My target immediately began to take evasive action, but at that moment I felt a hard blow against my back and one of the side windows in my canopy shattered. Instinctively, I tried to compress myself into the smallest possible space to take full advantage of the armour plate behind my seat, simultaneously kicking the rudder fully over and pulling back and over on the stick. My Mersu flicked over on its back, and I had a fleeting glimpse of an La-5 spitting shells at me and hanging on like a burr.

There was only one way to evade the nimble Lavochkin, and I pushed the Mersu into a tremendous vertical dive. My aircraft screamed down towards the ice at six hundred feet a second. I clung onto the control column with my right hand, winding the trim wheel furiously with my left. Warm blood was coursing from my nose as I plummeted thirteen thousand feet. My eyes misted over as I began to grey out, praying that I would be able to recover from the dive. Five hundred feet above the ice I was still heaving back on the stick with all my might, but the aircraft levelled off, forcing me down into my seat. The fuel-gauge needle was tapping against "zero", and the cannon shells from the La-5 had evidently wrought havoc in my Mersu, for the rudder control run was obviously severed, the radio equipment was a tangled wreck, and even the seat armour had been pierced. I thought that any moment I should have to make a forced landing, but somehow I struggled to the airstrip on the dregs of the fuel in my tank. I taxied to a standstill, elated at having notched up my twenty-ninth and thirtieth kills, and eased myself from the cockpit, but to my intense surprise my comrades grabbed me, hustling me into a car and saying something about the hospital. For some moments I couldn't understand what they were doing, and then it dawned on me: an aircraft riddled with holes and blood all over my face and my flying suit, they had assumed that I had been hit! In fact, the pull-out from that dive had cleared my blocked sinuses, and the accursed headcold had gone.

. . . . .

Spring was once more in the air, the snow melted rapidly, and we soaked up as much of the delightful sunshine as we could. During April we had received new fighters from Germany—Messerschmitt Bf 109G-6s with more reliable FuG 16 radio and greater firepower. The 7·9-mm. machine-guns of the Bf 109G-2 had been supplanted by 13-mm. weapons, and a pair of additional 20-mm. cannon had been slung in gondolas beneath the wings. The latter resulted in a serious reduction in manœuvrability and made the aircraft clumsy, and so we had the wing cannon removed, but the larger calibre machine-guns still gave us more firepower than we had had with the Bf 109G-2.

We received the Bf 109G-6s in small batches, and as they arrived we turned over our Bf 109G-2s to HLeLv 24. Again we were plagued by spares shortages, for much of the stock that we had built up for use with the earlier Messerschmitts could no longer be used for our new mounts, so this too had to be turned over to HLeLv 24. The ferrying of the new fighters from Germany severely taxed our already limited pilot roster, and those of us that remained were on standby from dawn until dusk.

As summer approached each day found us in our cockpits yet earlier, and on May 17th it was still not 04.00 hours as, loaded down with the usual paraphernalia, bright yellow Mae-Wests hung around our necks and maps bulging from our knee pockets, we walked across to the Command Post. Just under the window was the wingtip of my spanking new Mersu, MT-417, awaiting the day's events, the first rays of the sun glinting on its cockpit canopy. It was not until 10.29 hours that the sirens in Kotka began their mournful wailing, and jumping through the open windows, we swung ourselves into the cockpits of our Mersus. Seconds later six DB 605 engines were bursting into life, the mechanics were removing the wheel-chocks and protecting their ears from the thundering roars of the power plants, and then we were taxi-ing out one by one, the coveralls of the mechanics glued tightly to their legs by our slipstreams.

I raced down the runway, raised the undercarriage as soon as I was airborne, and began climbing steeply, at the same time pulling on my flying helmet with my left hand, fastening the 'chute straps and hooking on the safety belt, none of which I had had time for during the emergency take-off. As I climbed steadily into the blue sky the Command Post informed me that twenty-seven bombers and fifteen fighters were approaching Kotka from the south at an altitude of six thousand five hundred feet. Just then the sky immediately ahead and above became alive with bursts of flak. Olli Puhakka was flying alongside, but the other Mersus were still some distance behind us.

We flew straight through our own anti-aircraft barrage, attacking the bombers from beneath, hoping that they would not expect fighter interception from this quarter. No fewer than seven of the bombers fell to our guns, three of the kills being scored by Olli, and most of the survivors jettisoned their bombs into the sea. So rapidly had we got in among the bombers that they were going down like ninepins before the escorting fighters realised what was happening, and when they did finally come down to attack us we added three more Russians to our score. Ten kills in one sortie was really something, and we suffered only one loss, the aircraft ditching in the sea and the pilot being rescued by a gunboat.

The next day we did lose a pilot, however, as one of the newest members of our squadron, Lieutenant Lahti, crashed to his death in the woods near Utti while taking-off on a familiarization flight in a Mersu.

. . . .

Our operations were now becoming increasingly difficult as, owing to our successes, the Russians began to increase their fighter escorts which flew both above and below their charges, forcing us to fight our way through a fighter screen whichever way we attacked the bombers. I thanked our lucky stars that Ivan hadn't yet thought of sending part of the fighter forces to strafe our base *before* each raid. If they had come upon us while our handful of Mersus was taking-off we wouldn't have stood a chance. Russian thinking was indeed strange for, from the interrogation of prisoners-of-war, we knew that Ivan was only too well aware of the existence and position of our base, and the small number of fighters that it supported.

From time to time enemy shipping in the Gulf offered superb targets for dive-bombing, and so, during May and June, I trained ten pilots in the art of dive-bombing, and we fitted the Messerschmitts with racks for 110-lb. bombs which we dropped at low altitude in a 45-degree dive. We used a sixteen by twenty-seven yard target and consistently scored three direct hits out of every four bombs dropped. We were all anxious to have a go at the ships, but the authorities, unwilling to endanger much-valued fighter aircraft needed for the defence of towns and military installations, refused to give their permission, and the whole scheme had to be regretfully dropped.

As the summer reached its full glory, the character of the war changed radically. On the morning of June 9th, 1944, the immense Russian drive on the Karelian Isthmus began, the Russian forces being backed by a tremendous artillery barrage and afforded the cover of an aerial umbrella of hundreds of planes. The fighting raged furiously, and the Russians suddenly switched their main pressure point to the Gulf side of the Isthmus, temporarily disorganising our front. The next morning I was ordered to gather together all three flights and head for Immola to participate in the struggle. Hurriedly, our ground staff loaded trucks with servicing equipment and spares and left for our new base, but our fighters could not get away until the 12th owing to unfavourable weather conditions.

For the third time I found myself operating from Immola, but now the base was a scene of intense activity, with fighters from four squadrons preparing for what was to prove the beginning of the end.

Two days after our arrival at Immola our squadron participated in the furious battles over our main defences stretching from Vammelsuu through Kuuterselkä to Siiranmäki. The most ferocious hand-to-hand fighting was being waged beneath us, the battle ebbing and flowing, and positions changing hands time and time again. Our twelve-plane formation had been assigned the task of knocking down a pair of Makkara (Sausage) observation balloons that were accurately directing artillery fire against our troops. As we spotted them we also saw a score of enemy fighters whose task was obviously that of protecting the balloons. We were flying on a collision course with the Russian fighters, and I had only just time to waggle my wings to signal the attack before the two formations had become a whirling mêlée, my shells slamming into the fuselage of a Bell Airacobra which was squarely in my sights. As the distance between us closed to about three plane-lengths, my victim seemed to stagger, thin trails of fuel and smoke mingled as it fell away into a spin, and finally crashed into a ploughed field alongside the Kivennava-Kuuterselkä road.

Together with one of our other pilots who had also downed an Airacobra, I began climbing at full throttle in a south-westerly direction where most of our comrades were now occupied in a tremendous free-for-all. As we approached a Russian fighter plunged from the conflict, leaving a trail of black smoke, and, for a moment, an La-5 appeared in my sights, but my brief burst apparently failed to find its mark, for my target promptly put his nose down and headed for his own lines. Inadvertently, he had given me the advantage, for if he had gone into a tight turn I would have been unable to hold him, but now I had him. I overhauled the Ivan rapidly and was about to start firing when I realised that he was diving uncontrollably. My first burst must have found its mark after all, for the pilot made no attempt to recover, and the La-5 smashed into the trees below.

At the low altitude at which I was flying I could see one of the Makkara balloons silhouetted against the horizon. I had no doubt that some flak units had been positioned around the balloon and, in order to exercise the element of surprise, I climbed up into the sun. The vast city of Leningrad was spread before me, and just slightly to starboard was the fortress of

Kronstadt. The balloon was anchored near Terijoki and was flying at an altitude of about two thousand feet. I pushed down the nose of my Mersu and began diving on the Makkara, and although I was giving her only half-throttle, I was soon roaring down at more than 370 m.p.h., but firing at this stationary target offered no problems, and my first burst brought a puff of white smoke from the aft end of the Makkara. A tongue of flame appeared and in no time at all fire had enveloped the whole balloon which began to fall, the observation basket swinging wildly from side to side.

As soon as we had refuelled we were once again back over the Siiranmäki-Kuuterselkä area. Each sortie was a hectic battle, and there was never a shortage of targets, for in every direction there were Russian fighters or attack aircraft. The main problem was ensuring that oneself was not providing a target. By the end of the day our score was eleven aircraft and four observation balloons, and our only loss was Sergeant Saarni who hadn't returned to base and was listed as missing.

15

A CLOSE CALL

On June 16th the German forces began to arrive at Immola, and without any prior notice of their arrival, a continuous stream of transport aircraft began to disgorge ground personnel and servicing equipment. We arrived back from a mission just in the nick of time to rescue our personal belongings, the Germans evidently being under the impression that they were taking over the base. Focke-Wulf Fw 190s and Junkers Ju 87s began to arrive to participate in the Karelian defence, and so we decided to move over to the airfield near Lappeenranta where our sister squadron, HLeLv 24 joined us. We combined the move to our new base with an interception sortie over Uusikirkko, and in the fracas Captain Lauri Pekuri was forced to bale-out while attacking an Ilyushin Il-2, landing on the wrong side of the lines and instantly being made prisoner. Poke Pokela succeeded him as flight commander.

Previously the Lappeenranta field had been used only as an emergency base, and it was really too small for the operation of our Mersus, so almost immediately I began looking for a more suitable base. There was an airfield at Taipalsaari, about twenty-five miles to the north, and although it was by no means ideal, it would obviously be better than the Lappeenranta field after a little reconditioning. There was certainly nothing better available for many miles.

The continuous air activity soon took its toll of our fighting strength, and in no time we had only ten serviceable aircraft. Fortunately, replacements were arriving in a constant trickle from Germany, some of our pilots having been assigned to permanent ferrying duties. Reports from the ground forces were anything but encouraging. All the East Karelian reserve groups at Aunus were thrown into the Kannas in a vain attempt to stem the advance of the Russians, and by the 18th our troops had fallen back to a line running from Humallahti through

(*Above*) A Messerschmitt Bf 109G-6 on interception duty at Malmi. The Bf 109G-6s began arriving in Finland in April 1944, and HLeLv 34 turned its older Bf 109G-2s over to HLeLv 24. The G-6s had more reliable radio equipment than their predecessors and greater firepower, but the underwing 20-mm. cannon of this model were removed by the Finns as they drastically reduced the fighter's manoeuvrability. (*Right*) The Bf 109G-6 of Flight Sergeant Nuorala was one of a number of Messerschmitts involved in accidents resulting from too fierce application of the brakes on the soft turf of Finnish airfields. (*Below*) One of Karhila's victims, an Ilyushin Il-2 shot down near Tienhaara on June 21, 1944. The Il-2 was extremely heavily armoured and, in consequence, difficult to shoot down.

It has been said that the only major aircraft manufacturing country whose products were not represented in the Finnish Air Force was Japan! A large number of Russian aircraft captured by the Wehrmacht in the Ukraine were *sold* to Finland, and above is illustrated one such aircraft, an Ilyushin DB-3. (*Left*) One of several SB-2bis bombers that were operated, this particular aircraft (VP-10) being officially credited with the destruction of four Russian submarines. (*Below, right*) An SB-2bis pilot trainer.

The Blenheim was the Finnish Air Force's principal bomber, and thirty Blenheim Is (*below*) were acquired from Britain, and the type was manufactured under licence by the State Aircraft Factory which produced a further fifty-five machines of this type. In addition to these the Finns received twelve Blenheim IVs prior to the start of the "Continuation War". Finnish-built Blenheims were sometimes operated with fixed skis, and their bomb-bays were enlarged so that they could accommodate Swedish and American bombs. Their Mercury engines were manufactured by the Tampella Machine Works. Among units operating the Blenheim were PLeLv 46 and 48, the former converting to Dornier Do 17Z-2s in January 1942. The Blenheim was nicknamed "Pelti Heikki", or "Tin Henry" in Finnish service.

A CLOSE CALL

Römpötti, Summa, Muolaanjärvi, Yksjärvi, and Vuoksi to Taipale.

On the 19th, the eve of the fall of Viipuri, we were assigned the task of providing air cover for troops engaged in delaying tactics in the Äyräpää-Summa area. Our ten Mersus took-off at 10.25 hours, the dust clouds raised by the slipstreams from our airscrews swirling across the dry Lappeenranta airfield. It was already our second mission of the day, and we flew at low altitude as, although we would be at a disadvantage if bounced by a flock of Russian fighters, we could winkle out the enemy gun positions and spot troop movements more easily. Silhouetted against the horizon far to the south-east hung another of the detested Makkara balloons. No Ivans were visible in any direction. Although I was well aware that the Russians surrounded these balloons with plenty of flak units and that it was almost suicidal to attack other than from a dive out of the sun, I must have been in a particularly foolhardy mood for I told the rest of the pilots that I was going to attack the Makkara and ordered them to stay well out of range of the flak batteries that probably surrounded it.

I started my run on the Makkara at an altitude of less than two thousand feet. The Russians had high-speed winches and the habit of hauling down the balloons immediately an aircraft approached, so I had to make my firing pass as quickly as possible. I would have no further opportunity. At four hundred yards the Makkara was centred in my sights, but before I could fire all hell was let loose! The air around my Mersu was suddenly full of tracer and bursting shells—Ivan was certainly wide awake. I felt a severe shock in the starboard mainplane and my fighter skidded violently. I swung my machine back into line with the balloon. More throttle ... one fifty yards ... now!

A mass of flame and black smoke blossomed up in front of me, and for a fraction of a second my vision was obscured as I tore through the spot that only a moment before had been occupied by the Makkara. The flak was still bursting all round me, and then my Messerschmitt shuddered as if it had run into some unseen object. Pieces of metal torn from my engine cowling flashed past my canopy, and the engine began to back-fire heavily. Simultaneously my revs began to drop. Instinctively, I pulled up to two thousand four hundred feet with what little speed I had left and prepared to bale out. Flak continued to follow me. I shut off the fuel, for just behind my seat were about a hundred gallons of high octane.

I glanced around. I was about nine miles behind the Russian lines and I might well get short shrift from Ivan if I became his prisoner. The Mersu was gliding surprisingly well, although leaving a tell-tale trail of oily black smoke, and I recall thinking how odd it was to be sitting in my cockpit without the familiar bass roar of the Daimler-Benz. With any luck I might just reach our lines. I swung the gunsight over to one side, tightened my seat straps and dropped the seat to its lowest position so as to give my head some protection in case the Mersu turned over on its back. The fighter was now beginning to drop rapidly, and nine hundred feet below me there was nothing to be seen but a sea of treetops. There was not even a hint of an opening between the damned trees, and I was only too well aware that landing a Messerschmitt among the trees was sheer suicide.

With my right hand I held the canopy release handle. There was no sense in being trapped inside the cockpit with that hundred gallons of highly volatile fuel a few inches behind my back. I glanced to the west and saw the specks where my comrades were still circling calmly. I jabbed the R/T button and told them that I was going down in the woods. It must have been at that moment that I lost some of my calmness and indifference to my fate. The trees were rushing at me like an express train. A glance at my airspeed indicator showed 220 m.p.h. and, instantaneously, there was a loud crash as my starboard wing was sheered off by a tree as cleanly as if it had been a pat of butter cut with a knife. A split second later the same thing happened to my port wing without my Messerschmitt deviating even fractionally from its headlong course.

I tried to guide my wingless fuselage between the trees with the aid of the rudder and, somehow, the engine and cockpit got through but the rear fuselage snapped off immediately behind me as it struck one of the trees. All that remained of my Messerschmitt continued to plough on through the trees at about 60 m.p.h., then the engine struck the ground with a thud that jarred every bone in my body. Clods of dirt and sand flew in every direction but the wreckage had yet to finish its journey. I was thrown from side to side, only my seat straps holding me in the cockpit. Then, with a final lurch, all that was left of my fighter at last came to a standstill.

Silence. Blissful silence.

I crawled out of the pitiful heap of scrap metal that only a few minutes before had been a potent fighting craft. I flexed my fingers gingerly. I bent my arms and stamped my feet. I was alive and still in one piece. I fished a crumpled cigarette from my pocket, sat on a log and endeavoured to think coherently. In the middle of my smoke three Russian fighters flew low overhead, strafing the woods. The noise of firing from the front was close by, and artillery, either Russian or our own, began bracketing a small knoll less than a hundred yards away. Steel splinters whistled through the trees and ricocheted off the rocks. But finally the shelling died down, and I heard some voices approaching through the thick undergrowth. I flattened myself behind a bush, tugging the major's insignia from my shoulders and slipping my revolver from its holster. Then a Finnish lieutenant and his runner burst through the bushes. I had landed slap in the centre of no man's land!

We examined the wreckage of my fighter and discovered that it had received two direct hits from 40-mm. shells. I salvaged the tachometer and the clock from the instrument panel, slung my parachute over my shoulder, and headed for the battalion Command Post. Major Tapainen, the battalion commander, offered me tea, but just then a formation of about a hundred Russian aircraft flew over, heading north. I decided that I had better get back to my squadron without any delay. It appeared that the major's battalion was holding its own here in the Summa forests, although enemy armoured units had been seen along the road some twelve miles to the rear, as far as Kämärä. I was later to learn that this gallant force had been cut off that same day and, apart from a dozen or so men who succeeded in breaking through the Russian lines, was taken prisoner.

I hitched rides back to Lappeenranta, my first objective being Viipuri, some twenty-five miles to the north. Once, while riding aboard a guard truck, I had the unpleasant experience of suffering a strafing attack by four Il-2s, but despite the numerous firing passes and the number of small bombs that they dropped, neither the guard truck nor its occupants sustained a scratch. It seemed incredible that we could have survived the attack totally unscathed, and I began to wonder how many of the cat's proverbial nine lives I was going to use up that day. The truck eventually reached the guard station from where, with my 'chute still draped over my shoulder, I began hiking. I walked for about two and a half miles through the woods until I reached an artillery battery that was preparing to withdraw, and I hitched a ride aboard one of the light motorised guns to Colonel Pajari's headquarters from where I completed the remainder of my journey to Viipuri in the sidecar of a motor-cycle.

Many of the troops that we passed wore sad, disheartened expressions, and it seemed to me that their spirit was broken. Years of continuous fighting had sapped their energy, and this latest onslaught had been too much for them. Viipuri already seemed a city of the dead, and only one telephone line was still operating, but somehow I managed to get through to Lappeenranta to request that my car pick me up. While impatiently awaiting the car's arrival, I wandered around the city, meeting less than ten people. Nearly all the shops were still intact, their shelves piled high with goods, and in the large Starckjohan store the last of the personnel were preparing to leave. I offered them a lift out of Viipuri in my car, and so, when the car finally arrived, we piled cash registers high in the back. Soon after leaving Viipuri, on the Lappeenranta road, we were bogged down in a tremendous jam of marching troops, trucks, half-tracks, horse-drawn vehicles, in fact, all the paraphernalia of war, and it was not until evening that I eventually succeeded in getting back to the base.

After dinner in the mess I sat quietly considering the events of the day. I had to admit to myself that my rashness in attacking the Makkara in the manner that I had adopted was hardly deserving of my singular good fortune. It was still difficult to believe that I was alive and in one piece. I could only assume that it was the *high speed* of my Mersu when it crashed through the trees that had saved my life. If I had crashed into the trees at normal landing speed the very first contact with the treetops would have swung my Messerschmitt sideways, killing me instantly. The speed had enabled the fighter to plough through the trees in a straight line, and the big Daimler-Benz engine had provided frontal protection.

16

THE LAST ROUND

The following morning I was ordered by headquarters to take two weeks' leave, but I had to discover if my crash had affected my nerves or judgment, so on the 20th I took-off once more, this time in a borrowed machine, and bagged my fortieth kill—a beautiful Yak-4 fighter-bomber. How could I go on leave at this, the nineteenth hour? The skies were full of La-5s, Yak-9s, Airacobras, Pe-2s, Yak-4s and Il-2s, and every day had its share of furious dogfights. Sometimes the enemy aircraft came over in waves of hundreds; at other times they flew in small groups, but whatever time of day we took-off, we knew that we would not be carrying much ammunition when we landed once more. No, leave at this time was out of the question.

On the eve of Midsummer's Day eight of our Messerschmitts escorted a force of our bombers on a "night" raid on Tali between 00.40 and 01.55 hours, and we had just finished refuelling when, without warning, a force of twelve Il-2s scorched across the field, blazing away with all their guns and dropping dozens of small bombs, pitting the field with holes. Luck seemed to be on our side for, despite the fury of the attack, only three of our Mersus received slight damage and the only casualties among the personnel were two gunners of one of the anti-aircraft batteries who were wounded. By 03.00 hours the craters had been filled in and we were once more taking-off. Throughout the day we operated over the Viipuri area, knocking down five Ivans, and our last sortie was also our ferry flight to Taipalsaari as the rudimentary reconditioning of the field had now been completed.

Our nine-plane formation returned from the front and continued over Lappeenranta northwards, over the waters of the Saimaa sparkling in the rays of the sun which was now low on the horizon, to touch down at our new base. Our quarters were three miles away from the field, right on the beautiful

Saimaa beach, and away from the din of war we soon recovered from an exhausting day of almost continuous flying, enjoying the short twilight of Midsummer's Night.

The change of bases affected our routine in no way, and from dawn to dusk we were fighting in support of our retreating ground forces, escorting bombers and reconnoitring the enemy lines, but three hectic days resulted in serious deterioration of the dirt runway. The narrow-track undercarriage which supported over three tons of Messerschmitt soon had the runway surface as rutted as a ploughed field. During take-offs the Mersus bounced from side to side, the danger of digging in a wing ever present, and each fighter raised such a tremendous cloud of dust that the next had to wait an expensive minute or two until the dust had cleared sufficiently to permit its pilot to see. Again, other units were based at the field, their aircraft dispersed on either side of us, and there were many narrow escapes when an aircraft taking-off across the field all but collided with one of our Mersus taking-off hurriedly down field on an interception mission. Taipalsaari was totally unsuited for satisfactory Messerschmitt operations, and although we exercised extreme vigilance during take-off, and carefully graded the surface of the runway, these operations were fraught with danger. It is amazing that only one of our Mersus was seriously damaged during a take-off. Another was lost at this time on operations and, luckily, three replacements arrived from Germany. The pilots that ferried the new Mersus into our base could scarcely believe their eyes when they saw me for, somehow, a report of my death had reached their ears in Germany! Unfortunately, we had no time to adopt the Luftwaffe's practice of celebrating a "birthday" when someone survived a crash in which, logically, they should have been killed.

. . . . .

Bitter fighting continued. The first days of July were at hand and the front line was moving inexorably closer. There was no weakening of the enemy's air activity, and hundreds of Ivans roamed to and fro over our lines, but, as yet, despite their numerical superiority, the Russians had not achieved overall aerial superiority, and we continued pecking away at them, shooting one down here and another there.

On July 2nd we bagged eleven enemy aircraft for the loss of only one of our Messerschmitts, Lieutenant Silvennoinen baling out from his burning fighter near Ihantala after shooting down a Yak-9. Unfortunately, Silvennoinen pulled his ripcord too quickly, tearing some of the shrouds on the burning Mersu, and in consequence he came down too fast, severely injuring his back. The next day we added nine more Ivans to our score over the same area, but the newly-commissioned Lieutenant Yrjö Pallasvuo, a veteran of nearly two years of fighting, met his death in a duel with an La-5.

Unable to break through westward from Sorvali to Kivisilta, the enemy now occupied the southern islands in the Gulf of Viipuri, and on July 15th we fought a series of exceptionally intense battles when the Russians invaded the island of Teikari with between twenty and thirty assault craft. On the final mission of the day, while ten of our Mersus were covering our Blenheims attacking the assault craft, one of our fighters flown by Lieutenant "Pampsa" Myllylä was hit by flak. Pampsa, one of the squadron's most capable combat pilots, was forced to take to the silk, and landed in the woods near Hanhijoki, suffering only bruises and minor contusions.

At times it seemed incredible that our squadron could have suffered relatively so few casualties yet have knocked down more than a couple of hundred Ivans. In order to confirm a kill it was necessary to find the wreckage of the victim or, if the battle took place over enemy territory, the crash of the aircraft had to be witnessed by at least two pilots. So, if anything, our score was under-estimated, for so many other aircraft had been downed in individual combats when no witnesses were available to confirm the kills. There were several reasons for our success, apart from the fact that until 1944 many of the enemy pilots encountered had undoubtedly been novices with barely a hundred hours of flying time behind them. To my mind, the most important of these were our superior training, the almost daily bore-sighting of our guns combined with the fact that the average Finn is a born marksman and has keen eyesight, and the large formations so frequently employed by the enemy which tended to give their pilots a dangerously false sense of security.

The focal points of the battle raging on the ground changed

alternately north of the Ihantala area in the Kylä, Paakola and Äyräpää sectors, to the Central Karelian Isthmus where, on July 9th, the enemy succeeded in crossing the Vuosalmi. Occasionally we encountered Luftwaffe aircraft operating over the same area as ourselves, but for the most part all the aircraft we saw were Russian.

.   .   .   .   .

On the morning of the 13th we were assigned the task of escorting our bombers which were to attack the Russian supply dumps along the Vuoksi River. The bomber formation was to be large by our standards, and we had to make the most careful calculations, timing our fuel supply to the minute.[1] We climbed into the cockpits of our Mersus, and their engines roared into life almost in unison, their thunderous voices sending the birds fluttering from their roosts in the surrounding trees. One after another our fighters climbed through the swirling cloud of dust until all twelve were airborne, and as we made a circuit of the field we formed up in three groups of four, and then began climbing steadily on a south-easterly course. The weather was superb, and our field of view stretched for more than sixty miles in every direction. After fifteen minutes Viipuri was to starboard, although the city itself was hidden by a pall of grey-black smoke. The Karelian Heel lay spread beneath us like a toy landscape. Even the immense Lake Ladoga looked like nothing more than a large pond. Lake Saimaa and the inner Finnish lakes were little more than bright pinpoints, and even the Estonian coastline could be clearly seen to the south.

It was necessary to conserve our limited oxygen supply, and as we breasted the twenty thousand feet mark I began to feel slightly tight. As the instrument panel began to blur in front of my eyes I could delay no longer, and gulped down deep draughts of oxygen. We reached our rendezvous point over the church on the Vuoksi bank, and within less than a minute black specks on the horizon grew into forty Blenheims, Do 17Zs and Ju 88As. We split our force of Messerschmitts in two, six taking up position on each side of the bombers which seemed to rise and fall in undulating waves as their airscrews sliced through the rarefied atmosphere. They made a fine sight and,

[1] In clean condition, the Bf 109G-6 had an endurance of only fifty minutes.

with our greater cruising speed, we zig-zagged back and forth along the bomber formation.

Time seemed to pass extremely slowly. There was no sign of any Russian interceptors, but I was sure that it would not be long before a pack of Ivans would be clawing its way up towards us. The Vuoksi River was now below us, and the first bombers began a shallow dive towards their targets. It seemed an infinity before we saw the flashes of the first bombs exploding, and now the black specks of Russian fighters had appeared to the south. About a dozen fighters were approaching rapidly. "Eight above and to starboard," I yelled over the R/T, and eight of the Messerschmitts immediately turned towards the Ivans, four staying with the bombers.

We were soon whirling round and round with the Yak-9s, twisting and pirouetting as we endeavoured to keep the Russians away from our charges. The confused, tightly packed battle eddied to and fro, Russian and Finn firing at the least opportunity. Two Yak-9s spiralled down out of the mêlée, but our bombers did not get through completely unscathed, for one of the Blenheims was either hit by flak or by a fighter that succeeded in penetrating our screen, and went down trailing smoke.

The whole formation had now completed its bombing run and had turned for home, so we disengaged from the Yak-9s and also turned for home, keeping our fingers crossed that our fuel would last out. Over the Viipuri-Antrea railway line the fuel warning lights came on, indicating that we had a maximum of twenty minutes' supply left in our tanks, but eight of us succeeded in making the base, the other four landing at Lappeenranta to take on fuel.

Our ground staff had trained themselves to fill our tanks with hand pumps in record time while we pilots grabbed a sandwich and a glass of milk, but this time we hardly had lifted the glasses to our lips when we were ordered to get ready for an immediate scramble.

· · · ·

Throwing in all their reserves and with the aid of small German Panzer units, the Finnish Army succeeded in stemming the big Russian drive that had opened on June 9th, and on July 7th the Ihantala front had been stabilized, and nine days later the Vuosalmi front had also been stabilized. Between the middle of June and the middle of July we had flown one thousand and forty hours operationally, had participated in seventy-four major air battles, had used up twenty-five thousand rounds of 13-mm. and eleven thousand rounds of 20-mm. ammunition, and we had burned over fifty-five thousand Imperial gallons of fuel. I personally had added 18,630 miles to the distance that I had flown and seventeen confirmed kills to my score.

Eight young and eager lieutenants fresh from the war college reported for duty with the squadron and we soon had them checked out, thus giving us a small pool of reserve pilots, and enabling a few of us to take time off in rotation. In such off-duty periods the fish-filled waters of the Saimaa lured us, and I discovered that we had two Ladoga fishermen among our personnel. One night we took our motor-boat to Pönniälä, dropped our lines overboard baited with pieces of whitefish and began trolling. At dawn when we began pulling in our lines we found that our catch comprised about ninety pounds of pike.

The Luftwaffe's Focke-Wulf Fw 190 fighters and Junkers Ju 87 bombers left Immola on July 22nd for theatres in which the Wehrmacht was being gradually decimated. The operations of the Ju 87s in particular had aroused the greatest admiration in us, for their tight formations had been maintained through the heaviest flak barrages and the most vicious fighter attacks, and as they went down the others closed in to fill the gaps in the formation that they had left. Whatever the opposition, they always fought their way to the designated objective.

Day after day we took-off on interception and reconnaissance sorties, and sometimes we undertook search missions around the Estonian Gulf. It was during such a mission that Ture Mattila and I had our last encounter with Russian fighters. By chance we had flown over Narvi, Estonia, on August 5th. The day was delightful and my thoughts had begun to wander when Ture's voice came over the R/T informing me that he had spotted some enemy aircraft. A half-dozen Yak-9s were escorting a similar number of Il-2 ground-attack aircraft, and before the Russian fighters even knew that they no longer had the sky to themselves, we had shot two of the Yak-9s into the sea, multi-coloured patches of oil marking the spots where they hit the water. Little did I know then that my Yak-9, my fifty-fourth kill, would be the last Russian fighter to be on the receiving end of my Mersu's guns.

We undertook reconnaissance missions over Seiskari, Koivisto, Heinjoki and Terijoki; we escorted Do 17Zs to Taipale and other targets, but, strangely enough, we were opposed only by flak. We bounced across our airfield trailing tremendous clouds of dust, and took-off for a reconnaissance of Terijoki—my four hundred and fortieth combat mission. It was August 26th, and the midday sun was high in the sky, a few scattered white clouds sailing across the horizon like ships before a breeze. In order to avoid the worst of the flak, we climbed to nine thousand feet and flew south-east along the Rajajoki railway line. Between bursts of anti-aircraft fire we noted a number of enemy fighters dispersed along the boundaries of the Suulajärvi airfield; a freight train was in motion to the north-west of the field, and on the main road was a convoy of trucks heading towards the front.

On the return flight we approached the Jäppilä airfield, letting down over Koivisto for a low-level strafing run. As the field came into view we saw seven or eight fighters parked along one side, and a machine-gun opened up at us from the roof of our former headquarters. I sent a burst into the building from which frightened men ran, while Illu Juutilainen raked the line of fighters, and then we were over the Gulf. Although I did not know it at the time, I had completed my last operational flight against the Russians.

· · · · ·

Nine days later, on September 4th at 08.00 hours, hostilities against the Soviet Union ceased. We had been forced to sue for peace. One of the conditions of the truce was that all German forces should evacuate Finland within two weeks, and now our comrades of three years of fighting were, technically at least, our enemies to be expelled by force of arms. I was ordered to take the squadron to Selänpää airfield where, harbouring the most serious misgivings for the future, we awaited further orders. Our Armistice Commission journeyed to Moscow where a truce was signed, affording us temporary peace until the Finnish army had made an attempt to intern German forces still existing in northern Finland.

I had received orders to move the squadron once more to an airfield in the north, but I could find no suitable field until German forces left Kemi, so we flew our aircraft to Utti where they were temporarily stored. Finally, on November 11th, the reserves were discharged and for us the war was over. During its existence HLeLv 34 had scored two hundred and seventy confirmed kills for the loss of twenty-two Messerschmitts destroyed and a further seventeen damaged. Five of our pilots had received the much-coveted Mannerheim Cross for their efforts, and eleven had given their lives.

After four years of fighting its ending seemed an anti-climax. Aerial combat had become our life and everything had been subjugated to the task of fighting the war. Now the Messerschmitts stood around silently, shrouded in tarpaulins, and the bases seemed to languish in a heavy stillness. How were we to adapt ourselves to the staid existences of farmers, insurance agents and car dealers, reliving our battles in our dreams. We would hear the staccato chatter of machine-guns in every road drill; the deep-throated roar of our Mersus in every slow transport aircraft crawling across the sky, and every clear winter's night we would gaze up at the stars and remember.

APPENDIX I

OFFICIAL LIST OF THE AUTHOR'S AERIAL VICTORIES

Date	Type	Place
December 1, 1939	Tupolev SB-2	Koljola
December 23, 1939	Polikarpov R-5	Kämärä
January 6, 1940	Tupolev SB-2	Uomaa
July 8, 1941	Polikarpov I-153	Parikkala
August 18, 1941	Polikarpov I-153	Vuosalmi
August 30, 1941	MiG-3	Jäppilä
September 27, 1941	Polikarpov I-15	Petroskoi
October 6, 1941	Ilyushin DB-3	Wytegras
October 15, 1941	Tupolev SB-2bis	Aunus
November 7, 1941	LaGG-3	Lotinanpelto
May 1, 1942	Polikarpov I-153	Kuutilahti
July 27, 1942	Petlyakov Pe-2	Nr. Leningrad
August 6, 1942	Polikarpov I-16	Seiskari
August 31, 1942	Polikarpov I-153	Lavansaari
September 25, 1942	Petlyakov Pe-2	N. shore of Ladoga
October 22, 1942	(2) Polikarpov I-16	Kreivinlahti
October 30, 1942	Supermarine Spitfire V	Oranienbaum
October 30, 1942	Polikarpov I-16	,,
May 19, 1943	Polikarpov I-153	Peninsaari
May 21, 1943	Lavochkin La-5	Lavansaari
May 22, 1943	LaGG-3	,,
June 24, 1943	LaGG-3	Grasnaya-Gorka
July 16, 1943	Petlyakov Pe-2	Seiskari
July 20, 1943	(2) LaGG-3	E. of Suursaari
September 4, 1943	Lavochkin La-5	Seiskari
September 8, 1943	LaGG-3	Tytärsaari
October 27, 1943	Ilyushin Il-2	Lavansaari-Kotka
November 4, 1943	Lavochkin La-5	,, ,,
March 6, 1944	Lavochkin La-5	,, ,,
March 6, 1944	Petlyakov Pe-2	,, ,,
May 8, 1944	Petlyakov Pe-2	,, ,,

APPENDIX I

May 17, 1944	Petlyakov Pe-2	Kotka-Hamina
June 14, 1944	Captive balloon	Terijoki
June 14, 1944	(2) Lavochkin La-5	Kivennava
June 14, 1944	Bell Airacobra	Kuuterselkä
June 17, 1944	Ilyushin Il-2	Kämärä
June 19, 1944	Captive balloon	Perkjärvi
June 20, 1944	Yakovlev Yak-4	S. of Viipuri
June 21, 1944	Ilyushin Il-2	Tali
June 23, 1944	Ilyushin Il-2	Tienhaara
June 28, 1944	Polikarpov Po-2	Vammelsuu
June 30, 1944	Bell Airacobra	Ihantala
June 30, 1944	Lavochkin La-5	,,
July 3, 1944	Petlyakov Pe-2	,,
July 3, 1944	Ilyushin Il-2	,,
July 5, 1944	Ilyushin Il-2	Teikarsaari
July 5, 1944	LaGG-3	,,
July 9, 1944	Yakovlev Yak-9	Äyräpää
July 18, 1944	Bell Airacobra	Vuosalmi
July 25, 1944	Yakovlev Yak-9	Virolahti
August 5, 1944	Yakovlev Yak-9	E. end of Gulf

APPENDIX II

THE PRINCIPAL AIRCRAFT TYPES OPERATED OVER FINLAND
NOVEMBER 30, 1939–MARCH 13, 1940 AND JUNE 25, 1941–
SEPTEMBER 4, 1944

BREWSTER B-239

Conceived as a single-seat shipboard interceptor and fighter-bomber, the Brewster B-239 series was to have a singularly unfortunate operational career *except* in Finnish service. A mid-wing cantilever monoplane of all-metal construction with a flush-riveted metal stressed skin and metal-framed, fabric-covered control surfaces, the Brewster fighter was of relatively advanced concept when the prototype had been ordered by the U.S. Navy on June 22, 1936, as the XF2A-1, employing hydraulically-operated split flaps between the ailerons and the fuselage, and fully retractable main undercarriage members.

Designed around the single-row nine-cylinder Wright R-1820 Cyclone air-cooled radial engine, the XF2A-1, or Brewster B-139, flew for the first time in January 1938, with an XR-1820-22 engine rated at 950 h.p. for take-off and 750 h.p. at 15,200 feet. Evaluation trials were successful, and on June 11, 1938, the Brewster company received an order for fifty-four production machines powered by the R-1820-34 engine offering 940 h.p. for take-off and 750 h.p. at 17,000 feet. Designated B-239 by its manufacturers and F2A-1 by the U.S. Navy, the production model had empty and loaded weights of 3,785 lb. and 5,055 lb. respectively, attaining a maximum speed of 301 m.p.h. at 17,000 feet, an initial climb rate of 3,060 ft./min., a service ceiling of 32,500 feet and a normal range of 1,095 miles.

Production deliveries began in June 1939, and nine of the first eleven machines off the line were assigned to VF-3, the U.S. Navy's senior fighter squadron, operating from the U.S.S. *Saratoga*, but in December 1939, as a result of representations to the U.S. government and American sympathies for the Finns in their "David and Goliath" conflict with the Russians, the remaining B-239 fighters still to be delivered to the U.S. Navy

APPENDIX II

were officially declared surplus to requirements as a means of making them available for delivery to Finland. The B-239s were promptly shipped to Trollhättan in Sweden where they were assembled by volunteer mechanics from the Norwegian Air Force under the supervision of representatives of the Brewster company. Whereas the aircraft delivered to the U.S. Navy had been powered by the R-1820-34, the Finnish B-239s were fitted with an export version of the Cyclone purchased together with spares under a separate contract with the Wright Aeronautical Corporation. This engine, the R-1820-G5, offered 950 h.p. at 2,200 r.p.m. for take-off and 850 h.p. at 2,100 r.p.m. at 6,000 feet. Armament comprised two 0·5-in. Colt-Browning machine guns in the upper forward decking of the fuselage and two similar weapons in the wings.

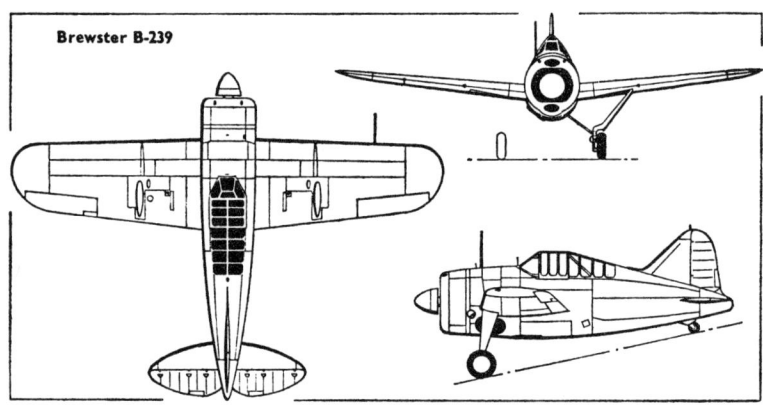

Brewster B-239

The B-239s were ferried from Trollhättan to Finland, HLeLv 22 being formed under Captain Erkki at Hollola on February 20, 1940, to operate the fighters. The personnel of HLeLv 22 included a considerable number of foreign volunteers, from Britain, Canada, Denmark, Poland, Spain and the U.S.A., but only five B-239s had arrived before the armistice terminated the "Winter War", and it was decided that the Brewsters would be operated by the more experienced pilots of HLeLv 24. HLeLv 22 was redesignated HLeLv 32 as part of a new Fighter Regiment (LeR 3) formed at Pori on the west coast of Finland during the summer of 1940, this unit taking over the "Winter War" D.XXI fighters of HLeLv 24.

(Above, left) Lieutenant Kale Tervo who lost his life in a Bf 109G-2 on August 20, 1943, while operating from Suulajärvi. He had nineteen kills to his credit. *(Above, right)* Lieutenant Pege Saalasti who lost his life in combat on May 21, 1943, when his Bf 109G-2 hit an I-153 Tchaika head on near the island of Lavansaari. *(Below)* Lieutenant Lauri Nissinen, a Flight Leader of HLeLv 24, who lost his life on June 17, 1944 when the wing of a Russian bomber shot down by another Finnish fighter struck his Messerschmitt. Nissinen had been awarded the Mannerheim Cross in July 1942, and at the time of his death he had scored thirty-two and a half kills.

(*Above*) The author in the cockpit of a Messerschmitt Bf 109G-6 during the closing stages of the "Continuation War". (*Left*) The emblem of HLeLv 34 here seen painted on the rudder of a Bf 109G-6. The emblem comprised a baby crow carrying a spiked club and wearing the author's cap. It was painted in black on a white background. (*Below*) The Pyry II tandem two-seat advanced trainer similar to that in which Major Olavi Ehrnrooth lost his life. Of Finnish design, the Pyry was powered by a 420 h.p. Wright Whirlwind R-975-E3 air-cooled radial engine. It was of mixed construction and normally carried an armament of one machine gun. It was relatively fast with a maximum speed of 205 m.p.h., but it was tricky to fly. Forty-one trainers of this type were built by the State Aircraft Factory.

APPENDIX II

HLeLv 24 received forty B-239s which were organised into four flights, and these were destined to become the backbone of Finnish fighter aviation, roaming far and wide over the whole battlefront, enjoying one of the best kill-to-loss ratios of any fighter. The Brewsters became extremely popular with their pilots who dubbed them *Taivaan Helmi* (Sky Pearl) and *Pylly Walteri* (Bustling Walter), remaining in service with HLeLv 24 until May 1944, when that unit received its first Messerschmitt Bf 109G-2s. The B-239s were then passed to HLeLv 26 as replacements for that unit's Fiat G.50s, continuing on operations until the end of hostilities.

It is of interest to note that the State Aircraft Factory at Tampere evolved its own version of the Brewster B-239 dubbed *Humu*, although, in the event, only a prototype was completed. The aim was to evolve a fighter possessing the desirable characteristics of the B-239 and using Finnish and captured Russian equipment. The nine-cylinder Russian M-63 air-cooled radial engine rated at 1,100 h.p. for take-off and 1,000 h.p. at 5,900 feet was selected for installation in the *Humu*, the fuselage was of metal construction, and the State Aircraft Factory, which had devoted considerable attention to investigating the suitability of national timbers for aircraft construction, designed a new wooden wing which was first flight tested on a *Pyry* advanced trainer.

The *Humu* had no fuel tanks or guns in the wings, all fuel being housed in a 79 Imp. gal. fuselage tank and the armament of three 12·7-mm. machine guns being mounted in the forward fuselage decking. All instruments were of Finnish manufacture, and overall dimensions were virtually identical to those of the B-239. With a loaded weight of 6,160 pounds, the *Humu* attained a maximum speed of 301 m.p.h., climbed to an altitude of 14,120 feet in five minutes, and had a service ceiling of 29,520 feet.

BRISTOL BLENHEIM

The Blenheim, greeted as a major step forward in combat aircraft design when it appeared in the summer of 1936, was one of the key types selected by the British Air Ministry for the re-equipment of the expanding R.A.F., and was the first modern all-metal cantilever monoplane of stressed-skin construction to be placed in production for that service. It was to prove woefully vulnerable to fighter attack, however, and all aircraft of this type had been withdrawn from first-line R.A.F. service by the end of 1943, although it remained the principal bomber serving with the Finnish Air Force until the end of hostilities.

The Blenheim's progenitor, the original Type 142, was designed as a high-speed eight-passenger transport with two 640 h.p. Bristol Mercury VI nine-cylinder air-cooled radial engines in 1934, and a prototype was ordered by Lord Rothermere, this flying for the first time on April 12, 1935. The official report of trials conducted with the Type 142 at Martlesham Heath in June 1935, revealed the fact that a maximum speed of 285 m.p.h. was attained at maximum loaded weight— 30 m.p.h. faster than the maximum speed of the Gloster Gladiator fighter which was to be ordered into production for the R.A.F. during the following month! In August 1935, the Air Ministry drew up a specification to cover a proposed bomber version of the aircraft, the Type 142M, and named Blenheim, the bomber flew less than a year later, on June 25, 1936.

Initially powered by Mercury VI-S.2 engines, this aircraft achieved 281 m.p.h. at 12,000 feet during trials at Martlesham Heath despite a 2,000 lb. increase in loaded weight over the original Type 142. The first production model was the Blenheim I with 840 h.p. Mercury VIII engines and, carrying a crew of three, its armament consisted of one forward-firing 0·303-in. Browning gun in the port wing and a Vickers "K" gun of similar calibre in a Bristol hydraulically-operated dorsal turret. A 1,000-lb. bomb load could be carried, and fully equipped, the loaded weight was 12,500 lb. Performance included maximum speeds of 269 m.p.h. at 10,000 feet, 285 m.p.h. at 15,000 feet, and 277 m.p.h. at 20,000 feet. Range fully loaded at 220 m.p.h. was 1,250 miles, initial climb rate was 1,540 ft./min., and service ceiling was 27,280 feet.

By March 1937, No. 114 Squadron of the R.A.F. had become the first unit to receive the Blenheim I, and the Finnish government was already evincing interest in the type, ordering eighteen machines and acquiring a licence for the manufacture of a further twelve Blenheim Is at the State Aircraft Factory. The Finnish Blenheim Is featured an enlarged bomb-bay capable of

APPENDIX II

accommodating Swedish or American bombs and could be operated from fixed skis, and the eighteen aircraft were delivered to Finland between July 1937 and June 1938, these equipping PLeLv 44 and PLeLv 46 of Bomber Regiment LeR 4, each unit having eight aircraft, the remaining two Blenheim Is being sent to the State Aircraft Factory to serve as pattern aircraft.

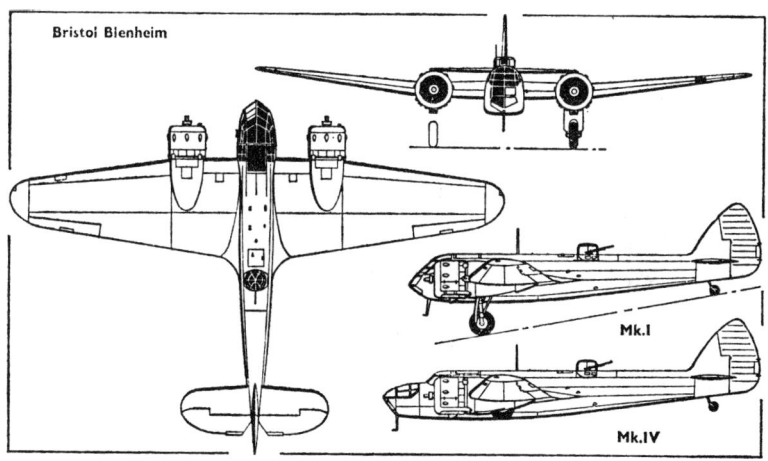

Bristol Blenheim

Mk.I

Mk.IV

Dubbed *Pelti Heikki* (Tin Henry) in Finnish service, the Blenheim operated from Luonetjärvi during the "Winter War", and in January 1940, twelve Blenheim IVs were despatched to Finland from Britain. Powered by 920 h.p. Mercury XV engines, the Type 149 Blenheim IV differed from the Mk. I in only two major respects—a new forward fuselage with a lengthened nose and stepped windscreen, and long-range tanks in the wings. One of the Blenheim IVs, together with its R.A.F. ferry crew, was lost en route to Finland, and another was severely damaged, but the ten remaining machines were issued to PLeLv 46 who promptly passed five of their Blenheim Is to PLeLv 44. Unfortunately, the bomb-bay of the Blenheim IV could only accommodate a 550-lb. load of Swedish bombs, and before the end of January four of the long-nosed Blenheims had been lost and a further three damaged in combat. Twelve more short-nosed Blenheim Is reached Finland from Britain in February 1940, these equipping a newly-formed unit, PLeLv 42.

The three Blenheim-equipped squadrons suffered heavy losses

during the "Winter War", one-third of their total strength being lost in action, and when fighting ended, only eleven Blenheims remained serviceable, eight others being in process of repair, and a further ten being at the State Aircraft Factory where some of them had to be virtually reconstructed. Production deliveries of the Blenheim I from the State Aircraft Factory at Tampere began in 1941, fifteen bombers being completed in that year, two further production batches of thirty and ten machines being completed in 1943 and 1944 respectively.

With the commencement of the "Continuation War", PLeLv 42 and PLeLv 44, each with nine Blenheim Is, operated from Siikakangas in support of the Second and Seventh Army Corps, and in July the former unit moved back to Luonetjärvi to support the Finnish forces advancing into East Karelia beyond Lake Ladoga, while the latter unit transferred to Mikkeli from where its Blenheims operated up and down the Karelian Peninsula and shores of Ladoga, supported troops attacking Petroskoi and, until the spring of 1942 when PLeLv 44 re-equipped with the Ju 88A-4, specialising in low-level strafing attacks along the Murmansk Railway and against enemy fighter fields. PLeLv 46, which began the "Continuation War" from Luonetjärvi with six Blenheim Is and the surviving three Blenheim IVs, operated as a long-range reconnaissance unit, although it was plagued by a shortage of aircraft. PLeLv 46's Blenheims were used to ferry fuel to the advancing Finnish forces during the Petroskoi assault and, early in 1942, the unit re-equipped with the Do 17Z.

PLeLv 42 retained its Blenheims until the end of hostilities, undertaking "Flying Guerilla" operations against the Murmansk Railway from Värtsilä. PLeLv 48, formed to take over the Blenheims of PLeLv 46 when that unit re-equipped with the Do 17Z, flew from Immola and Onttola after it became operational early in 1943, and on April 25, 1944, the Third Flight of TLeLv 12 converted to Blenheims from Fokker C.Xs for army co-operation and support. On June 9, 1944, immediately prior to the commencement of the big Russian offensive, PLeLv 42 had thirteen serviceable and five unserviceable Blenheims at Värtsilä, and PLeLv 48 had seventeen serviceable and two unserviceable at Onttola, but these units sustained extremely heavy losses during the last stages of the conflict, and

APPENDIX II

still more losses were sustained as a result of German flak during the brief but bitter fighting between Finnish and German forces after the Russo-Finnish Armistice. Thus, very few Blenheims remained when German forces finally retreated across the Norwegian border on April 25, 1945.

CURTISS HAWK 75A

The fantastic diversity of single-seat fighters available to the Finnish Air Force for the "Continuation War" against the Soviet Union was enlarged still further by the acquisition from Germany of a number of Curtiss Hawk 75A aircraft. All Twin Wasp-powered, the Hawk 75A fighters had been captured by German forces in France and Norway, most of them still in their shipping crates, then assembled by the Espenlaub Flugzeugbau, fitted with German instrumentation, and sold to Finland.

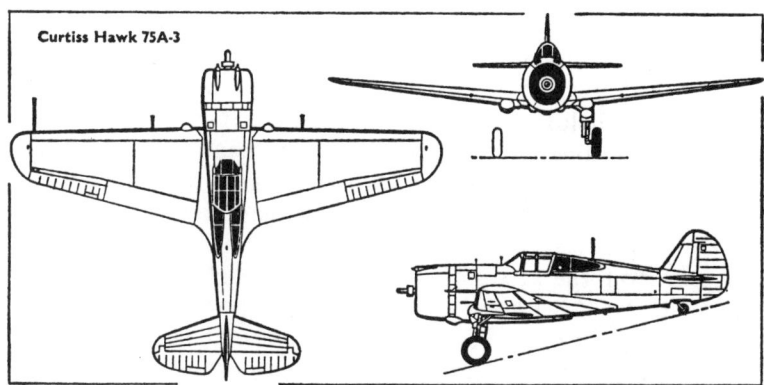

Curtiss Hawk 75A-3

The Curtiss fighter dated back to 1934, construction of the prototype Model 75 having begun in November of that year. Possessing a cantilever low-wing of multi-spar construction with Alclad skinning, an aluminium-alloy monocoque fuselage, an hydraulically-operated retractable undercarriage, fabric-covered control surfaces, and an experimental Wright XR-1670-5 two-row radial engine rated at 900 h.p., flight trials began in May 1935, but the XR-1670-5 engine proved unsatisfactory and was eventually supplanted by a single-row Wright XR-1820-39 Cyclone of 850 h.p. In this form, the prototype was known as the Model 75-B, and eventually, in July 1936, three service test examples of the fighter with a Pratt and Whitney R-1830 Twin Wasp fourteen-cylinder radial were ordered for the U.S. Army Air Corps under the designation Y1P-36. Official performance trials were completed on June 22, 1937, and on July 7th, 210 machines were ordered as P-36As.

In May 1938, within a month of the first P-36A having been delivered to the Army Air Corps, a French Purchasing Mission had placed an order with the Curtiss-Wright Corporation for one hundred examples of an export version, the Hawk 75A-1, the French government actually buying the machine tools and jigs for the manufacture of the aircraft at Buffalo. The Hawk 75A-1 was powered by an R-1830-SC3-G Twin Wasp engine rated at 1,050 h.p. for take-off. Armament comprised four 7·5-mm. F.N.-built Browning machine guns, two mounted in the forward fuselage decking and two in the wings, and for the first time in an American fighter, rudimentary armour protection was provided for the pilot. Metric-calibrated instruments were installed, a modified seat was introduced to accommodate a French Lemercier back-parachute, and a throttle which operated French-fashion (i.e., in the reverse direction to the throttle of British, German or American machines) was fitted. French equipment included a Baille-Lemaire gun-sight, a Radio-Industrie-537 radio, and a Munerelle oxygen supply system.

Apart from the first sixteen machines, the Hawk 75A-1s were assembled by the S.N.C.A. du Centre plant at Bourges, and in March 1939, the 4e and 5e Escadres de Chasse began conversion to the Curtiss fighter. Supplementary orders were placed by the French government for one hundred Hawk 75A-2s and 135 Hawk 75A-3s, the former differing from the A-1 in having two additional wing-mounted 7·5-mm. guns, and the latter having a similar six-gun armament and an R-1830-S1C3-G Twin Wasp engine rated at 1,200 h.p. for take-off and 1,050 h.p. at 7,500 feet. These orders were followed on October 5, 1939 by an order for no less than 395 Hawk 75A-4s, these having the Wright GR-1820-G205A Cyclone 9 nine-cylinder radial in place of the fourteen-cylinder Wasp and rated at 1,200 h.p. for take-off.

In the autumn of 1939, the Norwegian government had also

APPENDIX II

decided to purchase the Curtiss Hawk 75A, placing an order for twelve Hawk 75A-6s powered by the R-1830-SC3-G Twin Wasp engine and basically similar to the French Hawk 75A-1, armament comprising four 7·9-mm. machine guns. Only 291 Hawk 75A fighters were actually taken on strength by the Armée de l'Air before French resistance collapsed, all but a small number of these being Twin Wasp-powered. The Norwegian Hawk 75A-6s had reached Norway shortly before the German onslaught on that country began, and several of these had actually been assembled at Kjeller, although they had not been taken over by the Norwegian Army Air Force. Twenty-one Hawk 75A-3s captured in France and eight Hawk 75A-6s captured in Norway were, after overhaul and modification by the Espenlaub Flugzeugbau, sold to the Finnish government in 1941–2. Some of these were issued to TLeLv 14, but this unit soon exchanged its six serviceable Hawk 75A fighters for eleven Fokker D.XXIs from HLeLv 32, the latter being entirely equipped with the American fighter by August 1941, operating up and down the Karelian Peninsula as part of the 3rd Air Regiment (LeR 3) until, in May 1942, the unit became a part of the 1st Air Regiment (LeR 1). HLeLv 32 then transferred from Suulajärvi to Nurmoila with thirteen serviceable Hawk 75A fighters, but after a hectic summer operating along the Syväri River and subjected to frequent Russian attacks on its base, the unit had few fighters left until, early in 1943, fifteen more Hawk 75As acquired when German forces entered Vichy France were ferried in to Nurmoila.

The Hawk 75A was thought highly of by Finnish pilots, to whom it was known as the *Sussu* or *Kurtiksi*, as it possessed such excellent flying characteristics, and a number of pilots established first rate scores on this type, Lieutenant Kossi Karhila, for example, scoring his first ten kills with the Hawk 75A. The fighter handled extremely well and possessed beautifully harmonised controls. In a diving attack at 400 m.p.h., the Hawk 75A was even superior to the Spitfire owing to its lighter ailerons. In a dive at 400 m.p.h., the Spitfire pilot could not apply more than one-fifth aileron before the stick forces became excessive, whereas the pilot of the Curtiss fighter could apply three-quarter aileron. The Hawk 75A-3 had a maximum speed of 311 m.p.h. at 10,000 feet, cruising at 200 m.p.h. over a range of 820 miles. An altitude of 15,000 feet was attained in slightly under five minutes, and service ceiling was 33,700 feet.

DORNIER DO 17Z-2

The Dornier Do 17Z was the first version of the Do 17 series of bombers built in quantity to dispense with the clean, slender forward fuselage and hemispherical nose cap which had earned for its predecessors the popular appellation of "Flying Pencil". Experience gained with earlier Do 17s over Spain had led to the complete redesign of the bomber's nose section, the flight deck being raised and stepped above the upper fuselage contours, the lower portion being bulged to terminate in a rear-firing gun position, and the extreme nose being glazed with a series of small flat panels, or facets.

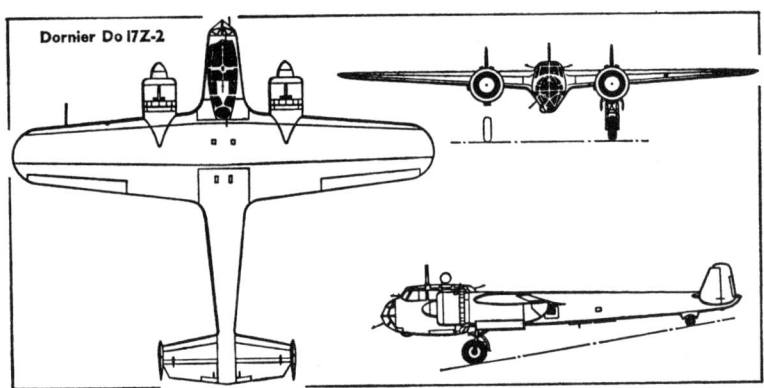

The first pre-production Do 17Z-0 and production Z-1 bombers began to leave the assembly line before the end of 1938, these having Bramo 323A-1 nine-cylinder radial air-cooled engines with which a maximum speed of 255 m.p.h. was attained at 13,120 feet. Four crew members were carried, defensive armament comprised three 7·9-mm. MG 15 machine-guns, and with a 1,100-lb. bomb load tactical radius was 380 miles. Relatively few machines had been delivered before, in the first weeks of 1939, the Do 17Z-2 made its début. This version switched to the Bramo 323P engine fitted with a two-speed supercharger and developing 1,000 h.p. for take-off and 940 h.p. at 13,120 feet. Bomb load was increased to 2,200 lb.

but fuel tankage had to be reduced correspondingly, tactical radius falling to 205 miles at 186 m.p.h. Maximum speed was also reduced, this being 224 m.p.h. at 13,125 feet and 186 m.p.h. at sea level. Although lacking the load-carrying capabilities of the Heinkel He 111 and the speed of the Junkers Ju 88, the Do 17Z was widely considered to be the best bomber in its category available to the Luftwaffe in quantity at the beginning of the Second World War. It was extremely manœuvrable and possessed an exceptionally sturdy structure which permitted it to approach its target in a shallow dive at speeds exceeding 370 m.p.h. It responded particularly well to all control movements, rendering it ideally suited for low-level, hedge-hopping attacks.

Although the fuel tanks were protected, no armour protection was provided for the crew members. On September 1, 1939, when German forces attacked Poland, a total of 212 Do 17Z-1 and -2 bombers had been delivered to the Luftwaffe, 188 of these being serviceable, but operational experience quickly revealed the inadequacy of the Dornier's defensive armament. Initially, an additional forward-firing MG 15 machine-gun was provided to bring the total armament to four 7·9-mm. weapons, but this was soon supplemented by two more flexible 7·9-mm. guns, one being mounted on each side of the wireless operator's position, and finally the defensive armament totalled eight 7·9-mm. guns, while rudimentary armour protection for the crew members was fitted at forward maintenance units.

Production of the Do 17Z was completed in 1940, and as more effective bombers became available some were passed to the Croat Air Force, while, early in 1942, Hermann Goering made a gift of fifteen ex-Luftwaffe Do 17Z-2 bombers to the Finnish government. These supplanted the Blenheims in PLeLv 46, joining operations during April 1942, and subsequently undertaking both day and night sorties with considerable success. During late 1943 and early 1944, the Dorniers of PLeLv 46 frequently operated in concert with the Junkers Ju 88A-4s of PLeLv 44, but when the Russian offensive began in June 1944, only five serviceable and four unserviceable Dorniers remained on strength, these being supplemented by three DB-3s and three Il-4s captured from the Russians, but most of PLeLv 46's equipment was lost during subsequent operations.

APPENDIX II

FIAT G.50 FRECCIA

The first all-metal single-seat fighter monoplane with a retractable undercarriage to be designed and built in Italy, the G.50 Freccia (Arrow) flew as a prototype on February 26, 1937, and thirty-five examples of this fighter had been ordered by the Finnish government before the first Russian attack on Finland. Designed by Ing. Giuseppe Gabrielli, the G.50 was a low-wing cantilever monoplane with an all-metal monocoque fuselage and a three-piece wing, the centre section of welded steel tubes and the outer sections having duralumin spars, the whole being covered by light metal skinning. The moveable control surfaces were fabric covered, and statically and aerodynamically balanced Frise-type ailerons and split flaps were fitted, these being interconnected so that the entire trailing edge could be depressed while retaining differential action of the ailerons. An hydraulically-operated, inward-retracting Messier undercarriage was fitted, and armament comprised two 12·7-mm. Breda-SAFAT machine guns with 300 r.p.g.

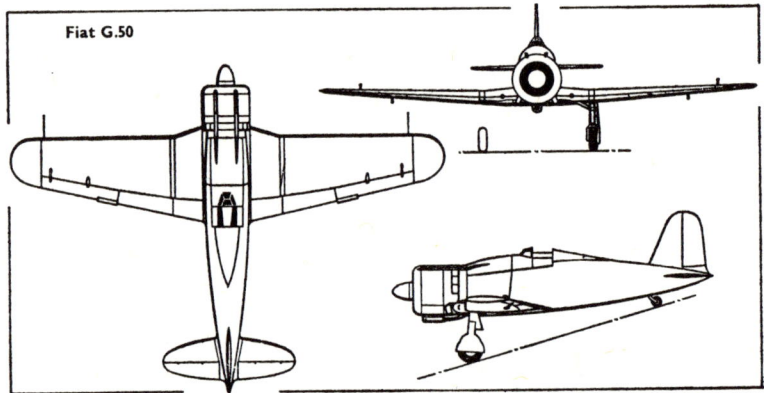

Fiat G.50

Twelve of the initial production batch of forty-five G.50s were sent to Spain in 1939 for testing under operational conditions, and the results of these trials led to an order for a further two hundred G.50s, these differing from the initial batch in having the sliding cockpit canopy deleted, the rear fuselage decking being built up to incorporate the turnover pylon. Power was provided by an 840 h.p. Fiat A.74 R.C.38 fourteen-cylinder radial air-cooled engine, and empty and loaded weights were 4,328 lb. and 5,295 lb. respectively. Maximum speed was 293 m.p.h. at 16,400 feet, cruising speed at seventy per cent power was 258 m.p.h., an altitude of 16,400 feet was attained in eight minutes, and service ceiling was 32,480 feet. Stressed for 14 g, the G.50 had an exceptionally sturdy structure, and on November 14, 1939, during acceptance trials at the Di Littoria Airport in Italy, the Finnish acceptance pilot, Lieutenant Tapani Harmaja, attained 515 m.p.h. in a terminal velocity dive in a G.50, the only damage suffered being a shattered windscreen.

Delivery of the thirty-five fighters to Finland was delayed by the German authorities, but in February 1940, fourteen G.50s were received by HLeLv 26 at Utti, a further twelve arriving during the following month. Unfortunately, these were too late to participate in the "Winter War". With the renewal of hostilities, HLeLv 26 began operations with twenty-five G.50s, flying mostly over the sectors around Lake Ladoga. Known as the *Fiiju* to the Finns, the G.50 was soon found to possess insufficient firepower, but, nevertheless, a number of pilots, such as Oiva Tuominen and Olli Puhakka, did extremely well with their Italian fighters owing to their outstanding marksmanship. However, the G.50 was never intended for Arctic warfare, and maintenance proved particularly troublesome under low temperatures. The G.50 continued in service with HLeLv 26 until, in May 1944, the unit took over the Brewster B-239 fighters of HLeLv 24.

FOKKER C.X

The Finnish Air Force's standard two-seat short-range reconnaissance and artillery observation aircraft, the Fokker C.X, dubbed *Franz Kalle* in Finnish service, was first produced in 1933 as a potential successor for the extremely successful Fokker C.V which, in its Mercury-powered C.VE form, had served in Finland for a number of years. Production deliveries of the C.X began in 1935, the standard Dutch model being powered by the 650 h.p. Rolls-Royce Kestrel V liquid-cooled in-line engine. The parent company produced twenty Kestrel-engined machines for the Netherlands Army Air Service and ten similar aircraft for the Air Division of the Netherlands Indies Army, and four C.Xs were also built for Finland.

APPENDIX II

The Finnish C.Xs were powered by the medium-supercharged Bristol Pegasus XII or XXI nine-cylinder radial air-cooled engine rated at 830 h.p. for take-off, 820 h.p. at 3,500 feet, and 890 h.p. at 6,000 feet, and a manufacturing licence for the type was acquired by the State Aircraft Factory where production was initiated in 1937, thirty Pegasus-engined C.Xs being delivered during the following year. When the "Winter War" began, TLeLv 10 at Lapeenranta had twelve C.Xs on strength as *dive bombers*! TLeLv 12 at Suur-Merijoki had thirteen C.Xs on strength for the reconnaissance-bombing and army co-operation roles, this unit operating in support of the Second Army Corps on the western side of the Karelian Peninsula, while TLeLv 14, which, based at Laikko, supported the Third Army Corps on the eastern side of the Peninsula, had four C.Xs as well as seven old C.VE aircraft, these being augmented in December 1939 by three C.VDs received from Sweden as a gift.

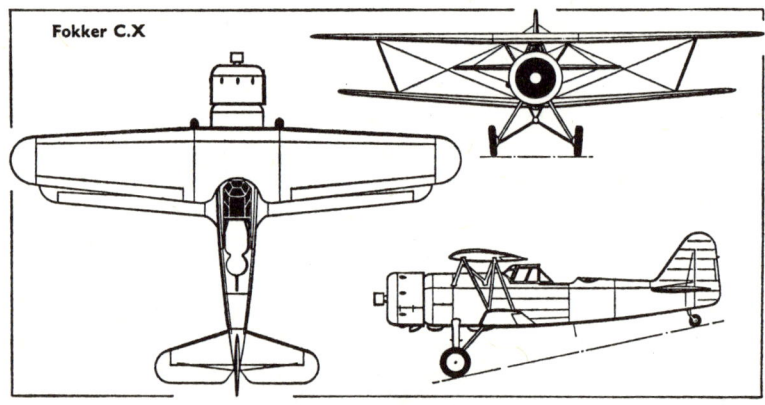

Fokker C.X

A single-bay staggered sesquiplane, the C.X had a welded steel-tube fuselage covered by light alloy panels forward and fabric aft, and wooden wings covered partly by bakelite-plywood and partly by fabric. The pilot and observer were seated in tandem, and both positions were enclosed by a sliding canopy. Defensive armament normally comprised a single fixed forward-firing 7·9-mm. machine-gun and a weapon of similar calibre on a swivelling mount in the observer's cockpit. Racks for flares or light bombs were attached beneath the lower wing. The Pegasus-engined C.X had empty and loaded weights of 3,410 and 5,500 lb. respectively, and performance included a maximum speed of 210 m.p.h. at 10,000 feet, and a cruising speed of 174 m.p.h. at the same altitude. Maximum range was 512 miles, an altitude of 9,840 feet was reached in five and a half minutes, and service ceiling was 27,400 feet.

The C.X was used extensively throughout the "Winter War" and proved capable of absorbing considerable punishment. Despite its apparent vulnerability, attacks by Russian fighters were frequently defeated by hedge-hopping tactics at minimum speeds, and when the "Winter War" ended, twenty-six of the thirty-four C.Xs with which the Finnish Air Force began fighting were still on strength, although nine of these were undergoing major repairs at the State Aircraft Factory.

When fighting was resumed in June 1941, only one flight of TLeLv 12 and one flight of TLeLv 16 were operating Fokker C.Xs. Two flights of TLeLv 12 were operating Fokker D.XXIs but the Third Flight had eight C.Xs for army co-operation duties, these operating in support of the Sixth Army Corps throughout its advance along the shores of Lake Ladoga, and during the assault on Petroskoi. TLeLv 16 had one flight of C.Xs, one flight of Westland Lysanders, and one flight of Gloster Gladiator IIs with which it supported the Seventh Army Corps and Group "O". Throughout the "Continuation War", the C.Xs were used for artillery spotting, short-range reconnaissance, liaison, and even night intrusion, and, surprisingly, the State Aircraft Factory resumed production of the type in 1942 when a further batch of five machines was completed. The C.X continued in Finnish service until January 25, 1958, when the last aircraft of this type was destroyed in an accident.

FOKKER D.XXI

The Fokker D.XXI was the most modern fighter serving with the Finnish Air Force when the first Russo-Finnish conflict began, but it was by no means modern by world standards. All the major aircraft-manufacturing nations were concentrating on all-metal stressed-skin monoplanes with fully retractable undercarriages and powerful liquid-cooled engines, but the D.XXI was of typical traditional Fokker construction with a radial air-cooled engine and a fixed, spatted undercarriage. Its design stressed simplicity of construction in order to ease field maintenance, an important factor when operating under conditions such as it was to experience in Finnish service. Its handling characteristics were, in general, extremely good with an experienced pilot at the controls, although it did not suffer novices gladly, and a number of aircraft were lost in training accidents, these usually occurring during the landing approach when, if the angle of attack was too high, the tail surfaces were partly blanketed and control inadequate. Nevertheless, the D.XXI in its Mercury-engined form was viewed with affection by most Finnish pilots by whom it was usually referred to as the *Isämokkeri* or *Ukkomokkeri*.

The D.XXI had a welded chrome-molybdenum steel-tube fuselage with detachable dural and aluminium sheets to a point level with the wing trailing edge and along the upper decking to the tail, the remainder being fabric-covered. The wing was built up on two wooden box spars with plywood ribs and bakelite-plywood skinning. The metal-framed, fabric-covered ailerons embodied trim tabs which were adjustable on the ground only, and hydraulically operated split flaps stretched across the centre-section trailing edges between the ailerons. The undercarriage comprised two fixed cantilever legs with oleo-pneumatic struts and light metal fairings. The cockpit was enclosed by a series of plexiglass panels, the whole canopy being jettisonable in an emergency and a hinged section on the port side providing access, and the main fuel tank of 77 Imp. gal. capacity was mounted immediately aft of the engine.

Powered by a 645 h.p. Bristol Mercury VIS nine-cylinder radial engine, the prototype D.XXI flew for the first time on February 27, 1936, having been developed to meet a Netherlands Indies Army requirement, but soon after the test programme began, the Netherlands Indies government decided to buy medium bombers instead of fighters, and in March 1936 it was suggested that the original contract should be taken over by the Netherlands Army Air Service. There were numerous objections to this proposal, one of the most important being the fact that the prototype attained only 249 m.p.h. at 12,470 feet, and this was considered totally inadequate by many. Among those against acquiring the D.XXI was the Commander of the Army Air Service, Colonel P. W. Best. Objections were finally overcome, however, and an order was placed for thirty-six D.XXI fighters powered by the more powerful Mercury VIII engine rated at 725 h.p. for take-off and 840 h.p. at 14,000 feet.

The final flight trials and ground tests with the D.XXI had taken place between November 25, 1936 and January 10, 1937, the official production order being placed shortly afterwards, the Finnish government placing an order for seven machines almost simultaneously, the first of these being, in fact, completed before the first D.XXI was handed over to the Netherlands Army Air Service on July 22, 1938. As well as purchasing seven complete D.XXIs, the Finnish government had acquired a manufacturing licence for the fighter, the State Aircraft Factory beginning preparations for production during 1938.

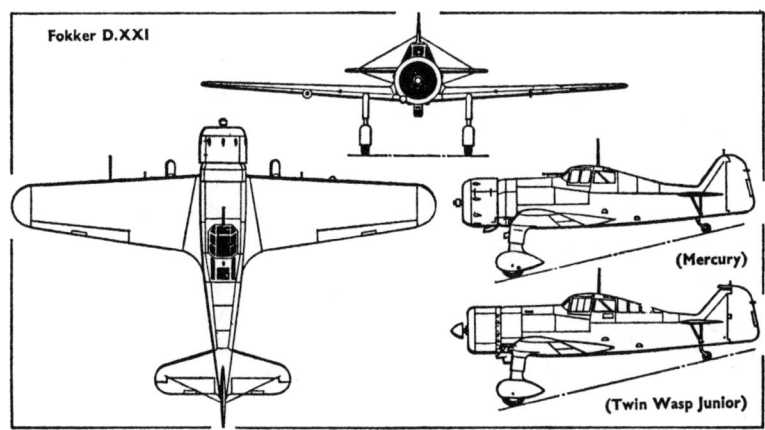

The Finnish D.XXI carried an armament of four 7·9-mm. F.N.-Browning M-36 machine guns with 300 r.p.g., and weighing 3,197 lb. empty and 4,519 lb. in normal loaded condition, the fighter attained a maximum speed of 286 m.p.h., cruised at 240 m.p.h. at two-thirds power and 212 m.p.h. at fifty-five per cent power, and had a range of 590 miles. An altitude of 3,280 feet was attained in 1·15 minutes, 19,685 feet being reached in 7·5 minutes, and service ceiling was 31,360 feet.

On November 30, 1939, thirty-one D.XXIs were serviceable with HLeLv 24 at Immola, five were undergoing overhaul, and a further five were at the State Aircraft Factory at Tampere.

HLeLv 24's D.XXIs provided the bulk of the Finnish fighter force throughout the months of the "Winter War", and when hostilities ceased twenty-two serviceable D.XXIs remained, while a further seven were undergoing overhaul or repair. No additional D.XXIs were manufactured during 1940 as the State Factory was preoccupied with the overhaul and repair of the surviving "Winter War" aircraft, but during 1941, fifty D.XXIs were completed. Mercury engines were being manufactured at the Tampella Machine Works, but output was inadequate for both Blenheim bombers *and* D.XXI fighters. However, eighty 825 h.p. Pratt and Whitney R-1535 Twin Wasp Junior SB4-G fourteen-cylinder two-row radials had been purchased from the U.S.A. in 1940, and it had been decided to adapt the D.XXI airframe to take the American engine.

The greater weight of the Twin Wasp Junior necessitated some shortening of the engine bearers to maintain the c.g., and, in consequence, the area of the vertical tail surfaces had to be increased to compensate. The same quartette of 7·9-mm. guns was installed, but the transparent panelling of the cockpit was extended to improve visibility to the rear. Heavier than the Mercury-powered model, the Wasp-engined D.XXI was somewhat underpowered, and manœuvrability had suffered. In consequence, it did not enjoy the same popularity with its pilots as the original version. Weighing 3,380 lb. empty and 4,820 lb. in normal loaded condition, the Wasp-powered D.XXI attained a maximum speed of 272 m.p.h. at 9,000 ft. and cruised at 221 m.p.h. at 525 h.p. at 14,000 feet.

When fighting was resumed in June 1941, HLeLv (later TLeLv) 30 was operating a mixture of Mercury-engined D.XXIs and Hawker Hurricanes, twelve of which had been supplied to Finland from Britain, and HLeLv 32 had seventeen Mercury-engined D.XXIs and nineteen Wasp-engined machines. Eleven of these were exchanged for six Curtiss Hawk 75A fighters from TLeLv 14, and by August 1941, this unit had completely re-equipped with the American fighter. The First and Second Flights of TLeLv 12 were equipped with Mercury- and Wasp-powered D.XXIs respectively, and continued to operate these until re-equipped with the indigenous Myrsky II fighter in August 1944, and TLeLv 14 continued to operate D.XXIs until

APPENDIX II 209

the end of the conflict, supplementing these in September 1943 with fourteen Morane-Saulnier M.S.406 fighters.

The State Aircraft Factory resumed production of the Wasp-powered D.XXI in 1944 with a batch of five aircraft, and also produced experimentally one example of a Wasp-powered D.XXI with an inward retracting undercarriage of its own design, although the relatively marginal improvement in performance did not warrant further development of this version.

GLOSTER GLADIATOR II

The fortunes of the Gladiator as a fighter during the Second World War ranged from the success of aircraft of this type defending Aden against Italian bombing attacks to the abysmal failure of this British biplane when flown by Finnish pilots against the Russians in February 1940. The Gladiator was already an anachronism when it reached Finland and totally unsuited for the operational conditions by which it was faced. Indeed, the Gladiator was already out-dated when the first production aircraft of this type was taken on charge by the R.A.F. on February 16, 1937! Its adoption reflected the uncertainty of the Air Ministry regarding the immediate future of the cantilever low-wing monoplane with retractable undercarriage and powerful liquid-cooled engine, but perhaps the most remarkable aspect of the Gladiator's history was the fact that this fighter, designed to meet the requirements of a specification framed in 1930, should remain in production until August 1939, long after the Hurricane and Spitfire had proved themselves.

Flown for the first time in September 1934 as the Gloster S.S.37, the prototype Gladiator was the only one of several competing aircraft capable of fulfilling the requirements of specification F.7/30, and attained 253 m.p.h. on the 645 h.p. furnished by its Bristol Mercury VIS.2 nine-cylinder air-cooled radial. The prototype was eventually taken on charge by the Air Ministry on April 3, 1935, and just over three months later, twenty-three aircraft were ordered. The Mercury VIS.2 was eventually supplanted by a Mercury IX rated at 840 h.p. at 14,000 feet, and a sliding cockpit canopy operated by a chain and sprocket gear from within the cockpit was introduced which, together with the hydraulically-operated flaps featured

o

by the production model, was the Gladiator's only concession to modernity.

The armament of the Gladiator I was specified as four 0·303-in. Browning machine guns, two mounted in troughs in the sides of the fuselage with 600 r.p.g., and two mounted below the lower wing with 400 r.p.g. Owing to a shortage of these weapons, however, the first Gladiator to be delivered with the Browning armament was the seventy-first aircraft off the production line. The structure of the Gladiator was orthodox, the wing comprising two high-tensile steel spars with duralumin former ribs, the whole covered by fabric, and the fuselage was a rectangular-section steel-tube structure with Warren-girder bracing in the side bays and faired to an oval section, skinning comprising detachable metal panels forward and fabric aft over a light metal structure in the form of hoops and stringers.

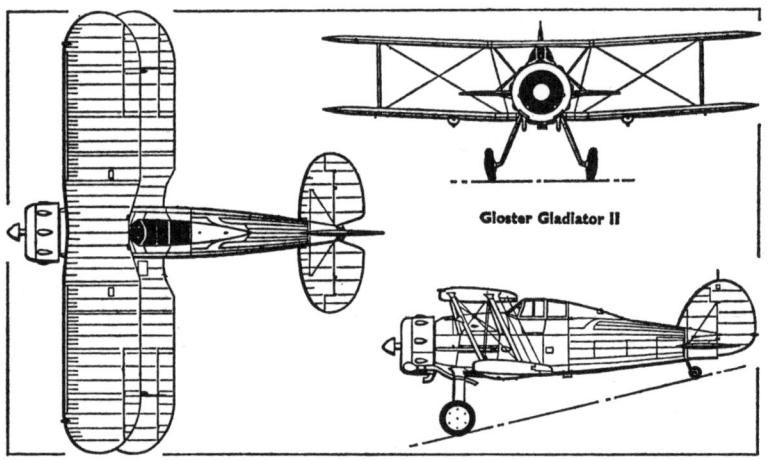

Gloster Gladiator II

Only 231 Gladiator Is had been built to Air Ministry contracts when production switched to the Gladiator II, this model standardising on a three-blade Fairey Reed metal airscrew in place of the Watts two-blade wooden airscrew, a Mercury VIII engine which, offering a similar performance to that of the Mercury IX, featured an automatic mixture-control carburettor and a Hobson control box, an accumulator for electric starting from the cockpit, a Vokes air filter and sand cleaners, and an instrument panel with a vacuum pump. The three-bladed metal airscrew and automatic mixture and boost controls of the Mercury VIII were mixed blessings. The metal airscrew was heavier than the Watts two-blader, resulting in the engine responding more slowly to throttle changes. The automatic mixture control limited the throttle opening when in the "weak cruising" position, but this amount of throttle was often insufficient to maintain patrol formation, so that the pilot was frequently changing from "weak" to "normal" and back again.

The Gladiator was, however, an extremely pleasant machine to fly. Take-off was extremely simple, and the flaps were only used in an emergency. Visibility from the cockpit was good, and the fighter performed all the standard aerobatics with ease, as well as quite a few others. Control response was extremely good, and the Gladiator was probably one of the last fighters capable of terminal velocity dives, this being a standard part of R.A.F. formation and battle practice, and from a wing-over at 25,000 feet the aircraft reached approximately 360 m.p.h. at 15,000 feet. Performance included maximum speeds of 231 m.p.h. at 10,000 feet, 241 m.p.h. at 13,000 feet, and 246 m.p.h. at 14,500 feet. Maximum cruising speed was 212 m.p.h. at 15,500 feet, range was 410 miles, and initial climb rate was 2,430 ft./min. Empty and normal loaded weights were 3,745 lb. and 4,790 lb. respectively, maximum loaded weight being 5,420 lb.

Air Ministry contracts were placed for a total of 350 Gladiator IIs, although sixty of these were transferred to the Admiralty as Sea Gladiators, and the last aircraft were taken on charge on August 30, 1939. Thirty Gladiator IIs were taken from storage and sold to Finland shortly after fighting began between Russian and Finnish forces, and these were promptly issued to HLeLv 26 at Utti, twelve arriving in January and the remainder in February 1940. The Finnish pilots, who promptly named the Gladiator II the *Gelli*, had nothing but praise for the flying characteristics of the fighter, but its début in Finnish service was little short of catastrophic, thirteen aircraft being lost within a few days! The quartette of 0·303-in. guns was ineffective against armoured bombers with self-sealing fuel tanks, and the Gladiator stood no chance in combat with the Russian fighters. It possessed no engine firewall and caught fire readily, and in consequence it was promptly withdrawn as a fighter and the surviving serviceable machines were issued before the end of February to the reconnaissance units, TLeLv 12 receiving eight and TLeLv 14 receiving six.

When fighting was resumed in 1941, one flight of TLeLv 16 was equipped with Gladiator IIs, operating them from Vitska in the Soviet Union during the summer of 1942 and part of the summer of 1943, and from July 1, 1943, the Gladiators of this unit operated from Hirvas until the Armistice. The Finnish Air Force's Gladiators were not, incidentally, the only fighters of this type to fly in the defence of Finland. During the "Winter War", a Swedish volunteer unit was formed with the authorization of the Swedish government, its equipment comprising twelve Gladiator IIs and four Hawker Harts. Designated Flygflottilj 19, the Swedish formation began operations on January 11, 1940, as a separate unit in Finland's Far North where the Finnish Air Force had only a few obsolete observation aircraft.

F 19 began operations from the surface of the frozen Kemi Lake, and was then divided into small sections operating from Oskar, Ulrik and Nora, as well as Kemi. The Swedes found, like the Finns a few weeks later, that the armament of the Gladiator was inadequate but, nevertheless, fought the Russians with spirit, and were operational for sixty-two days under appalling weather conditions, flying on all but two days and logging six hundred hours in the air. F 19 destroyed six Russian fighters and six Russian bombers for the loss of three Gladiators and three Harts, one of the Gladiators being lost as a result of an accident.

MESSERSCHMITT BF 109G

The Messerschmitt Bf 109G, the *Mersu*, was considered by most Finnish pilots to be the finest single-seat fighter in the world when it entered service with HLeLv 34 early in March 1943, and in its early sub-series the G-model of this fighter probably did represent the development peak of the basic Messerschmitt design. Externally, the early Bf 109G differed little from the preceding Bf 109F, the most important change being the introduction of the 1,475 h.p. Daimler-Benz DB 605A engine, this enjoying the benefits of GM 1 power boost—nitrous oxide being injected into the supercharger to boost power above the engine's rated altitude. Flying characteristics were generally similar to those of the Bf 109F, manœuvrability of early G-models not suffering as did later Bf 109G sub-series as a result of a substantial increase in combat weight without commensurate increases in power and lift. Care had to be exercised in steep turns, and the automatic slots opening at high speeds in manœuvres resulting in a high angle of attack invariably led to marked aileron shudder, although, in general, this shudder was harmless. Violent aileron shudder also resulted from the coarse use of the controls at high speed, and there was a tendency to drop a wing during take-off and landing, necessitating careful use of the rudder.

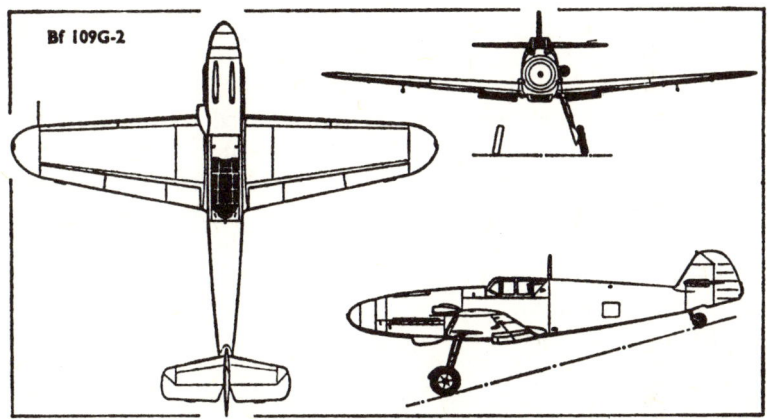

The initial production G-model, the Bf 109G-1, featured a pressurized cockpit, but the Bf 109G-2 produced in parallel and supplied to the Finnish Air Force had no pressure cabin. Armament comprised a single 20-mm. MG 151 cannon firing through the airscrew hub with 150 rounds and two 7·9-mm. MG 17 machine guns with 500 r.p.g. mounted over the engine in the forward fuselage decking, the gunsight being a Revi 16B. FuG 7 radio equipment was normally installed in the Bf 109G-2, although the Finns received no ground radio equipment for use with these sets, and were forced to use captured Russian RSB equipment.

The Finns purchased 48 Bf 109G-2 fighters which were operated for more than a year by HLeLv 34, flying from Malmi in defence of the capital, Helsinki, and from Utti, Suulajärvi, and Kymi before, in May 1944, the fifteen surviving airworthy fighters of this type were passed to HLeLv 24. HLeLv 34 then re-equipped with the Bf 109G-6, the first batch of which arrived in Finland in April 1944, and between June and August 1944, HLeLv 24 also re-equipped with this type, passing the well-worn Bf 109G-2s to one of the flights of HLeLv 28.

One hundred and fourteen Bf 109G-6 fighters were purchased by Finland, and although embodying numerous minor structural and equipment changes, the only major difference between this type and the G-2 was to be found in the armament, the MG 17 machine guns in the forward fuselage being supplanted by a pair of 13-mm. MG 131 weapons with 300 r.p.g., their installation necessitating the provision of bulged fairings over the gun breeches. When received by the Finns, the Bf 109G-6s also had a 20-mm. MG 151 cannon in a gondola beneath each wing, but their weight markedly reduced manœuvrability, and the tendency to swing pendulum-fashion in flight owing to the high axis which had been a characteristic of all G-models was seriously aggravated. Therefore, the Finns removed the underwing cannon from their aircraft, believing manœuvrability to be more important than the added weight of fire provided by the additional weapons. One other change was the introduction of the more reliable FuG 16 radio.

Prior to the removal of the underwing cannon, the Bf 109G-6 weighed 5,900 lb. empty, 6,950 lb. in normal loaded condition, and 7,500 lb. in maximum overload condition. Maximum speed ranged from 387 m.p.h. at 22,970 feet to 338 m.p.h. at sea level, an altitude of 19,000 feet was attained in six minutes, service ceiling was 38,500 feet, and range was 450 miles at 330 m.p.h. at 19,000 feet or 615 miles at 260 m.p.h. at the same altitude. The last Bf 109G-6 fighters were withdrawn from service with the Finnish Air Force during the early 'fifties.

MORANE-SAULNIER M.S.406

Known as the *Moraani* in Finnish service and used primarily by HLeLv 28 during both the "Winter War" and the "Continuation War", specialising in escort, low-level attack and close-support missions, the Morane-Saulnier M.S.406 was, like most other fighters acquired by Finland, already obsolescent when it entered Finnish service in January 1940.

APPENDIX II

The M.S.406 was the production model of the M.S.405, fifteen examples of which had been ordered in August 1936, although the first fighter of this type had actually flown a year earlier, on August 8, 1935. Each of the M.S.405s embodied various equipment and structural changes, and the most efficacious of these were embodied in the sixteenth machine, the first M.S.406 which was assembled by the S.N.C.A.O. plant at Bouguenais and flown in June 1938, three months after one thousand examples of the fighter had been ordered for the Armée de l'Air. Unlike most of its contemporaries, the M.S.406 did not employ an all-metal stressed-skin structure. The two-spar all-metal wing employed Plymax skinning (duralumin sheet bonded to plywood), and the fuselage, which had a duralumin tube frame, had wire-braced fabric-covering aft of the wings. Power was provided by an Hispano-Suiza 12Y-31 twelve-cylinder liquid-cooled engine rated at 830 h.p. for take-off and 860 h.p. at 10,660 feet, this driving a three-blade Ratier electric or Chauvière-351 pneumatic airscrew. The various systems were actuated mechanically, hydraulically, pneumatically and electrically, all at the same time, and in combat there were occasions when a bullet passing through the cockpit resulted in the undercarriage, the flaps, or even the armament functioning without any action on the part of the pilot!

Armament comprised a single 20-mm. HS-404 cannon firing through the airscrew hub with sixty rounds, and two wing-mounted 7·5-mm. MAC 1934 machine guns each with 300 rounds in drums, and in September 1939, light seat armour was fitted for the pilot's protection. Maximum speed ranged from 248 m.p.h. at sea level to 302 m.p.h. at 16,400 feet, cruising speed being 248 m.p.h. at the latter altitude. Initial climb was 3,543 ft./min., an altitude of 16,400 feet was attained in six minutes, and service ceiling was 30,840 feet. Empty weight was 4,189 lb., and normal and maximum loaded weights were 5,364 and 6,000 lb. respectively.

Thirty M.S.406 fighters were purchased by the Finnish government shortly after the beginning of the "Winter War", and these reached Finland in December 1939, being issued to HLeLv 28 which had been organised on the eighth of that month under the command of Major Jusu. The engine-mounted cannon had not been installed, only the wing armament being fitted but, nevertheless, after familiarization flying in January 1940, the M.S.406 joined operations in the following month from Säkylä (Turku), on Finland's west coast. Part of HLeLv 28 was deployed in defence of Viipuri and Kotka, and the M.S.406s strafed Russian forces advancing over the ice from the Estonian side of the Gulf of Finland.

Although the Finnish pilots found the flying characteristics of the French fighter to be extremely pleasant, and pronounced the M.S.406 an excellent aircraft for dog-fighting, it was highly vulnerable, minor damage invariably resulting in the failure of one or other system. Its reliability was poor as the pneumatic and hydraulic systems had not been designed to function under the Arctic conditions appertaining in Finland.

Between March 13, 1940 and June 25, 1941, the engine-mounted cannon were installed in the M.S.406s and the throttles were modified to operate in the conventional fashion. The light seat-armour had proved totally inadequate, being penetrated even by small-calibre Russian bullets, and a full-length back armour plate was introduced by the Finns, this adding 176 lb. to the fighter's weight. With the renewal of fighting, HLeLv 28 began operations from Joroinen with twenty-nine M.S.406s, the unit's primary missions being escort and low-level attack. By November 6, 1941, HLeLv 28 had transferred to the Petroskoi sector, and had become the Finnish Air Force's principal "train-busting" unit, operating continuously along the Murmansk Railway.

During the summer of 1942, HLeLv 28 ferried back from Germany thirty more M.S.406s which had been captured by the German forces in France and subsequently overhauled. Some of these had four or six belt-fed 7·5-mm. wing guns[1] in lieu of the engine cannon. By the beginning of 1943, the M.S.406s were finding themselves at an increasing disadvantage

[1] M.S.406 No. 1028 had been fitted with a strengthened wing housing four belt-fed 7·5-mm. guns in place of the standard pair of drum-fed weapons, resulting in the elimination of the characteristic bulged fairings on the wing leading edges. The modified aircraft, which was first test flown in May 1940, was redesignated M.S.410, and several similarly-modified machines were produced. It was intended to fit the modified wing to all damaged M.S.406 fighters at a centre established by the Ateliers Industriéls de l'Air, and a further seventy-four MS.406s were converted to M.S.410 standards with four or six wing guns after the Franco-German Armistice, some of these being supplied to the Croatian Air Force.

as more modern Russian fighters appeared over the Finnish Front in growing numbers. The French fighter could hold its own in combat with the I-16, and it was superior in a dog-fight to the LaGG-3 although, of course, appreciably slower. Previously, Finnish pilots had gained noteworthy successes while flying the M.S.406, despite the fact that their role was not primarily that of interception. Flight Master Jätti Lehtovaara, who was eventually to serve with HLeLv 34 and score forty-four kills, was but one example, gaining his first ten victories while flying the M.S.406.

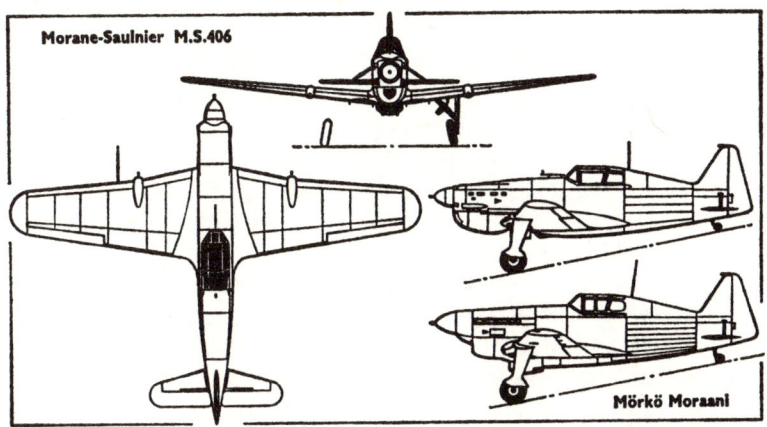

Morane-Saulnier M.S.406

Mörkö Moraani

The Wehrmacht had captured large numbers of unused Klimov M-105P engines in the Smolensk, Vitebsk and Brest-Litovsk areas, and as this power plant had the same dimensions and mounting points as the Hispano 12Y-31, being, in fact, a derivative of the French engine with increased cylinder volume and raised compression and pre-compression ratios, the captured engines were delivered to Finland, together with their VISh-61P three-blade constant-speed airscrews. The M-105P offered 1,100 h.p. for take-off and 1,150 h.p. at 13,120 feet, and had a mechanically-controlled two-speed blower, but the coolant and exhaust systems were missing. The problem of the missing components was eventually solved by the State Aircraft Factory which adapted the Bf 109G oil cooler and designed a new liquid cooler. The M-105P shaft had been bored out to accommodate a 20-mm. ShVAK or a 23-mm. VIa cannon, and it was found that a Mauser MG 151 could be fitted with relatively few modifications. Special thrust augmentation exhaust stacks were designed, and the conversion of the first M.S.406 airframe was begun in August 1943, and completed within the remarkably short period of fourteen days.

The flight-test programme with the modified M.S.406 was highly satisfactory, and apart from some minor changes to the liquid cooler installation, no modifications were called for. The aircraft was found to be slightly nose heavy, but this problem resolved itself when it was discovered that no stocks of the MG 151 cannon were available and that the captured Russian 12·7-mm. BS machine gun would have to be used in its place. Dubbed *Mörkö Moraani* or *Silakka Moraani*, the modified M.S.406 enjoyed a remarkably low power loading (5·07 lb./h.p.) which resulted in a marked improvement in the initial climb-rate, this being increased to 4,921 ft./min. Maximum speed and service ceiling were raised to 326 m.p.h. and 39,370 ft. respectively, and the excellent results gained by the installation of the Russian engine led to a decision to modify all remaining M.S.406 fighters in a similar fashion.

The *Mörkö Moraani* began to reach operational units in June 1944, the first batch going to the 1st Flight of HLeLv 28. In that month the long-awaited Russian offensive began, and the *Mörkö Moraani* saw considerable action over Karelia for the last two months of the Russo-Finnish conflict. Another unit still using the M.S.406 during the final stages of the war was TLeLv 14 which had received fourteen M.S.406s in September 1943.

BELL P-39 AIRACOBRA

Nicknamed the *Little Shaver* by the Russians, the highly unorthodox Airacobra was employed by the Soviet Air Forces with remarkable success, yet this single-seat fighter was to be referred to in the official history of the U.S.A.A.F. as "specially disappointing...!" The Airacobra *was* a poor interceptor and "practically useless over seventeen thousand feet", but as a low-level close-support fighter it excelled, and the Russians did not repeat the mistake of the U.S.A.A.F. in attempting to pit the aircraft against faster-climbing, more manœuvrable fighters with infinitely superior altitude performances. The Russians used the Airacobra primarily for

APPENDIX II

"shaving"—Soviet A.F. slang for ground strafing—large formations of these aircraft seeking targets of opportunity along and immediately behind the frontline. It possessed excellent low-level handling characteristics which, together with the American fighter's ability to absorb considerable damage from ground fire yet remain airborne, endeared the *Little Shaver* to the Russians.

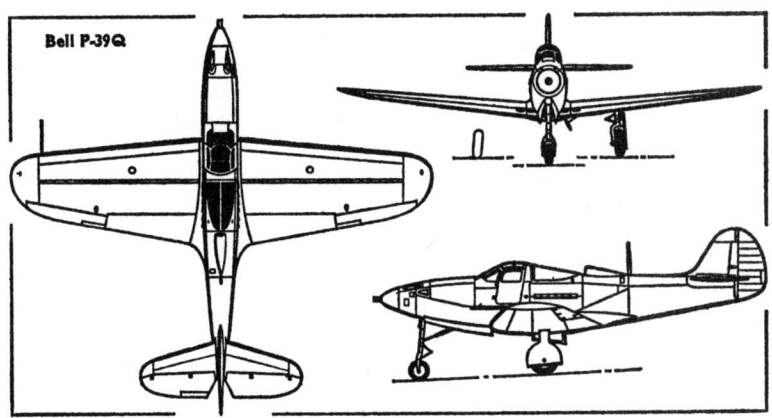

Design work on the Airacobra was initiated in June 1936 by the Bell Aircraft Corporation, the design team adopting the radical idea of mounting the engine behind the pilot and driving the airscrew by means of a 10-ft. extension shaft. This arrangement appeared to offer superior manœuvrability as the engine weight could be concentrated around the c.g. of the fighter, exceptional visibility for the pilot, and facilitated the concentration of heavy armament in the nose. A prototype was ordered by the U.S. Army Air Corps as the XP-39 on October 7, 1937, and this aircraft flew for the first time in April 1939, power being provided by a 1,150 h.p. Allison V-1710-17 with a B-5 supercharger. During initial trials, the XP-39 attained what was for that time the phenomenal maximum speed of 390 m.p.h. at 20,000 feet, this altitude being attained in five minutes. At this time, a service evaluation batch of twelve YP-39s and one YP-39A was ordered, and the prototype was subjected to numerous modifications as a result of proposals made by the N.A.C.A., these including the deletion of the turbo-supercharger and the installation of a V-1710-39 engine rated at

1,090 h.p. at 13,300 feet. The prototype was redesignated XP-39B and the many changes embodied by this model were incorporated in the service evaluation machines, the first of which flew in September 1940.

In the meantime, on August 10, 1939, a production order for eighty machines had been placed, and on September 14, 1940, this order was modified to allow for the introduction of self-sealing fuel tanks and wing guns on the twenty-first and subsequent production machines. The first twenty production Airacobras, or P-39Cs, were virtually identical to the service evaluation YP-39s, and the twenty-first aircraft was the first P-39D with four wing-mounted 0·3-in. machine guns with 1,000 r.p.g., two fuselage-mounted 0·5-in. machine guns with 200 r.p.g., and one 37-mm. cannon with thirty rounds. Internal fuel capacity was a 100 Imp. gal. and this could be supplemented by a 62·4 Imp. gal. drop tank. The bullet-proof windscreen and armour added to this model increased weight by 245 lb. The first P-39D Airacobras entered service with the U.S. Army Air Corps in February 1941, the Bell Aircraft Corporation evolving an export model simultaneously for the Armée de l'Air. Orders were also placed by the British government in April 1940, and no less than 675 Airacobras had been ordered for the R.A.F. before the first machine reached Britain in July 1941.

The R.A.F. model was powered by a 1,150 h.p. Allison V-1710-E4 (-35) engine and was essentially similar to the P-39D apart from having a 20-mm. Hispano M1 cannon in place of the 37-mm. weapon, and six 0·303-in. Browning machine guns. Trials with the Airacobra in Britain were extremely disappointing, and of the 675 machines scheduled to be delivered to the R.A.F., 212 were diverted to the Soviet Union, fifty-four were lost at sea, and 179 were taken over by the U.S.A.A.F. as P-400s. Airacobras appeared in Russian service over the Eastern Front during 1942, and in increasing numbers in 1943 when the improved P-39N and P-39Q began to reach the Soviet Union in really large numbers under Lend-Lease. The P-39N had a V-1710-85 (E19) engine developing 1,200 h.p. for take-off and 1,125 h.p. at 15,500 feet, and after completion of 166 Airacobras of this type, four fuel cells were removed to reduce the internal fuel capacity to 72·4 Imp. gal., reducing maximum permissible gross weight from 9,100 to 8,750 lb., and the last 695 of the 2,095 P-39Ns built had the total weight of armour reduced from 231 to 193 lb. and the bullet-proof glass behind the pilot replaced by a curved armour head plate.

The P-39N was followed in production by the P-39Q, 4,905 examples of which were built, the bulk of which were shipped to Russia. The principal change in the Q-model concerned armament, the four 0·3-in. wing guns being removed and a single 0·5-in. gun mounted beneath each mainplane. However, the Russians did not favour the underwing guns and retained only the fuselage-mounted armament which consisted of two 0·5-in. guns and one 37-mm. cannon. There were some differences in internal fuel tankage among early Q-model Airacobras, the P-39Q-1 production batch having 72·4 Imp. gal., the -5 having 91·6 Imp. gal., and the -10 reverting to the original 100 Imp. gal. Weight of armour also varied, but the P-39Q-5-BE which carried 193·4 lb. of armour attained maximum speeds of 330 m.p.h. at 5,000 ft., 357 m.p.h. at 10,000 ft., and 376 m.p.h. at 15,000 ft. Maximum range without external fuel was 525 miles at 10,000 feet at 250 m.p.h., and with a 145·7 Imp. gal. drop tank this was increased to 1,075 miles at 195 m.p.h. An altitude of 5,000 feet was attained in two minutes and 10,000 feet in four minutes, and empty and normal loaded weights were 5,645 and 7,600 lb. respectively, maximum loaded weight being 8,300 lb.

No less than 4,924 Airacobras were allocated to Russia from the 9,558 fighters of this type built, 4,758 reaching their destination. These began to appear on the Russo-Finnish Front late in 1943, and by mid-1944, the Airacobra was one of the most frequently encountered of Russian-flown aircraft.

ILYUSHIN DB-3

One of the principal medium bombers used by the Soviet Air Force elements engaged over Finland during the "Winter War", and used to a lesser extent during the "Continuation War", the DB-3 was evolved to meet a 1933 requirement for a fast, twin-engined, long-range bomber capable of carrying a metric ton of bombs over a 1,864-mile range, and attaining a maximum speed of not less than 217·5 m.p.h. A team led by P. O. Sukhoi, at that time a senior member of A. N. Tupolev's design collective, produced the ANT-37 to meet the official specification, the military designation DB-2 being allocated to the type, but the first prototype crashed during State Acceptance Trials, and although a second prototype was built, the Sukhoi bomber was not accepted for quantity production.

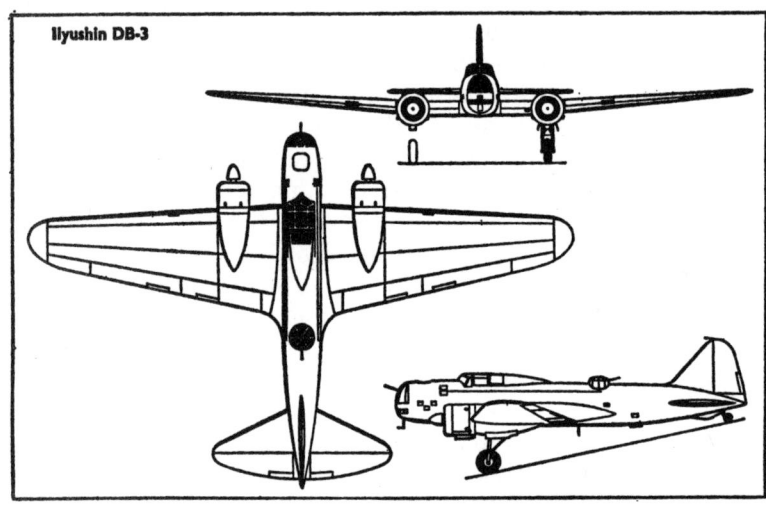
Ilyushin DB-3

The DB-3 was a competitive design evolved by Sergei V. Ilyushin, and built at Plant No. 39 in Moscow, the first prototype, which flew in 1935, was designated TsKB-26. This had two M-85 fourteen-cylinder radial air-cooled engines rated at 800 h.p. for take-off and 765 h.p. at 12,468 feet. It possessed an appreciably higher wing loading than the DB-2, and was 50 m.p.h. faster than the Sukhoi design. Carrying three crew members and of all-metal construction, it attained a maximum speed of 242 m.p.h. at 15,090 feet, and had a range of 2,485 miles with a 1,100-lb. bomb load cruising at 193–199 m.p.h. at the same altitude. An altitude of 16,400 feet was attained in 15·1 minutes, and service ceiling was 27,560 feet. The prototype rapidly passed its State Acceptance Trials and the DB-3 (DB indicating *Dalnii Bombardirovshchik*, or Range Bomber) was placed in production for the Soviet Air Forces. Test flying was in the charge of the well-known Russian pilot V. K. Kokkinaki who actually looped the prototype during a display at

Tushino, and subsequently established several payload-to-altitude and range-with-payload records with the aircraft for which he was awarded the title of "Hero of the Soviet Union".

Production deliveries of the DB-3 began in 1937, and powered by two M-85 radials, the bomber had a normal internal fuel tankage of 792 Imp. gal., although two supplementary 88 Imp. gal. tanks could also be carried. Three crew members were carried, and defensive armament comprised a single 7·62-mm. ShKAS machine gun with 1,100 rounds in the nose turret, a similar weapon in the manually-operated dorsal turret, and a third 7·62-mm. gun which, with 650 rounds, could be fired through a ventral trap. The normal bomb load comprised ten 220-lb. bombs or three 1,100-lb. bombs internally, but for short-range attack ten 220-lb. bombs could be carried internally and three 550-lb., 1,100-lb., or 2,200-lb. bombs externally. Performance included a maximum speed of 254 m.p.h. at 13,780 feet at a loaded weight of 16,833 lb., and range with a 5,510-lb. bomb load at 20,841 lb. was 808 miles at 217 m.p.h., or with a 1,100-lb. bomb load at 19,919 lb. was 1,865 miles at 186 m.p.h.

Late in 1937, the M-85 radials were replaced by M-86 radials in one production series, these offering 950 h.p. at 12,468 feet, and a few late-production aircraft had M-87A engines offering 950 h.p. at 16,420 feet and driving VISh-23 variable-pitch airscrews, although most DB-3s used over Finland during the "Winter War" had the earlier M-85s. During 1944, PLeLv 46 was employing three captured DB-3s to supplement its Do 17Z-2 bombers.

ILYUSHIN IL-4

During 1938, Sergei Ilyushin's team undertook an extensive redesign of the DB-3 bomber, this being designated DB-3F (the "F" suffix letter indicating *Forsirovanni*, or Boosted). Initially powered by M-87A radials driving VISh-23 airscrews, the DB-3F was aerodynamically cleaned up, and the nose turret was removed and replaced by a slim, extensively-glazed nose. State Acceptance Trials of the DB-3F were completed in June 1939, and deliveries to the Soviet Air Forces began in 1940, by which time the aircraft had been redesignated Il-4 under the new system adopted officially in that year.

The Il-4 provided the backbone of the Russian long-range bombing force from 1941 until the end of the war, this type remaining in production until 1944. The initial production series retained the M-87A, and the Il-4 was delivered both to the the Soviet Air Forces and the Soviet Naval Air Arm, and Russian sources claim that a formation of naval Il-4 bombers led by Colonel Preobrazhenskii undertook the first long-range attack on Berlin on the night of August 8, 1941. However,

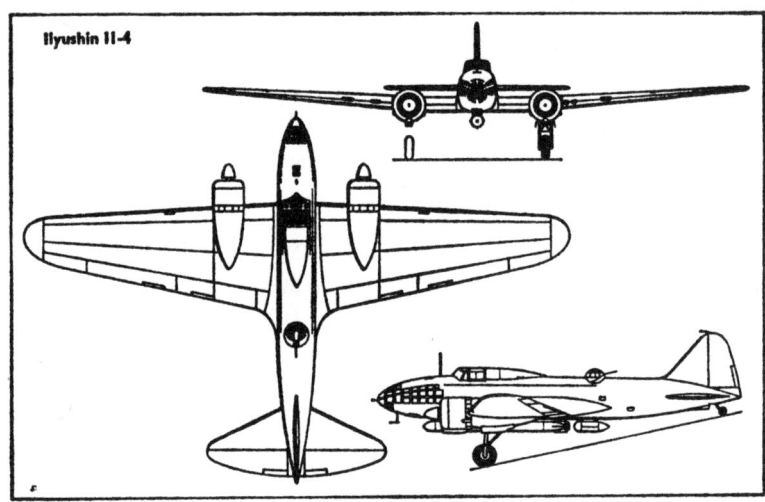

Ilyushin Il-4

during the early months of the Russo-German conflict, production of both M-87A engines and Il-4 airframes fell drastically owing to the need to withdraw from plants manufacturing these items. Shortages of light alloys also created serious problems, and late in 1941, Ilyushin's team began replacing many of the metal components in the Il-4's structure by wooden components, and during the summer of 1942, wooden ribs were introduced in the wing. Despite the increased weight resulting from the extensive use of wood, the Il-4's maximum speed fell by only 4 m.p.h., while the maximum range of this version at 163·4 m.p.h. was actually increased to 2,647 miles, range at 213 m.p.h. being 2,228 miles. At this time the M-87A engines were supplanted by M-88B fourteen-cylinder radials rated at 1,100 h.p. for take-off, maintaining this power to 13,120 feet, and giving 1,000 h.p. at 19,685 feet. With these power plants maximum speed ranged from 208 m.p.h. at sea level to 255 m.p.h. at 21,326 feet. Maximum range with a 2,204-lb. bomb load was 2,361 miles at 211 m.p.h., and empty and maximum loaded weights were 12,182 and 22,105 lb.

Defensive armament comprised three 7·62-mm. ShKAS machine guns disposed in the same fashion as those of the DB-3, and bomb loads were also similar, ranging from 2,200 lb. to 5,510 lb. with three 1,100-lb. bombs on racks beneath the fuselage. The naval version of the Il-4 could carry a 2,073-lb. 45-36-AN or -AV torpedo beneath the fuselage as shown by the accompanying general arrangement drawing. Together with its trio of captured DB-3s, PLeLv 46 operated a trio of Il-4 bombers during 1944.

ILYUSHIN IL-2

Known to its pilots as the *Ilyusha* and more widely as the *Shturmovik*, although the latter merely meant "Assaulter", the Il-2 armoured ground-attack aircraft was one of the most celebrated Soviet aircraft of the Second World War. Intended primarily for attacks against armoured vehicles, the Il-2's development began in 1938 when the collective led by S. V. Ilyushin completed the first prototype of an armoured two-seat assault aircraft, the TsKB-55 or BSh-2 (*Bronyirovanni Shturmovik*, or Armoured Assaulter) powered by an AM-35A twelve-cylinder liquid-cooled Vee engine rated at 1,350 h.p. for take-off and 1,200 h.p. at 19,685 feet.

Of mixed construction, the BSh-2 provided extensive armour protection for all vital components, and virtually the whole of the forward fuselage was an armoured shell weighing 1,543 lb. The rear fuselage was a wooden monocoque and the wings were of dural construction. Trials with the first prototype were somewhat protracted, and a modified second prototype joined the test programme on December 30, 1939, State Acceptance Trials of the BSh-2 taking place during the summer of 1940. The prototypes revealed a number of shortcomings, most of which stemmed from the inadequate power provided by the AM-35A engine. It also possessed poor longitudinal stability, and therefore Ilyushin's team undertook a complete redesign, producing a third prototype which, designated TsKB-57, or Il-2 under the new designating system, flew for the first time on October 12, 1940, with V. K. Kokkinaki at the controls.

The modified prototype employed an AM-38 engine in place of the AM-35A, the new power plant, although having a lower altitude rating than its predecessor, offering 1,600 h.p. for take-off and 1,550 h.p. at 6,560 feet. To increase the range, the gunner's seat had been removed to provide space for an additional fuel tank; the rear armour plate had been increased in thickness from 7-mm. to 12-mm., and weight of fire had been increased by replacing two of the four 7·62-mm. ShKAS machine guns by two 20-mm. ShVAK cannon. In addition, the new prototype had provision for eight 82-mm. rocket shells on rails beneath the wings. The problem of longitudinal stability was rectified by increasing the area of the horizontal tail surfaces and moving the c.g. of the aircraft. Bomb load ranged from 1,100 to 1,323 lb., and maximum speed was 292 m.p.h. at sea level.

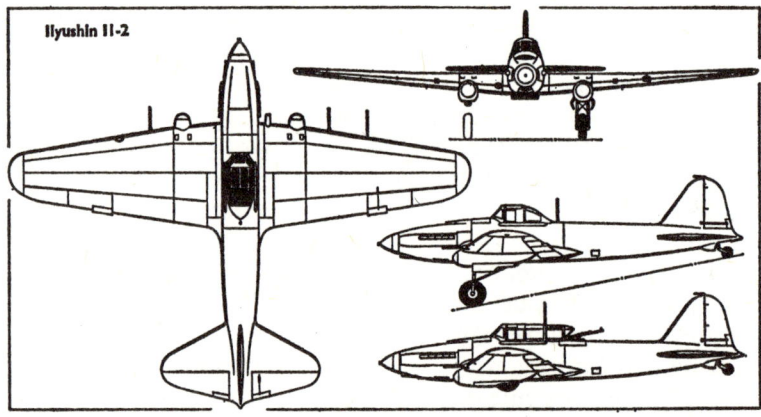

The Il-2 completed its State Acceptance Trials successfully in March 1941, by which time a pre-production batch of machines for service evaluation was already nearing completion, and these were, in fact, destined to be used operationally as they took part in the initial battles on the Central Front during July and August 1941. The successes achieved by these few aircraft, particularly during the battle for the approaches to Moscow in September and October 1941, resulted in Josef Stalin

APPENDIX II

sending a telegram on December 24, 1941, to the workers of plants preparing for the production of this ground-attack aircraft which said, "The Red Army needs the Il-2 as much as it needs bread!" The highest possible production priority was allocated to the Il-2 and its AM-38 engine, and substantial numbers of these aircraft began to reach the operational formations from mid-1942. Two hundred and forty-nine Il-2s had been completed by the end of 1941.

Several weaknesses in the Il-2 had been revealed during early operations with this type, and the units equipped with the assault aircraft requested that it be modified as a two-seater so that some rear defence could be provided. Heavier firepower and increased take-off power were also demanded, and all these requirements were embodied by a new version of the Il-2 which passed its State Acceptance Trials in July 1942. The modified Il-2 was a two-seater with a 12·7-mm. UBT machine gun on a swivelling mount for rear protection, the ShVAK cannon were replaced by VYa cannon which, although of the same calibre, had higher muzzle velocity, and the low-altitude performance of the engine was boosted. Designated AM-38F, this engine offered 1,700 h.p. for take-off, and the performance of the two-seat Il-2 at 12,947 lb. included maximum speeds of 231 m.p.h. at sea level and 250 m.p.h. at 4,920 feet. Armament comprised two 20-mm. VYa cannon and one 12·7-mm. UBT machine gun, and one of the most frequently used underwing loads was the 82-mm. RS (RS indicating *Raketny Snaryad*, or Rocket Projectile), four of which were normally carried beneath each wing. During the summer months of 1943, the PTAB-2,-5-1,5 anti-tank bomb or grenade based on the "hollow-charge" principle was also introduced by the Il-2, as many as two hundred of these being carried. At this time, the Wehrmacht introduced the PzKW VI Tiger and PzKW V Panther tanks around the Kursk salient, these being virtually impervious to the 20-mm. cannonfire of the Il-2. To counter these new tanks, a new variant of the Il-2 carrying two 37-mm. cannon made its début.

The two-seat Il-2, which first saw action on October 30, 1942, and appeared in numbers over the Russo-Finnish front early in 1944, created a serious problem for intercepting fighters. The extensive use of armour by the Ilyushin left few vulnerable spots, and the fact that the Russian aircraft invariably had to be attacked while hedge-hopping added to the fighter pilot's difficulties. German and Finnish pilots endeavoured to silence the rear gun during their first firing pass, and the Russian gunner frequently played dead in the hope of taking an unwary attacker by surprise when he closed to make the kill.

LAGG-3

One of the most frequently encountered Russian fighters during the first two years of the "Continuation War", the LaGG-3 stemmed from the same 1938 single-seat fighter specification as that to which the Yak-1 had been designed. Semyon A. Lavochkin, assisted by V. P. Gorbunov and M. I. Gudkov, completed the prototype of his fighter early in 1939, this flying for the first time on March 30th as the I-22. At this time, the Soviet Union was pitifully short of light metal alloys for aircraft construction, and the I-22 was, therefore, of wooden construction. The fuselage was built up on Siberian birch frames with a plywood skin impregnated with phenol-formaldehyde resin, the fin was integral with the fuselage, and the wings were two-spar wooden structures, all movable control surfaces being metal-framed with fabric covering. Power was provided by an M-105P twelve-cylinder Vee liquid-cooled engine rated at 1,100 h.p. for take-off and 1,050 h.p. at 13,120 feet, and armament consisted of one 23-mm. VYa cannon and two 12·7-mm. BS machine guns.

By comparison with the competitive Yakovlev fighter, the I-26, which had flown for the first time earlier in the month, the I-22 had the lower climb rate, the inferior service ceiling, and the poorer acceleration, although the maximum speeds of the two fighters were similar. The primary reason for the I-26's superiority was its lower structural weight which was partly due to its welded steel-tube fuselage. However, the Lavochkin team was already making a number of changes aimed at reducing structural weight and, at the same time, improving controllability, and in the meantime, the I-22 was placed in production under the designation LaGG-1. Weighing 6,543 lb. in normal loaded condition, the LaGG-1 attained maximum speeds of 320 m.p.h. at sea level and 376 m.p.h. at 16,240 feet, attaining an altitude of 16,400 feet in 6·2 minutes and having a service ceiling of 31,495 feet.

The various improvements that had been made in the design while the LaGG-1 was being readied for production were introduced on the assembly lines early in 1941, the modified fighter being redesignated LaGG-3. Loaded weight was reduced to 6,316 lb., and with the introduction of the M-105PF (the "F" suffix letter indicating *Forsirovanni*, or Boosted) engine rated at 1,210 h.p. for take-off, 1,260 h.p. at 2,625 feet and 1,180 h.p. at 8,860 feet, climb rate and service ceiling were improved, an altitude of 16,400 feet being attained in 5·6 minutes and service ceiling being 33,465 feet. The armament of this version was initially reduced to one 20-mm. ShVAK cannon and one 12·7-mm. BS machine gun, and maximum speed ranged from 309 m.p.h. at sea level to 353 m.p.h. at 12,795 feet. Five fuel tanks were provided, three in the wing centre section and one in each outer section, total fuel capacity being 105·6 Imp. gal., with which range was 404 miles at 280 m.p.h. Two 22-Imp. gal. auxiliary tanks could be carried beneath the wings to increase maximum range to 497 miles.

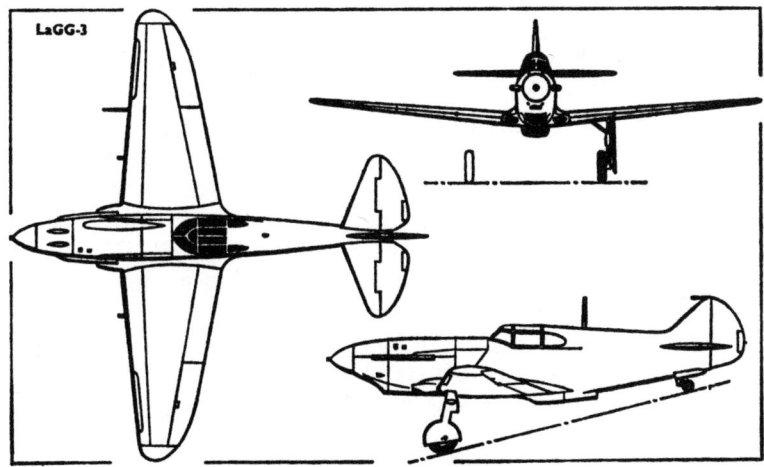

Various armament combinations were installed in the LaGG-3 as production progressed, these including a 20-mm. ShVAK cannon with 120 rounds, one 12·7-mm. BS machine gun with 220 rounds, and one 7·62-mm. ShKAS machine gun with 325

rounds, or one 23-mm. VYa cannon with 80 rounds plus two ShKAS and one BS, or three BS and two ShKAS, or one ShVAK and two BS guns.

In view of its extraordinarily robust structure, the LaGG-3 enjoyed a relatively low structural weight. Like the Bf 109, the LaGG employed automatic leading-edge slots, and to reduce fire risk, cooled and filtered exhaust gases were led into the fuel tanks, the air in the tanks thus being replaced by inert combustion gases consisting mainly of nitrogen and carbon dioxide. The only armour protection was a 9-mm. back plate for the pilot, and Finnish pilots found the most vulnerable parts of the LaGG-3 to be the coolant radiator and the wing fuel tanks. The normal armament could be augmented by six RS-82 missiles which could be carried by racks under the outer wing panels. Most Finnish pilots considered the combat qualities of the LaGG-3 to be good, although care had to be exercised in steep turns as the fighter had a tendency to go into a spin, and acceleration came in for some criticism. Three captured LaGG-3 fighters were used by HLeLv 32 for high-speed reconnaissance work.

LAVOCHKIN LA-5

The LaGG-3 fighter's performance had lagged behind that of the Yak-1 from the outset of development, and at the end of 1941 a LaGG-3 airframe was fitted with an M-82 fourteen-cylinder radial air-cooled engine. This engine had a better altitude performance than the M-105PF, developing 1,330 h.p. at 17,715 feet, but the increased drag of the radial power plant offset to some extent the performance improvement anticipated. Nevertheless, the M-82-powered LaGG-3 attained 373 m.p.h. at 21,160 feet, although climb was reduced, eighteen seconds more being needed to reach 16,400 feet, and production was started under the designation LaG-5 (this designation presumably indicating that either Gorbunov or Gudkov had left the design collective or had been demoted). The LaG-5s employed modified LaGG-3 airframes, but with the introduction of the boosted M-82F engine and cut-down rear fuselage with all-round vision canopy, the aircraft was redesignated La-5.

The M-82F engine developed 1,540 h.p. at 6,725 feet and the La-5 completed its State Acceptance Trials during May and June 1942, immediately being placed in series production, and making its operational début during the autumn operations in the Stalingrad area. However, the climb performance of the fighter still left something to be desired, being inferior to the Luftwaffe fighters by which it was opposed, and during the winter of 1942–43, the Lavochkin collective began development of what may be considered as the definitive version of the La-5. Normal loaded weight was decreased by 379 lb. by reducing the internal fuel capacity slightly and replacing the wooden wing spars by metal spars, and a further variant of the Shvetsov engine, the M-82FN with direct fuel injection, was installed, this offering 1,700 h.p. for take-off. Possessing an armament of two 20-mm. ShVAK cannon with 200 r.p.g., the La-5FN, as the new model was designated, attained a maximum speed of 402·5 m.p.h. at 21,000 feet, had a range of 475 miles, and climbed to 16,400 feet in 4·7 minutes.

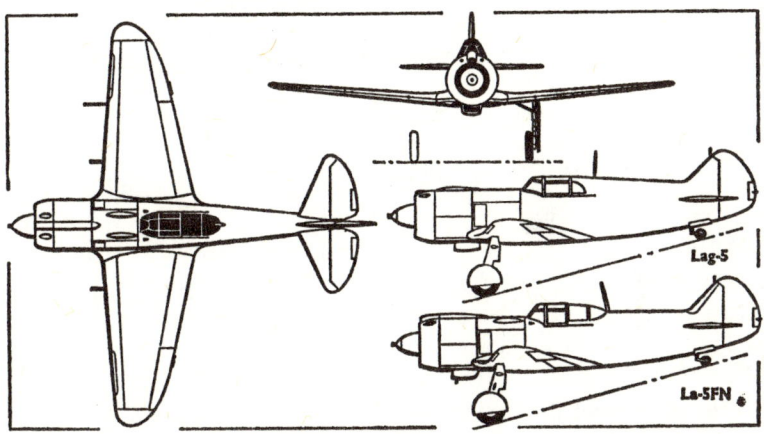

The La-5FN was employed in large numbers during the summer of 1943 over the Orel-Kursk area, and proved to be exceptionally manœuvrable. It could easily turn within the Bf 109G-2 and could out-climb the German fighter under most conditions, comparing favourably with most of its foreign contemporaries if somewhat less sophisticated.

MIG-3

Late in 1938, a requirement was conceived for a fighter offering maximum performance at altitudes exceeding 20,000 feet, and using the new Mikulin-design AM-35A twelve-cylinder liquid-cooled engine rated at 1,350 h.p. for take-off and 1,200 h.p. at 19,685 feet. The successful design was tendered by a collective headed by Artem I. Mikoyan and Mikhail I. Gurevich, and detail design and prototype construction were completed in the amazingly short time of four months! Initially designated I-61, the fighter accommodated the pilot in an enclosed cockpit over the wing trailing edge, and owing to the weight of the engine—830 lb.—only a relatively light armament could be mounted, this comprising one 12·7-mm. BS and two 7·62-mm. ShKAS machine guns. Mixed construction was employed, the forward fuselage being a welded steel-tube structure, the rear fuselage and tail assembly being of wood, and the wing centre section and outer panels being of metal and wood respectively.

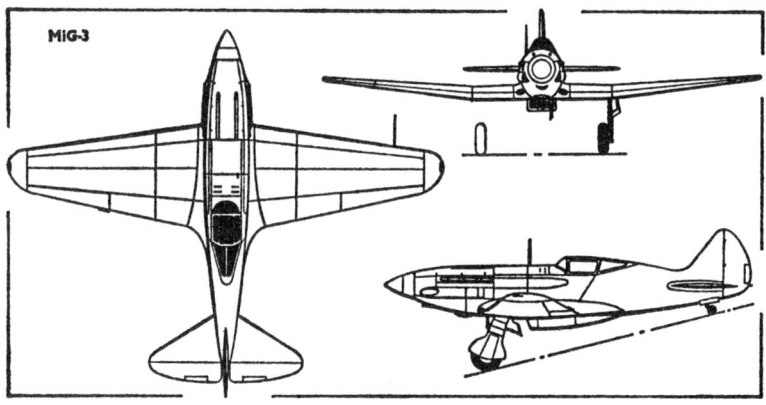

The I-61 was flown for the first time on April 5, 1940, by A. N. Yekatov, and during initial trials, the fighter attained a speed of 403 m.p.h. at 22,640 feet. State Acceptance Trials were completed by August, and the aircraft was ordered into series production immediately as the MiG-1. Owing to the poorer general finish of the production MiG-1s, maximum speed fell to 390 m.p.h. at 22,640 feet, maximum cruising speed and range being 280 m.p.h. and 454 miles respectively, an altitude of 16,400 feet being attained in 5·3 minutes, and service ceiling being 39,370 feet. Empty and normal loaded weights were 5,721 lb. and 6,770 lb., and maximum loaded weight was 7,290 lb. The AM-35A engine drove a VISh-22E, -22D-3 or

APPENDIX II 233

-22M three-blade constant-speed airscrew, and internal fuel capacity was 88 Imp. gal. The cockpit canopy of the prototype had been dispensed with, and the aircraft possessed poor longitudinal stability, while take-off and landing characteristics left much to be desired.

At the end of 1940, a certain amount of redesign work on the basic MiG-1 design resulted in the MiG-3. Like late-production MiG-1s, a 52 Imp. gal. supplementary fuel tank was installed beneath the pilot's seat, a sliding cockpit canopy was re-introduced, the dihedral of the outboard wing panels was increased to improve stability, a VISh-61Sh airscrew was fitted, and the ventral radiator bath was enlarged and extended forward. The MiG-3 attained a maximum speed of 398 m.p.h. at 25,590 feet, range was 776 miles at 342 m.p.h., an altitude of 16,400 feet was attained in 5·7 minutes, and service ceiling was 39,370 feet. Normal and maximum loaded weights were 7,385 and 7,695 lb., and initially the armament remained the same as that of the MiG-1, although soon after the MiG-3 entered service two 12·7-mm. BS machine guns were added beneath the wings.

Two thousand one hundred MiG-1 and -3 fighters were produced, but although possessing high maximum speeds, enjoyed poor manœuvrability and were at a distinct disadvantage when opposed by the latest Luftwaffe fighters, and when priority of the AM-38 engine for the Il-2 assault aircraft led to the termination of AM-35A production in November 1941, further work on the MiG-3 was abandoned, although a version powered by a fourteen-cylinder M-82A radial air-cooled engine was evolved to compete with the LaG-5. Designated MiG-5, this version was initially slower than the MiG-3, but the introduction of a new low-drag cowling raised performance appreciably. However, the MiG-5 possessed most of the shortcomings suffered by the MiG-3, and relatively small numbers of fighters of this type were completed.

PETLYAKOV PE-2

Employed extensively over Finland during the "Continuation War", the Pe-2 twin-engined mid-wing cantilever monoplane of all-metal construction was one of the best warplanes to serve with the Soviet Air Forces. It was a highly efficient aircraft, both aerodynamically and operationally, and Finnish fighters experienced more difficulty in intercepting the Pe-2 than any other Russian bomber. Design was initiated in 1938 by a collective supervised by V. M. Petlyakov, the aircraft being known initially as the VI-100 ("VI" indicating *Viisotni Istrebityel*, or High-altitude Fighter). The project had been started as a high-altitude, long-range fighter with a pressurized cabin, but before design details had been finalised its role had been changed to that of high-altitude bomber, and the first prototype—still designated VI-100—began flight trials in 1939 with Klimov-designed M-105 twelve-cylinder liquid-cooled engines with TK-3 turbo-superchargers.

The relatively poor results of high-altitude bombing trials with the first prototype dictated a reappraisal of the role of the aircraft, and in 1940, with the TK-3 turbo-superchargers removed and M-105R engines with normal two-speed superchargers installed, the VI-100 began trials as a dive bomber, dive brakes having been attached to the forward wing spar, outboard of the engine nacelles. In this form, the aircraft rapidly passed its State Acceptance Trials, and, in June 1940, entered quantity production as the Pe-2.

The Pe-2 was the first Russian combat aircraft to make extensive use of electrics, no fewer than eighteen electric-driven pumps being fitted. Four of these operated the radiator shutters and two the oil cooler shutters, there was one each for the hydraulic pump, a hydraulic valve, the dive brakes and the wing flaps, four were used to operate the various trim tabs, two for airscrew pitch changing, and two for the supercharger gear change. The twelve-cylinder Vee-type liquid-cooled M-105R engines were each rated at 1,100 h.p. for take-off and at 6,560 feet, and had a normal rated power of 1,050 h.p. at 13,120 feet, and three crew members were carried: pilot, radio operator who also acted as bombardier, and rear gunner. The pilot and radio operator were normally seated back-to-back, and the latter lay prone in the nose when performing the task of bombardier. When operating the ventral gun, the rear gunner lay prone, sighting the weapon by means of a 120-degree periscope. This ventral weapon employed an ingenious mount which permitted it to be extended and retracted, and was a 7·62-mm. ShKAS machine gun similar to the rear-firing weapon mounted

APPENDIX II

in the cockpit. Two additional ShKAS guns were mounted in the upper decking of the forward fuselage and fixed to fire forward. Normal bomb load was 1,320 lb., but this could be increased to 2,200 lb. by means of external racks, a typical load being ten 220-lb. bombs, six of which were carried internally and four on racks under the inboard wing sections.

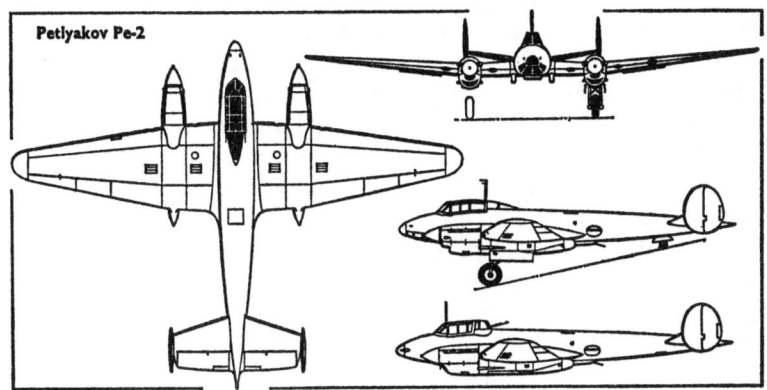

The Pe-2 possessed excellent diving characteristics, and handled extremely well with a competent pilot at the controls, although it was not a forgiving aircraft and spun readily if a faulty manœuvre was executed. It was extremely easy to land, and overall performance was very good indeed, maximum speed ranging from 335 m.p.h. at 16,400 feet and 314 m.p.h. at 6,560 feet to 286 m.p.h. at sea level. Normal cruising speed was 226 m.p.h. at 16,000 feet, and range with a 1,320-lb. bomb load was 746 miles. An altitude of 9,840 feet was attained in 3·5 minutes, and 16,400 feet in 7 minutes, service ceiling being 29,520 feet. Maximum diving speed with brakes extended was 372 m.p.h., maximum permissible diving speed being 450 m.p.h., and altitude lost in pulling out of a 50–70 degree dive was 2,000–3,000 feet. Empty weight was 12,900 lb., and normal and maximum loaded weights were 16,930 lb. and 18,730 lb. respectively.

During 1941, in which year 458 Pe-2s were produced, Petlyakov's collective carried out extensive modifications to convert the aircraft for the interceptor fighter role, the modified aircraft receiving the designation Pe-3bis. The Pe-3bis had the underwing dive brakes eliminated and leading edge slots installed in the wings to improve manœuvrability, and the nose glazing was eliminated, forward-firing armament being increased to two 20-mm. ShVAK cannon, 12·7-mm. BS machine guns being mounted in dorsal and ventral positions. Placed in production before the end of 1941, the Pe-3bis also served in the high-altitude reconnaissance role.

By the beginning of 1942, the Messerschmitt Bf 109F was being employed in substantial numbers by the Luftwaffe, and the first Bf 109Gs had made their operational début, and units operating the Pe-2 began to suffer higher casualties, resulting in the demand for improved defensive armament. A new dorsal gun turret known as the "FT" (FT indicating *Frontovoye Trebovaniye*, or Frontline Request) was hurriedly designed, and mounting a single 12·7-mm. UBT machine gun, this was installed in all first-line Pe-2s from June 1942 by special teams which undertook the modifications on the frontline airfields. Simultaneously, one of the nose-mounted ShKAS machine guns was supplanted by a 12·7-mm. BS gun on some machines, a 12·7-mm. gun was provided in the ventral position, and two hand-operated lateral 7·62-mm. ShKAS guns were fitted for protection against beam attacks. Supplementary armour protection was also provided for the crew members. However, the increased protection offered by these modifications was only effective for a short time as, with the Bf 109G appearing in ever-increasing numbers, it also became necessary to improve the overall performance of the Pe-2.

Thus, in February 1943, the Pe-2 was equipped with the M-105PF rated at 1,210 h.p. for take-off, 1,260 h.p. at 2,625 feet, and 1,180 h.p. at 8,860 feet. At the same time, a major "cleaning-up" process was embarked upon. The wing profile was slightly modified and the wing surface finish was improved; the aerodynamic shape of the oil cooler intake was modified; the landing flaps were redesigned to fit flush beneath the wings; the external bomb racks were removed and replaced by streamlined fairings, and the gaps between the movable and fixed surfaces were reduced. The net result was a 25·5 m.p.h. increase in maximum speed.

Among the most important variants of the Pe-2 were the Pe-2UT dual-control advanced trainer, the Pe-2R reconnaissance aircraft with increased fuel capacity, and the Pe-2I interceptor fighter (not to be confused with the Pe-3bis). The **Pe-2R** was equipped with an AK-1 automatic course device, carried three cameras for day-and-night vertical and oblique photography, and had two 64 Imp. gal. auxiliary fuel tanks which provided an increased range of 1,056 miles. The Pe-2I entered series production in 1944, and was fitted with the more powerful M-107A engine which, with injection-type carburettors, provided 1,620 h.p. for take-off and increased maximum speed to 408 m.p.h. at 18,700 feet. The Pe-2I could also be employed in the role of fighter-bomber, maximum bomb load being 6,614 lb., 4,409 lb. of this load being accommodated internally. Three captured Pe-2s were operated by PLeLv 48 for long-range photographic reconnaissance.

POLIKARPOV I-15BIS

One of the principal Russian fighters engaged during the "Winter War" but rapidly supplanted by the I-153, the I-15bis was flown for the first time in 1937, and embodied experience gained in aerial combat with the I-15 during the early months of the Spanish Civil War. The I-15 itself had been a logical successor to the I-5, and was designed by Nikolai N. Polikarpov who headed the central design bureau of the Aviatrust (TsKB). Work on the I-15 had commenced in February 1933, at which time the fighter was designated TsKB-3, the aim being to increase maximum speed, climb rate and manœuvrability of the basic I-5 design by means of aerodynamic improvements and the installation of a nine-cylinder Wright Cyclone SGR-1820-F3 radial. The specific wing loading was decreased from 12·92 lb./sq. ft. to 11·89 lb./sq. ft., and the TsKB-3 began trials in October 1933 with one of the best-known of Russia's pre-war pilots, Valerii P. Chkalov, at the controls.

The TsKB-3 was a sesquiplane of mixed construction with single streamlined bracing struts and cantilever undercarriage legs. The upper wing was of gull form, fairing into the fuselage decking to provide the pilot with an unimpeded forward view, and armament comprised two 7·62-mm. PV-1 machine guns in the forward fuselage. The aircraft evinced outstanding characteristics from the outset and, early in 1934, was accepted for series production as the I-15, the power plant being a Russian-built version of the Cyclone which, designated M-25, offered

715 h.p. at 10,000 feet. With this engine, the I-15 attained a maximum speed of 199 m.p.h. at sea level, 208 m.p.h. at 3,280 feet, and 224 m.p.h. at 9,840 feet. Normal loaded weight was 3,027 lb., a turn could be completed in eight seconds at 3,280 feet, and service ceiling was 29,530 feet. Normal armament was two PV-1 machine guns, but in overload condition the I-15 could carry two additional PV-1 weapons, and during 1935 these guns were replaced in some aircraft by the ShKAS of similar calibre but offering nearly twice the rate of fire.

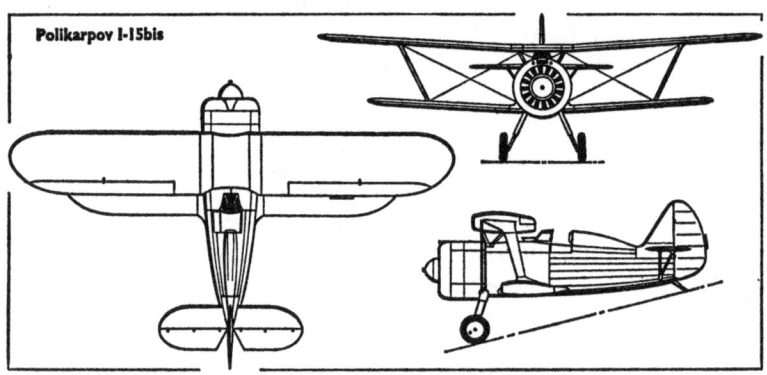

On November 29, 1935, V. K. Kokkinaki established a new altitude record[1] in the I-15 which, with armament, some instrumentation and equipment, and even the pilot's seat removed, attained an altitude of 47,820 feet. During 1936, production of the I-15 amounted to twenty-five per cent of that of all fighters in the Soviet Union, as the faster monoplane was already finding wide favour. However, during September and October of that year, a number of I-15 fighters together with I-16 monoplanes were sent to Spain, together with Soviet Air Force personnel, to aid the Republican forces. The I-16 fighter monoplanes had difficulty in combating the Fiat C.R.32 and Heinkel He 51 biplanes by which they were opposed and, in consequence, there was an immediate demand for an improved fighter biplane. Polikarpov's design collective immediately began work on an improved version of the I-15, the I-15bis which began flight trials early in 1937.

[1]This record was not recognised abroad as, at the time, the Soviet Union was not a member of the Fédération Aéronautique Internationale.

The I-15bis had a 750-h.p. M-25V engine rated at 750 h.p. at 9,500 feet and enclosed in a long-chord cowling. The centre section of the upper wing was raised on struts above the fuselage, and standard armament comprised four 7·62-mm. ShKAS machine-guns. The structure was of mixed steel and wood with fabric covering and essentially similar to that of the I-15, and the 68 Imp. gal. internal fuel tank could be supplemented by a pair of 22 Imp. gal. auxiliary tanks slung on the underwing bomb shackles. These normally carried two 110-lb. or four 55-lb. bombs. A 9-mm. armour plate provided the pilot with protection from the rear. The I-15bis attained a maximum speed of 230 m.p.h. and a maximum cruising speed of 186 m.p.h. at which range was 280 miles. With auxiliary tanks range was stretched to 497 miles at 174 m.p.h. Empty and normal loaded weights were 2,880 and 3,827 lb. respectively, maximum loaded weight being 4,189 lb.

The I-15bis began to reach Spain late in 1937 and, shortly afterwards, began to re-equip fighter units on the Manchukuoan border in time to participate in the fighting with Japanese forces during 1938. During the fighting over the Khalkiin Gol in the following year, the I-15bis used the RS-82 rocket missile operationally for the first time, six of these missiles being carried beneath the lower wing. The RS-82 was also used by I-15bis fighters in action against Finnish forces during the "Winter War".

POLIKARPOV I-153

Dubbed *Tchaika* (Gull) by its pilots, the I-153 single-seat fighter biplane featured a distinctive upper wing of gull configuration, and competed with the Italian Fiat C.R.42 for the distinction of being the last biplane fighter to enter production. Although the Soviet Union had been the first nation to introduce into service low-wing fighter monoplanes with retractable undercarriages, these had found themselves at some disadvantage in close combat with opposing biplanes during the Spanish Civil War, resulting in a similar renewal of Russian interest in the fighter biplane in 1938 as that two years previously which had resulted in the I-15bis, and a demand for a high-performance fighter of biplane configuration.

Accordingly, a senior member of Nikolai N. Polikarpov's

design bureau, A. J. Scherbakov, undertook the refinement of the 1937-vintage I-15bis to fulfil this new demand. Retaining the basic structure of the I-15bis, Scherbakov introduced a retractable undercarriage and resurrected the gull upper wing configuration of the earlier I-5 and I-15 fighters, this offering less drag than the braced centre section of the I-15bis, and designated I-153, the new fighter flew as a prototype late in 1938. Like the I-15bis, the prototype was powered by the M-25V nine-cylinder radial air-cooled engine, but the refinements had resulted in a noteworthy improvement in all-round performance, and to meet an urgent requirement for a fighter more manœuvrable than the I-16 to combat the Japanese Nakajima Ki.27 that was being encountered in the fighting over the Mongolian-Siberian-Manchurian border areas, the I-153 was rushed into production.

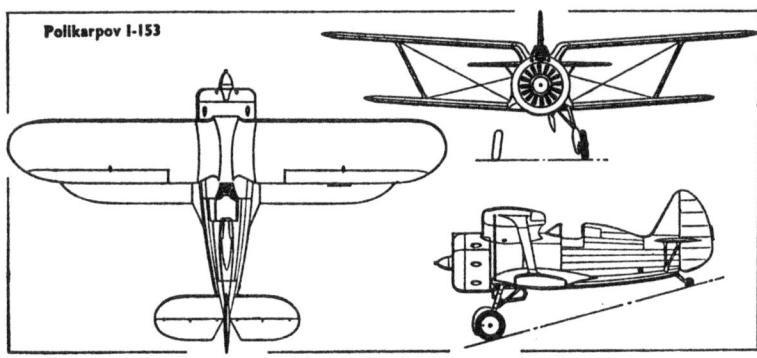

Polikarpov I-153

The production I-153 differed from the prototype in having a nine-cylinder M-62 radial developing 1,000 h.p. for take-off, 850 h.p. at 5,020 feet, and 800 h.p. at 13,780 feet. Armament comprised four 7·62-mm. ShKAS machine guns, two of which were mounted in the upper decking of the fuselage ahead of the cockpit, the others being mounted in the fuselage sides, these having 650 r.p.g. Provision was also made to mount six RS-82 projectiles on racks beneath the lower wing. The pilot's seat was protected by 9-mm. back armour, and the 68 Imp. gal. fuel tank was placed immediately behind the engine as in the I-15bis.

The first production I-153s appeared in the spring of 1939,

shortly before the temporary lull in the fighting between the Russo-Mongolian and Japanese forces developed into a full-scale war. I-153s reached the Khalkiin Gol in the late summer of 1939. According to Russian sources, the I-153s approached the combat area at cruising speed with their undercarriages extended and, as their pilots had anticipated, were mistaken by the Japanese for the very much less effective I-15bis fighters. As the Ki.27s approached, the Russians retracted their undercarriages, opened their throttles fully, and were through the Japanese formation before their startled opponents could take evasive action. The successes achieved by the I-153 in combat against the Japanese led to an immediate increase in the production of this fighter which, by 1940, had appeared with the more powerful M-63 engine which, rated at 1,100 h.p. for take-off, offered 1,000 h.p. at 5,900 feet and 900 h.p. at 14,765 feet.

The M-63-powered I-153 attained a maximum speed of 267 m.p.h. at 16,400 feet, cruising speed was 186 m.p.h., ceiling was 35,145 feet, and range with and without underwing auxiliary tanks was 560 miles and 298 miles respectively. Empty weight was 3,168 lb., and normal and maximum loaded weights were 4,100 and 4,431 lb. respectively. The I-153 was extremely manœuvrable, and in dog-fighting had a decided edge on the faster but less nimble Finnish fighter monoplanes, being able to turn well within the turning radius of the Brewster B-239. A number of I-153s were captured by the Wehrmacht in the Ukraine and were sold to the Finnish Air Force which, for want of better equipment, issued them to TLeLv 30 for reconnaissance duties. The Finns found the I-153's M-63 radial engine to be extremely unreliable, and several Finnish pilots lost their lives in consequence.

POLIKARPOV I-16

The I-16 possessed the distinction of being the first cantilever low-wing fighter monoplane with retractable undercarriage and enclosed cockpit to enter service with any air force. Designed by Nikolai N. Polikarpov, the first prototype of this fighter flew as the TsKB-12 on December 31, 1933, and the extremely small, barrel-like monoplane featured a circular-section wooden monocoque fuselage, a 450-h.p. M-22 (licence-built Gnôme-Rhône Jupiter) nine-cylinder radial air-cooled engine, an enclosed cockpit with a sliding canopy, a two-spar metal wing with fabric covering, split flaps, a manually-retracted undercarriage and an armament of two 7·62-mm. ShKAS machine guns.

Possessing a maximum speed of 225 m.p.h. at sea level and 202 m.p.h. at 13,120 feet, the production version of the TsKB-12 was designated I-16 Type 1, and weighed only 2,965 lb. in normal loaded condition. Deliveries of the I-16 Type 1 to Sov. A.F. squadrons began during the second half of 1934, and the new fighter was displayed publicly for the first time during the 1935 May Day celebrations. While preparations were being made to produce the I-16 Type 1, a second prototype, the TsKB-12bis, had been completed with a 700 h.p. M-25 and flew for the first time on February 18, 1934. Despite the outstanding performance displayed by the more powerful prototype—282 m.p.h. had been attained at 9,840 feet during the second test flight—eighteen months were to elapse before the M-25-powered model was ordered into production as the I-16 Type 4.

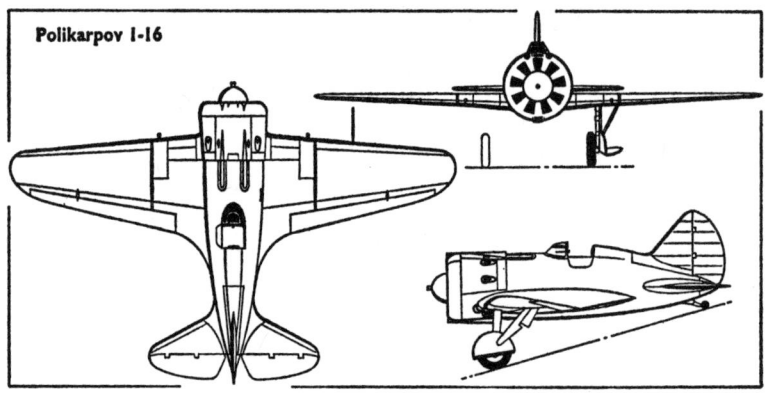

The I-16 was no novice's aircraft. The limited static stability under most conditions of flight and marked instability during climbing and turning made the aircraft somewhat unpopular. The oleo legs provided inadequate shock absorbing, the wheel brakes were ineffective, and there was a tendency to bounce indefinitely after touching down, a dangerous nose-up attitude being adopted. The nose also rose alarmingly when the flaps

APPENDIX II

were lowered for landing, and it was difficult to wind up the undercarriage. A training version, the UTI-4, was therefore produced to verse pilots in the idiosyncrasies of the fighter monoplane. The I-16 Type 4 retained the twin-ShKAS armament of the initial production model, and weighing 3,135 lb., its maximum speed ranged from 248 m.p.h. at sea level to 283 m.p.h. at 9,840 feet. An altitude of 16,400 feet was attained in 5·9 minutes, service ceiling was 30,440 feet, and maximum cruising speed and range were 224 m.p.h. and 510 miles respectively. The I-16 Type 5 introduced 9-mm. seat armour for the pilot's protection, and the Type 6 switched to the 730 h.p. M-25A engine, the latter being the first model to see operational service, making its début over Spain on November 5, 1936, in support of the offensive against Nationalist forces advancing in Valdemoro, Seseña and Esquivias.

The I-16 was dubbed *Mosca* (Fly) by the Republican forces and *Rata* (Rat) by the Nationalists, but to Soviet Air Force pilots it was unofficially the *Ishak* (Donkey). Continuous development of the basic design was undertaken, and in 1937 the I-16 Type 10 with two additional 7·62-mm. ShKAS guns made its appearance, this version having the cockpit canopy deleted. Experiments aimed at increasing the fighter's firepower by the inclusion of cannon in its armament had begun in 1938, and in that year the I-16 Type 17 was placed in production, this variant retaining the two fuselage-mounted ShKAS guns but replacing the similar weapons in the wings with two 20-mm. ShVAK cannon which raised loaded weight to 3,990 lb. By this time, the M-25 engine had reached the limit of its development, and in 1937 A. D. Shvetsov had evolved a new engine based on the earlier power plant, the M-62. This power plant had a two-speed supercharger and offered 1,000 h.p. for take-off and 850 h.p. at 5,000 feet.

The first production model to be fitted with the M-62 engine was the I-16 Type 18 which appeared in 1939, and which was encountered frequently by the Finns during the "Winter War". Loaded weight had risen to 4,034 lb. despite a drastic reduction in the capacity of the fuselage fuel tank (from 93·5 to 56 Imp. gal.), and armament comprised four 7·62-mm. ShKAS machine guns, but the similarly-powered I-16 Type 24 had two fuselage-mounted 7·62-mm. guns and two wing-mounted 20-mm. cannon, this being built in larger numbers than any other version of the fighter. Weighing 3,285 lb. empty and 4,215 and 4,546 lb in normal and maximum loaded condition respectively, the I-16 Type 24 attained maximum speeds of 286 m.p.h. at sea level and 326 m.p.h. at 14,765 feet. Range on internal fuel was 248 miles at 199 m.p.h. at 3,280 feet, and with two 22 Imp. gal. auxiliary tanks was 435 miles at 186 m.p.h. An altitude of 16,400 feet was reached in 5·8 minutes, and service ceiling was 29,530 feet.

The I-16 fighter bore the brunt of the combat on the Eastern Front during the first year of fighting, and remained in widespread service until the Russian counter-offensive in the Stalingrad area at the end of October 1942. Long after this the rotund Polikarpov fighter was encountered on the Russo-Finnish front, eventually being withdrawn from first-line service in 1944.

POLIKARPOV R-5

Although designed initially as a light bomber and reconnaissance two-seater, the R-5, which first flew in 1928, was probably manufactured in more variants and for more widely differing roles than any comparable type, and more than six thousand machines of this type were built between 1931 and

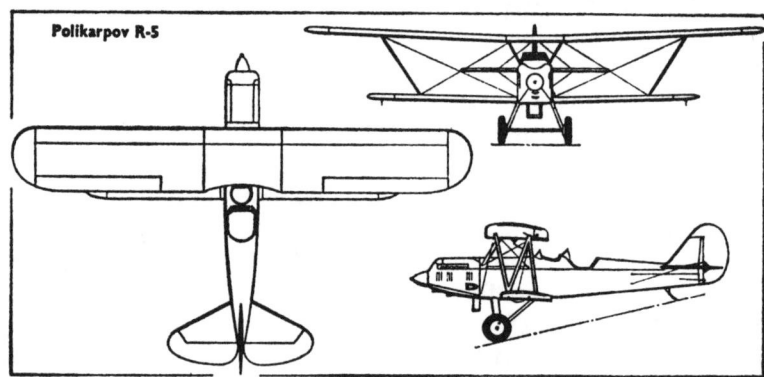

1937. Although obsolete, the R-5 was still standard Soviet Air Force short-range reconnaissance equipment during the "Winter War", and also undertook such roles as ambulance, liaison, night intruder, and artillery observation post.

Designed by N. I. Polikarpov, the R-5 was of mixed construction and, in its most widely-used form, was powered by an M-17 liquid-cooled engine with a nominal rating of 500 h.p. Defensive armament comprised one fixed forward-firing 7·62-mm. PV-1 machine gun and a similar weapon or a 7·62-mm. ShKAS machine gun on a swivelling mount for the observer. Racks beneath the lower wing could accommodate a 550-lb. bomb load, or, in overload condition, 880 lb. of bombs. Easy to fly and simple to maintain under operational conditions, the R-5 had a maximum speed of 143 m.p.h. at 9,845 feet, a cruising speed of 132 m.p.h. at 13,125 feet, and a range of 684 miles. An altitude of 9,845 feet was attained in ten and a half minutes, and service ceiling was 21,000 feet. Empty weight was 4,222 lb., and loaded weight ranged from 6,514 to 7,378 lb.

The R-5 was first used operationally over Spain where it was dubbed *Natasha*, but during the "Continuation War" this type had been largely relegated to the role of nocturnal nuisance raider.

TUPOLEV SB-2

A. N. Tupolev's SB-2 provided, together with Ilyushin's DB-3 and its derivative, the Il-4, the mainstay of the Soviet Air Forces' medium bomber force throughout the Second World War, and it was used in larger numbers than any other medium bomber over the front on which Finnish forces were engaged. A contemporary of the Heinkel He 111, the Martin 139, and the Savoia-Marchetti S.M.79, the SB-2 was of advanced concept, and was one of the best aircraft in its class at the time of its service début. Design of the SB-2 had been initiated by Tupolev's design collective in the summer of 1933 to meet an official requirement for a "frontal" bomber—a three-seat, high-speed aircraft of relatively short range suitable for co-operation with land and naval forces.

Possessing the design bureau designation ANT-40, the project marked a complete departure from previous Russian bomber design practice, and such was the promise seen in the aircraft that preparations for quantity production were begun in April 1934, shortly after work had begun on the construction of two prototypes. The two prototypes differed in several respects. The first, intended specifically to meet the demands of the official requirement, was powered by two M-25 nine-cylinder radial air-cooled engines with single-speed superchargers which offered 730 h.p. for take-off and 700 h.p. at rated altitude, and its fuel capacity of 207 Imp. gal. was intended to provide the specified range of 435 miles with a 1,100-lb. bomb load. This aircraft was flown for the first time on October 7, 1934, and, at a loaded weight of 10,398 lb., attained a maximum speed of 202 m.p.h. at 13,124 feet, ceiling being 22,310 feet.

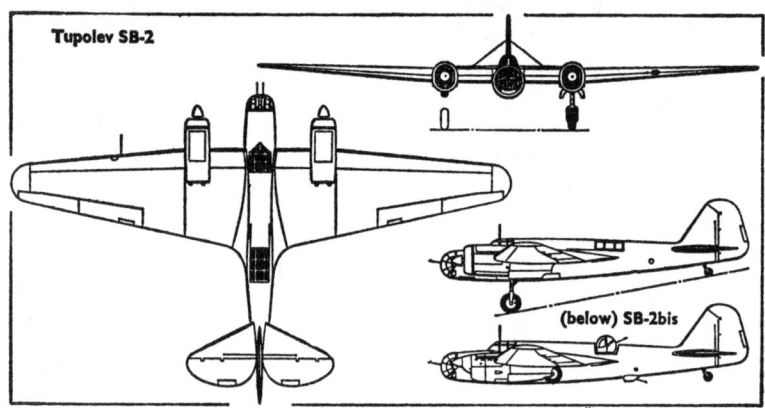

The second prototype, which flew on December 30, 1934, embodied changes which the design bureau considered to increase the operational flexibility of the aircraft, the principal differences being the installation of 750 h.p. M-100 twelve-cylinder Vee liquid-cooled engines with single-speed super-chargers and a substantial increase in internal fuel capacity. The M-100 engines, which provided 830 h.p. for take-off and 750 h.p. at 14,107 feet, were licence-built versions of the French Hispano-Suiza 12Ybrs with shuttered frontal-type radiators, these offering appreciably less drag than the larger radial cowlings of the M-25s, and total fuel tankage was 376 Imp. gal. This prototype attained a maximum speed of 251 m.p.h. at 16,405 feet despite an increase in normal loaded weight of 624 lb.

The initial production version of the bomber was based on the second ANT-40 prototype, and was designated SB-2 (SB indicating *Skorostnoi Bombardirovshchik*, or Fast Bomber). State Acceptance Trials were completed in July 1935, and so important was the new bomber considered that assembly lines were prepared at several factories simultaneously. The first SB-2s began to reach the squadrons during the first quarter of 1936, and by the early summer a daily production rate of twelve machines had been attained.

Anxious to evaluate the new warplane under operational conditions, the Russian government sent a number of SB-2 bombers to the aid of the Spanish Republican Government within a few weeks of the outbreak of the Spanish Civil War, and in October 1936, manned by "volunteers" who were, in fact, serving members of the Soviet Air Forces, these began attacks on Nationalist-held towns. Two hundred and ten SB-2s were eventually sent to Spain where the bomber was dubbed *Katiuska* by the Republicans and *Sofia* by the Nationalists.

With the signing of the Non-Aggression Pact between the Soviet Union and the Chinese Central Government, a number of SB-2s were delivered to China for use against the Japanese in 1937, and during the same year a manufacturing licence for the SB-2 was negotiated by the Czechoslovak government. The SB-2 thus became the first Russian aircraft of indigenous design to be manufactured abroad. The Aero plant began production of the SB-2 in 1938, the designation B-71 being applied to the Czech-built version which had Avia-built Hispano-Suiza 12Ydrs engines.

By this time, the SB-2 had been fitted with the improved M-100A engine which produced 860 h.p. at 10,826 feet, this power plant increasing maximum speed marginally, reducing climbing time to 16,400 feet by one minute, and permitting the normal bomb load to be raised from 1,100 to 1,320 lb. The M-100A-powered version had a loaded weight of 12,636 lb., a maximum speed of 263·5 m.p.h. at 13,125 feet, and a ceiling of 30,365 feet. Like the earlier production model, it was of all-metal construction with a dural monocoque fuselage and a two-spar wing. All fuel was housed in the wings, an 88-Imp. gal. fuel tank being mounted in each centre section half, and a 79-Imp. gal. tank being positioned immediately outboard of each engine nacelle. The internal fuel could be supplemented by an 82-Imp. gal. drop tank between the fuselage and each engine. The internally-housed bomb load comprised six 220-lb. bombs, two 550-lb. bombs or one 1,100-lb. bomb, and defensive armament consisted of four 7·62-mm. ShKAS machine guns, a pair of these being mounted in the extreme nose but only capable of movement in the vertical plane, and the others being mounted in ventral and dorsal positions.

Further development of the basic design produced the SB-2bis powered by M-103 engines providing 960 h.p. each at 13,125 feet, and driving the new VISh-22 three-blade variable-pitch airscrews. An additional 7·62-mm. ShKAS machine gun was fitted, and fuel capacity was again increased, maximum range with overload fuel and a 1,100-lb. bomb load being extended to 1,429 miles, loaded weight being 17,195 lb. On September 2, 1937, an SB-2 flown by M. Yu. Alekseyev established a new load-to-altitude record by lifting a 2,204-lb. payload to 40,181 feet. The SB-2bis possessed a maximum speed of 279·6 m.p.h. at 13,452 feet at a loaded weight of 14,330 lb., normal range was 995 miles at 186 m.p.h., and service ceiling was 27,890 feet.

Several variants of the SB-2bis were produced, including a pilot training version with an open cockpit for the pupil ahead of the normal cockpit, and the glazed panelling for the bombardier removed. A dive bomber model designated Ar-2 was evolved from the basic design by a team headed by A. A. Arkhangelskiï. Production of the SB-2bis terminated in 1941, late models featuring a revolving dorsal turret with a single 7·62-mm. ShKAS gun in place of the sliding transparent hatch and hand-held gun, and a ventral gun-bath housing a similar weapon. A substantial number of Czech-built SB-2s served with the Luftwaffe in the crew training and target-tug roles, and several captured SB-2 and SB-2bis aircraft, some purchased from Germany, were used by TLeLv 6 for maritime reconnaissance and anti-submarine duties, one SB-2bis of this unit being credited with the destruction of four Russian submarines.

YAK-1

Flown for the first time in March 1939 by Yv. I. Pyontkovsky as the I-26, the Yak-1 single-seat fighter designed by Alexander S. Yakovlev was, without question, the most successful Russian aircraft in this class for the first two years in which the Soviet Union participated in the Second World War, and progressive developments of the basic design were to serve with the Soviet Air Forces into the 'fifties. Work on a pre-production batch

APPENDIX II

of fighters was begun almost immediately after the first flight of the I-26, and the first of these emerged at the beginning of 1940, by which time the aircraft had been redesignated Yak-1.

The Yak-1 had a one-piece two-spar wing of wooden construction with plywood skinning, and the fuselage was a welded steel-tube structure, the forward portion of which was covered by detachable metal panels and the aft section by plywood which, in turn, was covered by doped fabric. The control surfaces were metal-framed and fabric-covered, and the retractable undercarriage was operated hydraulically. Power was provided by an M-105PA twelve-cylinder liquid-cooled engine which drove a VISh-61P airscrew and was rated at 1,100 h.p. for take-off and 1,050 h.p. at 13,120 feet. Armament comprised one 20-mm. ShVAK cannon firing through the airscrew hub and two 7·62-mm. ShKAS machine guns in the upper decking of the forward fuselage.

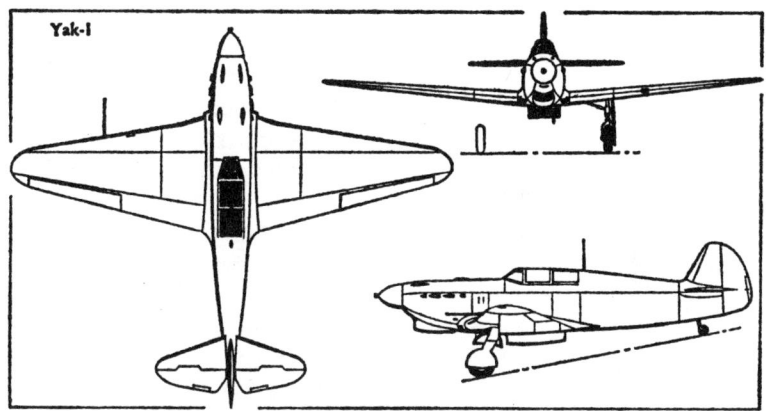

Various changes were introduced on the pre-production Yak-1 fighters, and these were not entirely free of teething troubles, but in June 1941, the fighter had passed its final acceptance trials at the State and Air Force test centres, and had been cleared for mass production, although deliveries were delayed by the need to move the main Yakovlev assembly plants from the vicinity of Moscow to Kamensk/Uralsk, and in consequence the Yak-1 did not reach operational units in worthwhile quantities until the late spring of 1942.

The first production model of the Yak-1 attained maximum speeds of 311 m.p.h. at sea level and 363 m.p.h. at 15,740 feet. Economical cruising speed was 155 m.p.h. at sea level and 149 m.p.h. at 9,840 feet, and maximum range was 510 miles, the fuel tanks between the wing spars having a total capacity of 89 Imp. gal. Empty and loaded weights were 5,137 and 6,217 lb. respectively. As production progressed, a number of modifications were introduced, one of the most important changes being the installation of the M-105PF engine driving an automatic VISh-105SV airscrew, this power plant providing 1,210 h.p. for take-off. The M-105PF had the disadvantage that the second speed of the supercharger engaged at 8,860 feet as compared with 13,120 feet for the earlier M-105PA. The introduction of the new engine was accompanied by a deeper ventral radiator bath which was moved forward to a point just aft of the mainwheel wells, and shortly afterwards the twin 7·62-mm. ShKAS weapons were supplanted by a single 12·7-mm. BS machine gun. Loaded weight rose to 6,382 lb., and time to 16,400 feet was increased from 4·5 to 5·4 minutes, but maximum speed was raised to 372 m.p.h. at 11,150 feet.

At an early stage in the fighter's development, a two-seat conversion training model had been evolved, this flying for the first time in 1940 as the UTI-26 and entering production during the following year as the Yak-7V. Various improvements were made to the controls and, apart from repositioning the radio and other equipment aft of the original cockpit to provide space for the instructor's seat, minor changes were introduced in the structure. Some of the modifications embodied in the Yak-7V trainer, together with the progressive improvements introduced during Yak-1 production, were standardised in a new single-seat fighter model, the Yak-7A. Externally, this differed little from the late-production Yak-1 apart from slightly modified upper fuselage contours aft of the cockpit.

At the end of 1941, a further change was made in the two-seat Yak-7V—the rear fuselage was cut down to improve rear vision. At this time, the Yak-7A fighter was undergoing some refinement during which the internal ducting was redesigned and the ventral bath improved aerodynamically and returned to its original position as on the early Yak-1. With these changes and the first-all-round vision canopy, the Yak-7A became the

APPENDIX II

Yak-7B, and the result was a net gain of 8 m.p.h. in maximum speed which was raised to 381 m.p.h. Armament was the same as that of late-production Yak-1s, and the internal fuel capacity of 91 Imp. gal. provided a maximum range of 516 miles. The loaded weight of the Yak-7B was increased to 6,636 lb.

YAK-4

One of the less successful of the designs evolved by the collective headed by Alexander S. Yakovlev was the Yak-4 two-seat short-range high-speed bomber which appeared in small numbers over the Finnish Front during the "Continuation War", and was also encountered occasionally by the Luftwaffe during the first year of fighting on the Eastern Front. Intended as a successor to the KhAI-designed R-10 and Polikarpov R-5, the Yak-4 was a progressive development of the generally similar Yak-2, design of which had begun late in 1938 as the BB-22. Flown for the first time in 1939, the BB-22 entered production in 1940 as the Yak-2.

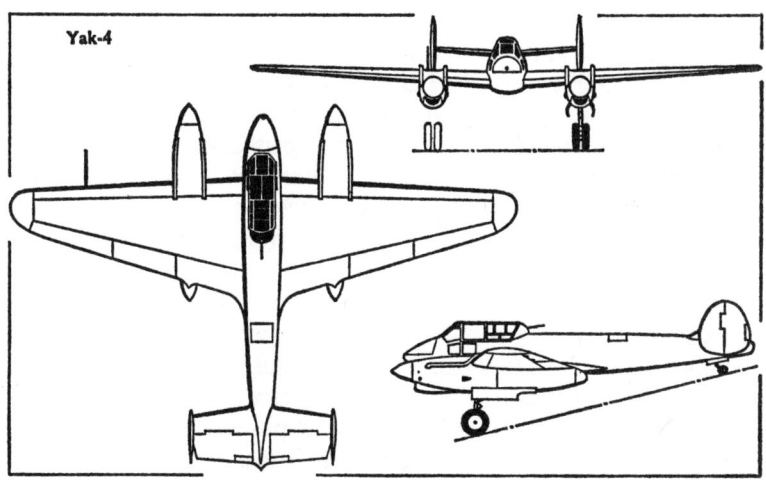

The Yak-2 possessed exceptionally clean lines, and was powered by two M-103 liquid-cooled engines which, driving VISh-22 three-blade variable-pitch airscrews, were each rated at 960 h.p. at 13,125 feet. All fuel was housed in six wing tanks which had a total capacity of 154 Imp. gal., and the small internal bomb-bay accommodated eight 55-lb. bombs. Four racks under the wing roots and immediately outboard of the engine nacelles each carried a single 220-lb. bomb, and defensive armament comprised one fixed forward-firing 7·62-mm. ShKAS machine gun, and a similar weapon on a flexible mount in the rear cockpit. Mixed construction was employed, and the main undercarriage members, which could be fitted with either wheels or skis, retracted rearward into engine nacelle wells.

Shortly after deliveries of the Yak-2 commenced, M-105R engines rated at 1,100 h.p. for take-off and 1,050 h.p. at 13,125 feet were introduced and, at the same time, twin-wheel main undercarriage members supplanted the single-wheel units. With these changes, the aircraft was redesignated Yak-4, and entered service with the Soviet Air Forces during 1941. The offensive load and defensive armament of the Yak-4 were similar to those of the Yak-2, and performance included a maximum speed of 352 m.p.h. at 15,740 feet, a ceiling of 39,000 feet, a range of 497 miles with an 880-lb. bomb load, and a maximum range without bomb load of 995 miles. Maximum loaded weight was 11,465 lb.

Combat experience with the Yak-4 during the opening stages of the Russo-German conflict revealed serious deficiencies in the aircraft, and the type was promptly taken out of production, those already in service being used primarily in the reconnaissance role for which the Yak-4's high speed and good ceiling particularly suited the type. The author destroyed an aircraft of this type South of Viipuri on June 20, 1944.

YAK-9

During the summer of 1942 supplies of steel alloys and light metals for the Soviet aircraft industry began to improve, and the wooden spars of the Yak-7B fighter's wing were replaced experimentally by light alloy spars, although the wooden ribs and plywood skin were retained. The use of metal spars resulted in appreciable weight saving and provided more space within the wing for fuel. This modified variant was initially known as the Yak-7DI (DI indicating *Dalnii Istrebityel*, or Range Fighter), but this designation was changed to that of Yak-9 when the new model entered production. By comparison with the Yak-7B, the Yak-9's useful load was increased by 324 lb., although normal loaded weight rose by only 110 lb. to 6,746 lb. Fuel capacity was raised by 7·7 Imp. gal., increasing range to 565 miles. The Yak-9 was placed in large-scale production in the late summer of 1942, and appeared operationally over the Stalingrad Front during that October. The M-105PF engine was retained, and maximum speed was 367 m.p.h. at 16,400 feet, and at a loaded weight of 6,334 lb. an altitude of 16,400 feet was attained in 4·9 minutes, range at this weight being 528 miles.

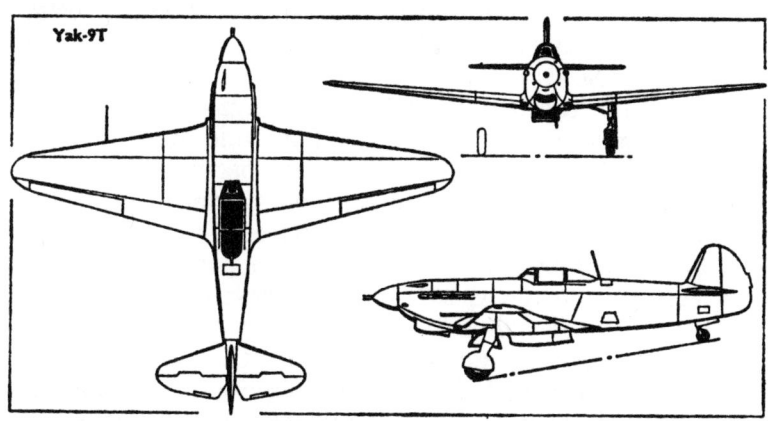

Yak-9T

Armament of the initial production version of the Yak-9 remained one 20-mm. cannon and one 12·7-mm. gun, but the Yak-9M (M indicating *Modificatsion*—Modification) featured a second 12·7-mm. gun in the forward fuselage, while the Yak-9B (B indicating *Bombardirovshchik*, or Bomber) had the lower portion of the second fuselage bay adapted as a bomb-bay with racks for an 880-lb. internal bomb load. Early in 1943, the wing fuel cells were once again enlarged to provide a total capacity of 143 Imp. gal. and a maximum range of 882 miles at 177 m.p.h. at 3,280 feet, or 655 miles at 248 m.p.h. at 9,840 feet, and this version entered production as the Yak-9D. With the demand for a still greater range to suit the fighter for long-range escort duties, in 1944 the maximum fuel load was raised to 187 Imp. gal. to provide a maximum range of 1,245–1,365 miles, this variant being designated Yak-9DD.

Evolved in parallel with the long-range Yak-9D, was the Yak-9T (T indicating *Tyazholy*, or Heavy, and referring to the armament) which had a hub-mounted 37-mm. Type 11-P-37 cannon with thirty-two rounds of ammunition. To accommodate this large cannon, it was necessary to move the cockpit aft by 1 ft. 3¾ in. to the second fuselage bay. The 12·7-mm. gun was retained for aiming purposes, and this model proved particularly efficacious against Mk.3 or Mk.4 tanks, armoured troop carriers and self-propelled guns. Later, the Yak-9T was also built with the 20-mm. MPSh-20, 23-mm. MP-23-VV and even the 12·7-mm. UBS gun in place of the 37-mm. weapon, being used for the combined low-level interception and close-support roles, and frequently using RS-82 rocket projectiles for the latter task.

The 37-mm. cannon of the Yak-9T did not prove entirely effective against the armour of the Tiger and Panther tanks, however, and in 1944 the Yak-9K appeared with a hub-mounted cannon of no less calibre than 45-mm.! Some units were equipped with a mixture of Yak-9T and Yak-9K aircraft. Still further developments of the Yak-9 appeared during the war years, such as the M-107A-powered Yak-9U (U indicating *Usilennui*, or Strengthened, and referring to the increased power of the engine), but these later models did not appear over the Russo-Finnish front before the end of the conflict, and were so extensively modified that they were virtually new aircraft.

Reprinted 1992 from the 1963 edition.
Cover design © 1989 Time-Life Books Inc.
All rights reserved.

Library of Congress Cataloging-in-Publication Data

Luukkanen, Eino Astere.
[Hävittäjälentäjänä kahdessa sodassa. English]
Fighter over Finland / Eino Luukkanen.
p. cm. — (Wings of war)
Translation of: Hävittäjälentäjänä kahdessa sodassa.
Originally published: London : Macdonald, c1963.
ISBN 0-8094-9620-8 (trade) — ISBN 0-8094-9621-6 (library)
1. Luukkanen, Eino Astere.
2. World War, 1939-1945—Aerial operations, Finnish.
3. Russo-Finnish War, 1939-1940—Aerial operations, Finnish.
4. World War, 1939-1945—Personal narratives, Finnish.
5. Fighter pilots—Finland—Biography.
I. Title. II. Series.
D792.F5L83 1992   940.54'21897'092—dc20   91-40911 CIP
[B]

Cover photograph © Carl Purcell
Endpapers photograph © Rene Sheret/After Image